WITHDRAWN

EPHREM THE SYRIAN

SELECT POEMS

◆

EASTERN CHRISTIAN TEXTS

Volume 2

Neal A. Maxwell Institute for Religious Scholarship
Brigham Young University

This publication was funded through the support of the U.S. Congress and the Library of Congress

Ephrem the Syrian

Select Poems

Vocalized Syriac text with
English translation, introduction, and notes by

Sebastian P. Brock & George A. Kiraz

Brigham Young University Press • Provo, Utah • 2009

LIBRARY OF CONGRESS CATALOGING-IN-PUBLICATION DATA

Ephraem, Syrus, Saint, 303–373.
[Poems. English & Syriac. Selections]
Select poems / Ephrem the Syrian ; vocalized Syriac text with English translation, introduction, and notes by Sebastian P. Brock and George A. Kiraz.
p. cm.—(Eastern Christian texts ; v. 2)
Includes bibliographical references and index.
ISBN: 978–0–934893–65–7 (alk. paper)
1. Christian poetry, Syriac. 2. Ephraem, Syrus, Saint, 303–373—Translations into English. 3. Christian poetry, Syriac—History and criticism. I. Brock, Sebastian P. II. Kiraz, George Anton. III. Title. IV. Eastern Christian texts (Provo, Utah) ; 2.
PJ5671.E7A2 2006
892′.3—dc22 2006013629

PRINTED IN THE UNITED STATES OF AMERICA

09 10 11 12 13 14 9 8 7 6 5 4 3 2

Contents

Abbreviations

Cycles of Ephrem's *Madrashe*

Azym.	*de Azymis (On Unleavened Bread)*
Cruc.	*de Crucifixione (On the Crucifixion)*
Eccl.	*de Ecclesia (On the Church)*
Fid.	*de Fide (On Faith)*
Ieiun.	*de Ieiunio (On the Fast)*
Jul.	*contra Julianum (Against Julian)*
Nat.	*de Nativitate (On the Nativity)*
Nis.	*Carmina Nisibena (Nisibene* Madrashe*)*
Par.	*de Paradiso (On Paradise)*
Res.	*de Resurrectione (On the Resurrection)*
Virg.	*de Virginitate (On Virginity)*

Additional Abbreviations

ANP	Andrew N. Palmer (see p. ix)
Aphrahat, *Dem.*	J. Parisot, ed. and trans., *Aphraatis Sapientis Persae Demonstrationes,* 2 vols., Patrologia syriaca 1–2 (Paris: Firmin-Didot, 1894–1907)
CSCO	Corpus Scriptorum Christianorum Orientalium (Leuven)
Ḥudra	T. Darmo, ed., *Ḥudra,* 3 vols. (Trichur: Mar Narsai Press, 1960–62)
Mosul Fenqitho	C. J. David, ed., *Breviarium iuxta Ritum Ecclesiae Antiochenae Syrorum,* 7 vols. (Mosul: Dominican Press, 1886–96)
Pampakuda Fenqitho	A. Konat, ed., *Fenqitho d-Ḥudro shattonoyo,* 3 vols. (Pampakuda: Mar Julius Press, 1962–63)

General Introduction

Ephrem justifiably has the reputation of being a wonderful poet and at the same time a profound theologian. Although there are now a number of English (and other) translations of his works available for the general reader, there is no easy access for anyone who wants to go on to read him in the original Syriac. The excellent standard edition of his poetry, by Edmund Beck, remains daunting to all but the more expert Syriacist, seeing that the text is unvocalized and in the *estrangela* script. We have long felt the need for a selection of Ephrem's poems in vocalized *serto* script[1] that would serve to provide a stepping-stone, as it were, towards using Beck's edition. If this selection of poems encourages people to explore further Ephrem's poetry in its original language, then it will amply have served its purpose. In no way does this edition seek to advance scholarship on Ephrem.

The poems are deliberately arranged according to the outline of Ephrem's concept of salvation history, commencing with Paradise and continuing through the course of the incarnate life of Christ to the sacramental life of the Church.

We take the opportunity to thank Kristian Heal for much assistance, and in particular for seeing to the entering of our vocalized Syriac texts on computer. We are also grateful to our two readers, Dr. Andrew Palmer and Dr. David Taylor, for their valuable comments and corrections. Andrew Palmer very kindly provided us with numerous good observations on metrical matters, as well as other suggestions, many of which we have with gratitude adopted (in the text and notes these are indicated by the initials ANP).

1. For transcriptions, however, we have retained the older East Syriac vowels.

Life and Writings

Little for certain is known of Ephrem's life. He must have been born in the early years of the fourth century, in or near Nisibis, on the eastern edge of the Roman Empire. On the basis of the internal evidence of his own writings, it is likely he was born to Christian parents (in contrast to the later Life, which presents his father as a pagan priest). It was in Nisibis that he spent most of his life, as a deacon serving under a succession of bishops—Jacob, Babu, Vologeses (Walgash), and Abraham. Both on internal evidence and on the authority of Jacob of Serugh's panegyric on him,[2] he wrote many of his poems to be sung by women's choirs. In 363, as part of the peace treaty with the Persians, Nisibis was handed over to the Sassanian Empire and the Christian population had to leave. Ephrem ended up for the last ten years of his life in Edessa (modern Urfa, in southeast Turkey), where he found himself much more involved in the theological controversies of the time. He evidently acquired a surprisingly good knowledge of Greek philosophical concepts,[3] even though he expresses these in an essentially un-Greek way. He died in 373, very probably on June 9 of that year.

The scarcity of reliable biographical information about Ephrem served as an invitation to later generations to remedy this in an imaginative way. Thus, for example, by the mid-sixth century, when the influential Syriac Life of Ephrem was probably composed, he had anachronistically been transformed into a monk who paid visits to famous contemporaries in Egypt (Bishoi) and Cappadocia (Basil).[4]

Ephrem's extensive works fall into four main categories: in verse there is both stanzaic poetry (the *madrashe,* the sole category represented here) and the narrative couplets *(memre)*; and in prose there is both ordinary prose and artistic prose.[5] Famous names are liable to attract works by other people, and the corpus of writings under Ephrem's name includes many pieces that have been falsely attributed to him.[6]

---

2. Edited by J. Amar (1995).

3. This has been well brought out recently in Possekel 1999.

4. For the development of the biographical tradition, see Griffith 1989–90, Amar 1992, and Brock 1999c (appendix).

5. A list of editions will be found in Appendix 1.

6. Of the texts in CSCO listed in Appendix 1, the following partly or wholly contain poems which cannot be genuine: *de Epiphania, Soghyatha, Sermones I–IV, de Abraham Qidunaya, de Juliano Saba,* and *Nachträge.* The problem is even more acute in the very large corpus of works attributed to Ephrem in Greek.

As far as the *madrashe* in the present selection are concerned, however, one can be reasonably assured that they are all genuine.

Although Ephrem never offers a systematic presentation of his theology, it is clear that his writings are based on a clearly thought-out theological worldview, and different presentations of this can be found in de Halleux 1973 and 1983, Murray 1975–76 and 2004, Bou Mansour 1988, Brock 1992, and Griffith 1998. General information may be found in Ortiz de Urbina 1965, Beck 1960a and 1962a, Leloir 1963a, and Murray 1982 (for Ephrem Graecus, see Hemmerdinger-Iliadou 1960, Geerard 1974–87, 2:366–468, and Geerard and Noret 1998, 227–50).

Transmission

The survival of any of Ephrem's poems in a complete state is due to the preservation of fifth- and sixth-century manuscripts from the Syrian Monastery in the Nitrian desert, protected by the dry climate of Egypt. It is likely that the person who was originally responsible for collecting these was the monastery's abbot, Moses of Nisibis, in the early tenth century. In the eighteenth and nineteenth centuries these manuscripts were acquired by the Vatican Library and the British Museum (the latter are now in the British Library). The importance of these early manuscripts lies in the fact that they alone preserve the *madrashe* in their full form, seeing that later manuscripts invariably abbreviate them, or even run together stanzas from different *madrashe*.[7]

In these fifth- and sixth-century manuscripts the *madrashe* are grouped into collections, or cycles, entitled "volumes" *(penqyata),* and it is by the titles of these cycles that the *madrashe* are regularly referred to. Within several of the cycles there are smaller groups, such as "On Oil and the Olive" in *de Virginitate,* and "On the Pearl" in *de Fide.* Whether the gathering of the poems into larger cycles goes back wholly, or in part, to Ephrem himself is uncertain. There is, however, definite evidence that the grouping into "volumes" was already in existence in the late fifth century, since references to several of them feature in an anthology of texts produced by Philoxenus of Mabbug in his *Discourses*

7. On this later transmission see Gribomont 1973, Brock 1997, and Ibrahim and Kiraz 1999. This situation is also reflected in the modern printed liturgical editions (the West Syriac Mosul Fenqitho and Pampakuda Fenqitho, and the East Syriac Ḥudra), as can be seen from the excerpts in these from Texts 8, 11, 12, 13, and 15 (*Res.* 1, *Azym.* 3, *Cruc.* 2, *Nis.* 41, and *Res.* 2).

against Habbib, which can be dated to ca. 482–84. Much more detailed information about the various "volumes" is to be found in an elaborate index to the *qale,* or melodies (see below), used for Ephrem's *madrashe,* preserved in Sinai Syr. 10. From this index the following list of nine volumes and their contents can be extrapolated:[8]

I. Of the Nativity (59 *madrashe*)
II. Of the Fast (67)
III. Of Nisibis (77)
IV. Of the King's Bride *(kallat malka),* against the Jews (66)
V. Of the Church (52)
VI. Of the Church (52)
VII. Of Faith (87)
VIII. Against Erroneous Doctrines and On Paradise (56 and 15)
IX. Of the Confessors and Departed

Of these, III, V, VII, and VIII correspond exactly with the surviving cycles in the early manuscripts; VI will be the extant *de Virginitate.* I and II are both much larger than the surviving cycles under those names (even if *de Azymis, de Crucifixione,* and *de Resurrectione* are included, as seems likely, in II). IV is completely unknown, though one incipit can be identified as a *madrasha* edited by Lamy. IX is also almost entirely lost, though it will include those *madrashe* on Abraham of Qidun and Julian Saba which are genuinely by Ephrem (some of those in the surviving collection cannot be by him). What emerges most clearly from this evidence is that a considerable number of Ephrem's *madrashe* have been lost.[9]

Dating the cycles is problematic. The small collection *de Paradiso* is usually thought to belong to the earlier part of his life in Nisibis, before 363, and many of the *madrashe* in the cycle on Nisibis (including Text 19 [*Nis.* 1]) will also date to this period, since they are clearly written in Nisibis; others, however, in the same cycle (notably 26–34) must have been written at Edessa. It seems very likely that the cycles *de Fide* and *contra Haereses* were also written during the last ten years of his life in Edessa.

8. On this subject see de Halleux 1972 and 1974, and Brock 1997.

9. It is of course possible that some stanzas from these lost *madrashe* are in fact preserved in the medieval liturgical collections.

Meters

The basic metrical principle of Syriac poetry lies in the syllable, rather than length or stress. There are two basic forms of poetry, the stanzaic and the couplet, and Ephrem makes use of both, the former being entitled *madrashe* (sometimes translated "teaching poems") and the latter *memre*. Ephrem employs the *memra* for narrative poetry, and the meter he uses (and which came to be known by his name) consists of couplets, each of 7+7 syllables. A number of other meters for *memre* are found in later writers, a particularly favored one consisting of 12+12 (or rather, 4+4+4 4+4+4) syllables, associated with the name of Jacob of Serugh (d. 521).

All the poems in the present collection, however, are stanzaic *madrashe*. In the *madrasha* every stanza in a poem follows the same metrical pattern, where regular word breaks, or caesuras, provide the demarcation between syllabic units. Thus in a simple meter such as that used in Text 11 (*Azym.* 3), the syllabic pattern for each stanza is four syllabic units, here set out in two lines each with two units, the first of five syllables and the second of four syllables (the whole stanza thus being designated as 5+4 5+4). Thus, for example, in stanza 3:

netqol wa-npaḥḥem neṣḥanayhon
d-haw ᵓemar (ᵓ)raza w-ᵓemar qushta

In modern editions the *madrashe* are normally set out in lines, usually with two syllabic units to a line (depending on the length of the syllabic unit). The syllabic units mostly consist of 3, 4, 5, 6, or 7 syllables, though occasionally 2- or 8- (and even, rarely, 9- or 10-) syllable units are found. Especially in the case of the more complex meters, the way in which the syllabic units are separated out into lines in modern editions depends on the editor's decision; in the present collection we have followed Beck's line divisions and layout, though we have altered it tacitly in a few cases where his line divisions are manifestly wrong (examples are in Text 17 [*Fid.* 10], stanzas 20 and 22, and Text 18 [*Fid.* 14], stanzas 8 and 9). A notable instance of how the same editor can set out the same meter in two different ways is provided by Texts 16 and 19 (*Virg.* 7 and *Nis.* 1).

Ephrem employs some forty-five different stanza patterns in his *madrashe*, ranging from simple to highly complex syllabic patterns. In contrast with the practice of modern editions, Syriac manuscripts do not set out poetry in lines, but present it written continuously, with points denoting the metrical breaks.[10] With *madrashe,* the demarcation between stanzas is almost always clearly marked (e.g., by points in red), but the internal syllabic structure of a stanza, consisting of various syllabic units, may well be inadequately, or ambiguously, indicated, seeing that points may be omitted or misplaced. Furthermore, since points designate both metrical and sense breaks (which may not always coincide), there is yet further scope for confusion. However, it is only with the long and complicated meters that serious problems arise; an example of this can be found in Text 9 (*Ieiun.* 3), where it remains unclear exactly how the syllabic structure of the meter should be analyzed (and thus, how it should best be set out in lines).

An added complication is that there is a certain degree of metrical license, in that the vocalic *shwa* (historically representing a lost full vowel) can be treated as a full vowel for metrical purposes (e.g., *nṣur* in stanza 2 of Text 12 [*Cruc.* 2] is treated metrically as if it were *neṣur*). It is also likely that in the case of a cluster of three consonants an epenthetic vowel may be inserted in certain conditions (see Nöldeke 1904, §52B). Conversely a full vowel in certain circumstances is discounted from a metrical point of view—this is especially frequent with verbs whose first radical is *alaph* (thus in Text 17 [*Fid.* 10], stanza 12, *ʾekalton* is treated metrically as *ʾkalton*). In the introductions to the individual poems attention is drawn to some (but by no means all) of these cases of metrical license. It should be noted, however, that for the present edition we have normally provided the standard vocalization, even when this goes against the meter. It should also be kept in mind that the rules of Syriac versification have as yet been very little studied; furthermore, even though the text of Ephrem comes down to us in sixth-century manuscripts, it may well already have suffered from corruption in places.

Madrashe were sung (and still are in liturgical use), and in the manuscripts the melody, known as the *qala,* is regularly given: this consists of the opening words of a particular *madrasha* using the meter in question (the same practice is often used for western hymn tunes). In some, but not all, cases the *madrasha* that provides the *qala* title can be identified as one of Ephrem's own poems. Sometimes the same meter (and indeed

10. Palmer 1995, 161–76, argues (conjecturally) that the cycle *On Faith* in its original form was set out by lines.

the same poem) may have more than one *qala* indicated: whether these are alternative titles for the same tune or represent different tunes that fit the same meter is not entirely clear. In practice, the *qala* title also serves as a way of indicating the meter.[11] An index of the *qale* employed in the present selection is given in Appendix 2.

Alphabetic acrostics already occur in the Hebrew Bible (e.g., Pss 111–12, 119; Lam 3–4). Ephrem employs a variety of different forms of acrostic (Palmer 2002, 278), several of which are represented in the present collection. Alphabetic acrostics of different kinds feature in the following poems:

Text 6 (*Eccl.* 37): This has the first six letters of the Syriac alphabet (*alaph* to *waw*); stanza 6, however, begins with *beth* (though British Library Add. 14574 tries to remedy the situation by prefacing it with *waw*—but against the meter). ANP nicely suggests that, since stanza 6 belongs closely with stanza 5 (and so is not likely to be an interpolation), the break in the pattern is deliberate and symbolizes "the failure of humanity, created in the sixth day, to live up to the perfection symbolized by the number six."

Text 18 (*Fid.* 14): The stanzas run from *zayin* to *nun,* but then *alaph* and *waw* follow.

Text 19 (*Nis.* 1): This provides alternate letters of the alphabet, *alaph, gamal, he,* etc.

In three other poems in the collection there are acrostics which provide Ephrem's own name *(ʾPRYM):*

Text 3 (*Fid.* 49): Here we have only *ʾPPRR,* but the rest of the name is to be found in *Fid.* 50 *(YMMMMMMM).*

Text 8 (*Res.* 1): The first five stanzas provide *ʾPRYM,* and *M* continues on from stanza 6 to the end, apart from a break in the sequence in stanzas 18 and 19, which begin with *lamadh* and *sadhe.*

Text 10 (*Ieiun.* 6): Here the first and last letters of his name are doubled: *ʾʾPRYMM.*

Irregularities in acrostic poems, such as some of those found in the poems mentioned above, may sometimes serve as indicators of later interpolations, although in other cases there may well be a specific reason lying behind the irregularity (as in Text 6 [*Eccl.* 37]). On this topic see Palmer 1995 and (especially) Palmer 2002; since these are

11. Beck provides basic information in the introductions to his text editions about the different meters employed.

problems that require detailed discussion, they are not dealt with further in the present collection.

The Present Edition and Translations

The texts are based on E. Beck's critical editions in CSCO, though in a few places we have preferred readings to be found in his apparatus. Beck's layout of the poems in lines has also been followed, though with a few modifications (see above). The translations are set out in lines corresponding to those of the Syriac texts. Although the translations have generally aimed to keep fairly closely to the originals, they avoid being overly literal. Wherever it has been thought helpful for the sake of the general sense, a few expansions have been made or names added (in brackets). The convention of using capital letters for personal pronouns referring to God (i.e., You, He, etc.) has been adopted since this often helps clarify the sense. Notes to the translation are simply meant to clarify what might otherwise have been obscure, and by no means are they intended to represent a commentary. For the sake of brevity, references in the notes (and elsewhere) to modern studies are by means of author's name and date of publication; the full bibliographic references will be found in the bibliography.

EPHREM THE SYRIAN

SELECT POEMS

◆

TEXT 1

On Reading the Paradise Narrative (*Par.* 5)

In his cycle of fifteen poems on Paradise, Ephrem creatively explores various aspects of the narrative of Gen 2–3. Though he treats the topic in a manner that is very different from his exposition in the *Commentary on Genesis,* a reading of the latter provides some helpful insights into his much more poetic treatment of the biblical text in the poems (a complete English translation of the cycle, along with the relevant sections of the *Commentary,* is to be found in Brock 1990b).

Ephrem opens the present poem by comparing the biblical text with the miraculous rock that accompanied the Israelites in the wilderness (Exod 17:7): if treated rightly it comes alive, and from it flow streams of vivifying water (1 Cor 10:4). Ephrem then describes his own experience of being transported to Paradise, with the verses leaping out of the text to embrace him as he reads the narrative concerning Paradise in Genesis. Once transported in spirit to Paradise, Ephrem wonders whether Paradise is really capacious enough to contain all the righteous (stanza 7), but learns the answer from analogies in the New Testament (Mark 5:9; stanza 8) and in the natural world and the human heart (stanzas 9–10). Once back in this world after having experienced something of the beauty of Paradise, Ephrem reflects on the paradox that people lament departing from this world when in fact death should really be seen as a process of being born out of this world into "the Garden of splendors."

Meter

All fifteen of the *madrashe* in the cycle *On Paradise* are in the same meter, for which the *qala* is given as *dina d-sharbata,* which is also found for *Eccl.* 21 and 28. In other cycles where Ephrem uses this meter, different *qale* are given: (1) *ʾestmek(w) ʿal qushta* (=opening of a single *madrasha* printed by Beck at the end of his edition of *de Paradiso*): thus *Jul.* 1–4; (2) *bayyaʾ(w) b-mulkane* (=opening of *Par.* 7): thus *Fid.* 31, 39–48 and *Nat.* 3; (3) *pardaisa* (=title of the cycle *de Paradiso*): thus appendix to *Ieiun.* and *Nat.* 3 (according to two manuscripts). In later *madrashe* collections, *pardaisa* is the normal *qala* given.

The metrical pattern is as follows: 5+5 5+5 5+5 5+2 5+5 5+5. It will be observed that there are a few irregularities, with six syllables instead of five (e.g., stanza 3, line 2; stanza 4, line 1). It should be noted that the meter indicates that *alaph* preserves its consonantal character in *wa-pʾe* (stanza 5) and *ba-mʾa* (stanza 8). In stanza 5, *ʿden* is treated as a dissyllable.

Text

The cycle *On Paradise* is preserved in three sixth-century manuscripts: British Library Add. 14571 (of 519 CE; Beck's D), Vatican Syr. 111 (of 522 CE; Beck's B), and Vatican Syr. 112 (of 551 CE; Beck's G). For this poem Beck also uses one later manuscript, British Library Add. 17141 (of eighth or ninth century; Beck's E), but like almost all manuscripts later than the sixth century, it preserves only select stanzas (1–2, 6–7, 12, 14–15).

ܥܠ ܩܠܐ ܕܙܘܚܐ ܕܡܫܒܚܬܐ

1. ܒܫܒܝܠܗ ܕܒܪܝܬܐ   ܚܙܝܬ ܘܐܬܕܡܪܬ
ܒܟܐܦܐ ܕܥܡ ܥܡܐ   ܘܗܠܟܬ ܥܡܗ ܒܒܪܐ
ܕܠܗ ܡܢ ܐܬܚܫܒܬ   ܕܡܝܐ ܢܒܥܝܢ ܗܘܘ ܒܗ
ܢܫܬܐ ܠܗܘܢ ܥܡܡܐ   ܡܨܗܝܢܐ
ܒܗ ܟܣܐ ܗܘܐ ܡܝܐ   ܘܡܬܝܬܐ ܢܦܩܘ ܡܢܗ
ܐܝܟ ܡܠܬܐ ܕܒܪܐ   ܒܬܪܐ ܡܢ ܠܐ ܡܕܡ

ܒܥܘܬܐ : ܫܘܒܚܐ ܠܟ ܒܪܐ ܕܡܪܐ   ܕܐܬܐ ܠܦܘܪܩܢ

2. ܒܪܝܬܐ ܕܥܝܢܐ   ܒܫܦܪܗ ܠܝܬ ܡܘܡܐ
ܕܢܚܙܐ ܠܒܪܝܬܐ   ܥܝܢܐ ܐܦ ܫܦܝܪܐ
ܥܝܢܐ ܒܣܘܟܠܗ   ܠܒܐ ܒܦܘܪܫܢܗ
ܫܘܦܪܐ ܕܡܬܚܙܐ   ܒܟܠ ܐܬܪ
ܫܟܝܚܝܢ ܒܟܠ ܐܬܪܝܢ   ܐܡܝܢܝܢ ܒܟܠ ܙܒܢܝܢ
ܡܫܚܝܢ ܒܟܘܪܐ   ܕܠܐܡ ܒܒܪܝܬܐ

1. I considered the Word of the Creator, and likened it
to the rock that marched with the people of Israel in the wilderness; Exod 17:6; 1 Cor 10:4
it was not from the reservoir of water contained within it
that it poured forth for them glorious streams:
there was no water in the [rock], yet oceans sprang forth from it,
just as the Word which fashioned created things[1] out of nothing.

Refrain: Blessed is that person accounted worthy
to inherit Your Paradise.

2. In his book Moses described the creation of the natural world,
so that both Nature and Scripture[2]
might bear witness to the Creator: John 8:17
Nature, through [man's] use of it, Scripture, through his reading of it.
These are the witnesses which reach everywhere;
they are to be found at all times, present at every hour,
confuting the unbeliever who defames the Creator.

---

1. created things (*ᶜbade*): One of the manuscripts instead reads *ᶜebraye*, in which case the previous verb is best taken as *debrat* rather than *da-brat*, i.e., "led the Hebrews"; the text and translation given here, however, are preferable (and alone fit the meter).

2. Nature and Scripture: Compare *Haer.* 28.11:
Once Nature and Scripture had cleansed the land
they sowed in it new commandments
—in the land of the heart, so that it might bear fruit,
praise for the Lord of Nature,
glory for the Lord of Scripture.

3. ܒܪܶܡܙܶܗ ܕܗܰܘ ܦܰܓܪܳܐ ܩܪܶܝܬ ܕܗܘܶܝܬ ܘܰܐܬܠܰܒܫܰܬ
ܕܶܐܣܛܽܘܟܣܰܘܗܝ ܐܘ ܚܽܘܫܒܰܘܗܝ ܦܶܪ̈ܨܽܘܦܰܝ ܕܩܢܽܘܡܶܗ
ܘܰܡܕܺܝܢܬܳܐ ܕܰܚܙܳܘܳܐ ܢܰܦܫܶܗ ܐܰܘܕܥܰܬ ܠܒܰܪ ܐܰܒܽܘܗ̇
ܘܟܰܕ ܡܫܰܠܡܳܐ ܠܗܰܘ ܚܶܙܘܳܐ ܕܒܶܗ ܚܳܙܶܐ
ܦܰܓܪܶܗ ܕܦܰܪܨܽܘܦܳܐ ܗܘ ܕܗܘ ܡܣܬܟܠ ܘܚܳܙܶܐ
ܡܶܢ ܒܢܰܘܗ̈ܝ ܕܗܰܘ ܦܰܓܪܳܐ ܠܒܰܢܰܘܗ̈ܝ ܕܦܰܪܨܽܘܦܳܐ

4. ܒܢܰܘܗ̈ܳܐ ܐܰܝܟ ܕܰܒܦܰܓܪܳܐ ܟܝܳܢܳܐ ܘܰܐܠܳܗܽܘܬܳܐ
ܒܒܰܪ ܗܽܘ ܘܰܟܽܠ ܐܰܚܺܝܕ ܒܦܰܓܪܶܗ ܕܦܰܪܨܽܘܦܳܐ
ܕܟܝܳܢܳܐ ܠܰܐܠܳܗܽܘܬܳܐ ܐܰܥܒܪܶܗ ܒܦܰܓܪܳܢܳܐ
ܘܰܚܙܶܝܬ ܐܘ ܠܰܐܠܳܗܽܘܬܳܐ ܐܶܬܚܰܙܝܰܬ
ܒܟܝܳܢܳܐ ܡܶܢ ܦܰܓܪܳܢܳܐ ܕܟܰܕ ܐܶܬܦܪܰܥ ܦܰܓܪܳܐ
ܚܙܳܐ ܗܘܳܐ ܒܟܝܳܢܳܐ ܘܰܟܡܺܠ ܠܰܐܠܳܗܽܘܬܳܐ

5. ܒܦܰܓܪܶܗ ܘܰܐܦ ܠܰܐܒܽܘܗ̇ ܕܡܶܢܶܗ ܕܦܰܪܨܽܘܦܳܐ
ܐܰܚܘܝܰܬ ܒܗܰܘ ܦܰܓܪܳܐ ܘܰܒܒܪܳܬܳܐ ܘܰܒܟܽܠܶܗ ܒܶܗ
ܟܝܳܢܳܐ ܒܒܰܪ ܦܰܫܛܳܐ ܘܰܐܠܳܗܽܘܬܶܗ ܒܶܗ ܒܟܽܠܶܗ
ܦܳܪܰܫ ܕܰܐܦܽܘܬ ܒܶܗ ܕܠܳܐ ܠܗܘ
ܗܰܘ ܕܗܘ ܙܰܘܥܳܐ ܦܰܫܛܳܐ ܡܶܬܟܰܠܰܠ ܒܳܐ ܘܦܳܐܐ
ܠܗܳܐ ܡܶܢܝܰܢ ܒܶܢ ܕܙܰܘܥܳܐ ܗܘ ܕܟܽܠ ܠܫܽܘܦ̈ܪܶܐ

3. I read the opening of this book   and was filled with joy,
for its verses and lines   spread out their arms [to welcome me];
the first rushed out and kissed me,   and led me on to its companion;
and when I reached that verse   wherein is written
the story of Paradise,   it lifted me up and transported me
from the bosom of the book   to the very bosom of Paradise.

4. The eye and the mind   traveled over the lines
as over a bridge, and entered together   the story of Paradise.
The eye as it read   transported the mind;
in return the mind, too,   gave the eye rest
from its reading,   for when the book had been read
the eye had rest,   but the mind was engaged.

5. Both the bridge and the gate   of Paradise
did I find in that book.   I crossed over and entered;
my eye indeed remained outside   but my mind entered within.
I began to wander   amid things not described.
This is the serene height,   clear, lofty and fair:
Scripture named it Eden,   the summit of all blessings. Gen 2:8

6. ܐܝܟ ܚܙܝܬ ܗܘܝܬ ܠܗܘܢ   ܒܥܝܢܐ ܕܐܪ̈ܙܐ
ܐܬܒܢܝ ܒܡܫܝܚܐ   ܦܢܝ ܒܪܚܡܐ
ܡܫܬܪܟ ܒܐܪܥܬܐ   ܡܬܟܠܟ ܒܩܘܪܒܐ
ܐܝܟ ܒܥܠܡܗ ܕܐܢܫ ܗܘܐ   ܡܬܠܟܠܗ
ܐܝܟ ܕܡܛܐ ܒܪܟܝܢܗ   ܘܐܝܟ ܕܡܦܪܚܐ ܒܡܦܪܝܢܗ
ܐܝܟ ܕܦܩܘܐ ܒܫܘܢܗ   ܘܐܝܟ ܕܢܚܝܐ ܒܡܚܝܢܗ

7. ܡܠܟܐ ܘܐܦ ܗܘܐ   ܕܐܢ ܗܘ ܕܦܪܘܫܐ
ܦܩܕ ܒܐܪ̈ܙܐ   ܟܠܗܘܢ ܕܒܗ ܢܛܪܘܢ
ܡܠܟܐ ܕܠܐ ܠܡܛܐ   ܘܠܟܠܗ ܒܪܩܠܡܝ
ܚܙܐ ܟܡ ܒܗܘ ܥܒܪܐ   ܕܒܗ ܡܪܐ
ܥܡܘܢܐ ܕܟܠ ܡܠܘܝ   ܒܗ ܗܘܐ ܘܠܐ ܡܬܒܥܝ
ܕܚܝܠܐ ܗܘ ܕܐܦ ܡܢܗ   ܕܢܩܡܐ ܡܢܐ ܘܦܝܫ

8. ܗܢܐ ܩܡ ܗܘ ܚܝܠܐ   ܟܠܗ ܚܒܝܫ ܒܩܘܡܬܐ
ܚܒܝܫ ܒܥܘܒܐ ܡܢܗ   ܗܘܐ ܡܢܐ ܘܦܝܫ
ܦܓܪܐ ܕܐܪ̈ܙܐ   ܡܠܐ ܕܡܢܗ ܘܐܬܢܣܒܘ
ܕܡܘܬܐ ܗܘ ܕܪܘܚܢܐ   ܡܡܠܠܐ
ܕܐܢ ܙܟܐ ܦܫܩ ܘܐܬܝܒ   ܘܐܢ ܙܟܐ ܡܦܫ ܘܐܟܪ
ܐܢ ܡܦܫ ܗܘܐ ܒܪܘܚܐ   ܘܐܢ ܦܫܩ ܗܘܐ ܒܟܠ ܕܐܝܟ

6. There too did I see the bowers of the righteous
dripping with unguents and fragrant with scents,
garlanded with fruits, crowned with blossoms.
In accord with a person's deeds, such was his bower:
thus one was lowly in its adornments,
while another was resplendent in its beauty;
one was but dim in its coloring, while another dazzled in its glory.

7. I enquired into this too, whether Paradise
was sufficient [in size] for all the righteous to live there.
I asked about what is not written [in Scripture],
but my instruction came from what is written there:
"Consider that man in whom there dwelt
a legion of all kinds of demons; Mark 5:9;
they were there although not apparent, Luke 8:30
for their army is of a stuff finer and more subtle than the soul itself.

8. "That whole army dwelt in a single body.
A hundred times more refined and subtle
are the bodies of the righteous
when they are risen, at the Resurrection:
they resemble the mind which is able,
if it so wills, to stretch out and expand,
or, should it wish, to contract and shrink:
if it shrinks, it is in some place, if it expands, it is in every place.

9. ܗܟܢܐ ܐܦ ܐܚܪܢܝܬܐ ܘܐܝܟ ܕܢܘܗܪܐ
ܘܛܠܠܐ ܕܐܝܠܢܐ ܡܢܗ ܒܗ ܒܝܬܐ
ܘܙܠܓܐ ܕܫܡܫܐ ܡܢܗ ܒܗ ܒܗܘܐ
ܘܟܕ ܡܢܗ ܒܠܒܘܫܬܐ ܕܡܝܐ ܗܘ ܠܗܘܢ
ܕܢܬܦܪܫܘܢ ܠܟܠܗܘܢ ܘܗܟܢ ܐܦ ܦܪܘܫܘܬܐ
ܟܕ ܡܠܐ ܡܢ ܕܡܝܐ ܕܡܝܢ ܗܘ ܠܦܘܪܫܢܐ

10. ܡܢܗ ܐܦ ܣܘܟܠܐ ܕܠܐ ܡܫ ܘܠܐ ܡܬܡܫ
ܒܟܠܐ ܕܐܒܘܪ ܡܢ ܒܘܠܐ ܟܕ ܠܗܘܢ ܘܪܚܝܩ ܡܢ ܟܠ
ܠܐ ܡܬܟܪܝܢ ܠܗ ܘܠܐ ܐܦ ܡܬܐܟܪܝܢ
ܒܗܐ ܟܝܬ ܦܪܘܫܘܬܐ ܡܫܟܚܐ
ܢܦܩܘ ܒܪܘܚܬܐ ܡܬܟܠܐ ܕܠܐ ܡܬܟܠ
ܐܦ ܠܐ ܗܘ ܣܘܟܠܐ ܕܢܦܫܘܩ ܡܬܦܫܩܗܘܢ

11. ܡܟܝܠ ܒܗܐ ܕܦܫܝܛ ܘܡܫܝܛ ܗܘܐ ܕܐܦܩܘ
ܘܟܠ ܕܟܪ ܡܢ ܡܕܡ ܟܠܗܘܢ ܕܦܪܘܫܘܬܐ
ܘܐܝܟ ܗܘ ܕܡܬܪܢܝܐ ܡܟܝܠ ܕܡܫܩܘܪܐ
ܟܠܐ ܠܐܟܠܐܝܬ ܡܟܝܢܐ
ܘܬܠܝܬ ܠܟܘܠܐ ܡܬܐܟܠܐ ܟܠܗܘܢ
ܫܒܪܐ ܕܪܘܐ ܗܘܐ ܘܡܬܒܥܝܬ ܕܪܟܝܢ ܗܘܐ

9. "Listen further and learn
how lamps with thousands of rays can exist in a single house,
how ten thousand scents can exist in a single blossom:
though they exist within a small space, they have ample room
to disport themselves. So it is with Paradise:
though it is full of spiritual beings,
it is amply spacious for their disportment.

10. "Again, thoughts, infinite in number, dwell
in the smallest [organ] of all, the heart,[3] yet they have ample room:
they neither constrict each other, nor are they constricted there.
How much more will Paradise the glorious
suffice for the spiritual beings that are so refined in substance
that even thought cannot touch them!"

11. I gave praise as far as I was able and was on the point of departing
when, from the midst of Paradise,
there came a sudden thunderous sound,
and, like the blare of trumpets in some camp,
voices crying "holy" thrice over. Isa 6:3
Thus I knew that the Divinity received praise in [Paradise]:
I had supposed it was empty,[4]
but I learn otherwise from the thunderous sound.

---

3. heart: In biblical and early Syriac anthropology the heart is the center of the intellectual faculties as well as of the emotions.

4. empty: Since body and soul will not be reunited (and so able to enter Paradise) until the final Resurrection.

12. ܛܘܒ ܡܪܝܚ ܬܓܪ ܒܢܦܫܗ ܐܝܟ ܕܒܡܘܦܪܗ
ܒܗ ܗܘ ܡܟܝܠ ܡܘܦܪܐ ܕܠܐ ܐܝܬ ܒܗ ܡܘܡܐ
ܒܗ ܗܘ ܗܪܐ ܡܢܐ ܕܠܐ ܐܝܬ ܒܗ ܩܢܛܐ
ܠܡܘܒܠܘܗܝ ܠܟܠ ܕܡܛܐ ܕܢܣܒܝܘܗ
ܐܠܐ ܠܚܐܪܘܬܐ ܘܐܦ ܠܡܠܟܘܬܐ
ܘܐܠܐ ܠܒܝܬ ܡܠܟܐ ܐܦ ܠܒܝܬ ܕܘܝܐ

13. ܐܡܬܝ ܕܢܣܒ ܬܓܪܐ ܐܣܛܠܗ ܕܦܪܙܡܐ
ܦܫܛ ܘܦܫܛ ܗܘܐ ܒܩܢܝܐ ܕܫܘܒܚܢܐ
ܘܡܢ ܡܫܝܚ ܠܒܣܪܐ ܕܐܘܪܚܐ ܐܝܟ ܕܒܩܘܒܠܐ
ܦܫܛ ܟܝ ܬܐܓܐ ܘܫܢܝܐ ܕܟܠ ܢܦܫ
ܬܟܦܠ ܕܒܗ ܐܦܪܬܐ ܗܘ ܐܠܗܝ ܬܒܥܘ ܗܘ
ܫܪܝܪܐ ܕܒܗ ܟܠܢ ܡܠܐ ܕܢܩܦ ܡܢܗ

14. ܐܡܬܝ ܕܐܦ ܒܡܠܐ ܟܠܢ ܒܡܥܡܘܕܝܬܗ
ܟܠܢ ܕܡܢ ܫܡܝܐ ܢܩܦܝܢ ܠܒܣܪܐ
ܘܡܢ ܠܗ ܣܢܝܩܘܬܐ ܢܩܦܝܢ ܠܗ ܐܟܚܕܐ
ܘܟܢ ܐܦ ܡܘܬܐ ܠܟܠܟܠܐ
ܙܥܘܪܐ ܗܘ ܕܡܘܒܠܐ ܟܠܢ ܕܡܢܠܟܢ
ܡܢ ܐܟܚܕ ܐܝܟ ܕܫܡܝܐ ܠܟܢܫܐ ܕܫܠܝܘܬܐ

12. [Paradise] delighted me as much by its peacefulness as by its beauty:
in it there resides a beauty that has no spot;
in it exists a peacefulness that knows no fear.
How blessed is that person accounted worthy to receive it,
if not by right, yet at least by grace;
if not because of labors, yet at least through mercy.

13. I was in wonder as I crossed the borders of Paradise
at how well-being, as though a companion,
turned round and remained behind.
And when I reached the shore of earth, the mother of thorns, Gen 3:18
I encountered all kinds of pain and suffering.
I learned how, compared to Paradise, our abode is but a dungeon;
yet the prisoners within it weep when they leave it!

14. I was amazed at how even infants weep as they leave [the womb]—
weeping because they come out from darkness into light
and from suffocation they issue forth into this world!
Likewise death, too, is for the world
a symbol of birth, and yet people weep because they are born
out of this world, the mother of suffering,
into the Garden of splendors.[5]

5. splendors: Lit. "luxuries." Behind this term there evidently lies an awareness of the Septuagint's translation of the Garden of Eden as "the Garden of luxury" *(truphē)*.

15. ܐܕܡ ܒܟ ܢܦܩ   ܡܢܗ ܕܦܪܕܝܣܐ
ܘܐܢ ܗܘ ܕܟܬܒ ܦܪܘܣ   ܕܐܥܠ ܠܦܪܕܝܣܢ
ܐܡܘܚ ܐܦ ܡܢ ܒܪ   ܠܒܪܝܐ ܕܒܫܝܢܗ
ܒܘܗ ܢܗܪܐ ܦܠܓ   ܡܝܐ
ܘܦܐܪܐ ܕܒܫܝܢܗ   ܡܢ ܒܪ ܐܝܟ
ܢܬܪܘܢ ܒܢܝܫܐ   ܕܢܣܘܢ ܒܡܫܘܬܦܝ

15. Have pity[6] on me, O Lord of Paradise,

and if it is not possible for me to enter Your Paradise,

grant that I may graze outside, by its enclosure:

within, let there be [spread] the table for the "diligent,"[7]

but may the fruits within its enclosure
drop outside like the "crumbs" Matt 15:27; Mark 7:28

for sinners, so that, through Your grace, they may live!

◆

6. have pity: The verb normally means "thunder" (as in stanza 11), but it can also have the meaning "feel sorry for." Alternatively, one might emend to *traḥḥem,* "have mercy" (ANP).

7. diligent: Although this term does not feature in any of the Syriac Gospel versions, it is regularly used by early Syriac writers in connection with the parables of the laborers in the vineyard (see Text 10 [*Nis.* 1.9] below) and of the talents.

TEXT 2

On Human Language about God
(*Fid.* 31)

This *madrasha* is of particular importance for the light it sheds on Ephrem's understanding of how the biblical text is to be understood, for it sets out to describe how God speaks to humanity through the biblical text, allowing himself, as it were, to become incarnated into human language. The starting point is the dilemma: how can human beings speak about the Godhead, seeing that the human mind is not capable of crossing the ontological gap (or "chasm," as Ephrem often calls it) which exists between Creation and its Creator? This might suggest that a holy silence is all that is possible. Ephrem, however, has a solution to the problem: God, stirred by love for his creation, has himself crossed this gap and entered the created world, allowing himself to be described in human terms and in human language in the Bible. Thus, before becoming incarnate in the human body, he first became incarnate in human language, or, in Ephrem's own homely metaphor of clothing, "God put on names," or metaphors, in the Old Testament, just as subsequently he "put on a body" at the incarnation. Of great importance for Ephrem in all this is the fact that God is not forcing himself on humanity; rather, he is deliberately encouraging the use of his gift to humanity of free will (stanza 5). Ephrem then goes on, with a delightful sense of humor, to compare God's action, in teaching humanity about himself, to that of a man teaching a parrot how to talk, using a mirror to deceive the parrot into thinking that it is a fellow parrot talking to it.

Humanity, on its part, must not abuse this divine condescension by taking literally these "names" or metaphors with which God has clothed himself; to understand these terms literally would be a total misunderstanding of biblical language. The very fact that the biblical text moves from one metaphor for God to another should be a sufficient warning against any such misconception. Thus, instead of fixing one's mind on the literal meaning of the metaphors, one should allow these metaphors to act as pointers upwards, as it were, towards the hiddenness of God, whose true nature cannot be described by, let alone contained in, human language.

As usual, Ephrem employs many subtle verbal allusions to a variety of different biblical passages; amongst these it is interesting to find the "sapphire brick," which is a reference to Exod 24:10, a passage which gave rise to a great deal of mystical speculation among both Christian and Jewish writers.

An excellent study of Ephrem's approach to reading the biblical text is provided by Griffith 1997.

Meter

The *qala* is given as *bayya*ʾ*(w) b-mulkane,* the opening words of *Par.* 7. This is the widely used *pardaisa* meter, for which see on Text 1 [pp. 2–3].

Text

The cycle *On Faith* is preserved in four sixth-century manuscripts: British Library Add. 12176 (Beck's A), Vatican Syr. 111 (dated 522; Beck's B), Vatican Syr. 113 (Beck's C), and British Library Add. 14571 (dated 519; Beck's D). The opening of the present *madrasha* is lost in C (which begins at stanza 9), and the whole poem is absent from D.

ܥܠ ܩܠܐ ܕܥܠܘ ܒܡܫܘܚܬܐ

1. ܢܘܪܐ ܠܒܫܝ ܕܠܒܫ ܡܫܘܚܬܐ ܕܗܘܡܠ
ܐܘܪܚܐ ܕܡܫܟܗ ܠܗ ܕܢܠܦ ܕܡܫܟ ܠܝ
ܟܢܫܐ ܕܟܢܫ ܠܗ ܕܢܗܘܐ ܕܝܠܐ ܠܝ
ܡܫܘܚܬܐ ܕܪܒܘܬܐ ܠܟܠ ܠܚܘܕ
ܘܟܕ ܥܡܗ ܒܐܝܩܪܗ ܫܡܫܐ ܘܬܘܬܐ ܢܥܡܐ
ܠܟܠ ܗܘܐ ܡܫܘܚܝܢ ܡܛܠ ܡܫܝܚܘܬܢ

ܥܘܢܝܬܐ : ܒܪܝܟ ܗܘ ܕܒܟܠ ܙܒܢܝܢ ܐܬܚܙܝ ܠܐܢܫܘܬܢ

2. ܢܫܒ ܕܝܠܗ ܠܐ ܠܟܠ ܗܘܐ ܡܫܘܚܝܢ
ܘܡܠܘܢ ܕܪܒܘܬܐ ܠܐ ܐܬܡܪܝ ܡܠܠ
ܟܡܘܢ ܕܐܢܫܘܬܢ ܒܝܠܟ ܡܢܟ ܙܐܘܝ
ܡܫܘܚܬܐ ܠܟܠ ܕܝܠܟ ܕܢܠܒܫ
ܘܡܠܗ ܒܗܘܢܬܐ ܐܫܟܚ ܡܠܠ ܘܠܟܠ
ܘܐܝܟ ܐܝܠܐ ܟܡ ܡܠܘܪܐ ܡܠܠ ܟܡ ܡܟܪܘܬܢ

1. Let us give thanks to [God] who has clothed Himself
   in the names of the [body's] various parts:

   [Scripture] refers to His "ears," to teach us that He listens to us; Ps 34:15

   it speaks of His "eyes," to show that He sees us. Ps 34:15

   It was just the names of such things that He put on,

   and—although in His true Being there is no wrath or regret— Gen 6:6; 1 Sam 15:29

   yet He put on these terms because of our weakness.

   Refrain: Blessed is He who has appeared to our human race
   under so many metaphors.

2. We should realize that, had He not put on the names

   of such things, it would not have been possible for Him

   to speak with us humans. By means of what belongs to us
   did He draw close to us:

   He clothed Himself in our language, so that He might clothe us

   in His mode of life. He asked for our form and put this on,

   and then, as a father with his children,
   He spoke with our childish state.

3. ܗܘ ܗܘ ܕܡܘܬܢ ܠܒܫ ܠܒܫܗ ܘܠܐ ܠܒܫܗ
ܡܟܝܟ ܘܠܐ ܡܟܝܟ ܟܕ ܒܟܠܗ ܡܟܝܟ ܗܘܐ ܠܗ
ܠܒܫܗ ܒܥܘܕܪܢܐ ܘܡܟܝܟܗ ܒܡܫܘܚܬܐ
ܟܕ ܠܒܫ ܡܟܝܟ ܘܒܥܝܢ ܒܟܠ ܕܡܘ
ܟܠܗ ܕܠܗ ܗܘ ܗܘ ܕܡܘܬܢ ܘܐܠܗܘܬܗ
ܘܟܣܝܐ ܗܝ ܐܠܗܘܬܗ ܪܘܙܗ ܒܐܢܫܘܬܐ

4. ܗܘܐ ܒܕܘܟ ܐܝܟ ܣܒܐ ܘܡܠܦ ܠܣܦܪ̈ܐ
ܗܘܐ ܬܘܒ ܐܝܟ ܓܒܪܐ ܚܟܝܡܐ ܘܡܪܒܝܢܐ
ܒܫܢܝܐ ܗܘܐ ܣܒܐ ܒܓܘܐ ܗܘܐ ܚܟܝܡܐ
ܒܕܘܟܐ ܐܝܟ ܡܣܟܢܐ ܘܙܠ ܗܘܐ
ܒܕܘܟܐ ܗܘܐ ܠܐܝܐ ܒܕܘܟܐ ܗܘܐ ܕܡܟܐ
ܒܕܘܟܐ ܗܘܐ ܣܢܝܩܐ ܒܟܠ ܦܪܘܣ ܠܗ ܕܢܥܬܪܢ

3. It is our terms that He has put on—
    though He did not literally do so;

He then took them off—without actually doing so: when wearing
    them, He was at the same time stripped of them.

He puts on one when it is beneficial,
    then strips it off in exchange for another;

the fact that He strips off and puts on all sorts of metaphors

tells us that the metaphor does not apply to His true Being:

because that Being is hidden,
    He has depicted it by means of what is visible.

4. In one place He was like an Old Man and the Ancient of Days,[1] Dan 7:9

then again, He became like a Hero, a Valiant Warrior. Exod 15:3

For the purpose of judgment, He was an Old Man,
    but for conflict He was valiant.

In one place He was delaying; elsewhere, having run,

He became weary. In one place He was asleep, Isa 7:13; Ps 44:23; 78:66

in another, in need: by every means
    did He weary Himself so as to gain us.

1. Ancient of Days: In Ephrem the Ancient of Days designates the Father (*Nis.* 4.7; *Haer.* 32.5), whereas in later Syriac (and Greek) poetry it more frequently refers to the Son: this is due to the indirect influence of the Old Greek text of Dan 7:13, where "a son of man" does not come *to* the Ancient of Days (so the Aramaic, Peshitta, and standard Greek Text ["Theodotion"]), but is "like" him.

5. ܗܘܝܘ ܓܝܪ ܛܘܒܐ ܕܒ ܡܪܐ ܕܟܘܡܪܐ
ܢܣܦܪܢ ܕܠܐ ܟܡܠܐ ܒܡܠܠܐ ܒܟܠܐ ܦܘܪܫܢ
ܘܢܣܦܪ ܒܪܒܘܬܗ ܘܐܢܫܐ ܚܕܘܪ ܣܘܦܪܢ
ܒܫܡܫܬܐ ܕܚܐܪܘܬܢ ܡܟܝܢܐ
ܘܐܦ ܗܘ ܡܪܟܒܬ ܠܟ ܒܪܟܒܐ ܗܘ ܕܡܢ ܐܢܫܝ
ܘܐܣܪ ܒܫܡܫܬܗܘܢ ܪܐܙ ܡܪܟܒܬ ܠܗ

6. ܘܐܦ ܗܘ ܕܡܠܟ ܠܗ ܡܫܝܚܐ ܒܦܪܝܫܬܐ
ܒܫܠܘܢܗ ܘܡܫܬܐܠܬܐ ܛܒܐ ܘܡܠܟ ܠܗ
ܗܘܝܘ ܗܐ ܕܦܬܟ ܠܒܪܗ ܕܗܘ ܡܫܝܚܐ
ܘܡܢܬܗ ܡܢ ܟܬܒܗ ܡܫܝܚܐ
ܘܫܒܪܐ ܕܫܒܪܬܗ ܗܘ ܡܫܬܘܪܐ ܒܫܡܗ
ܘܡܢܬܗ ܐܬܐ ܡܘܕܥܗ ܕܗܘ ܡܫܝܚܘܬܗ ܐܬܟ

7. ܗܘ ܕܝܢ ܦܪܝܫܬܐ ܡܫܝܚܐ ܗܘ ܒܟܪܝܗܐ
ܘܟܕ ܠܒ ܐܣܝܘܬܐ ܗܘ ܐܝܟ ܗܘ ܕܢܘܒܪܝܢ
ܠܗ ܟܗ ܫܒܠܐ ܘܠܟ ܟܘ ܗܘ ܡܠܐ ܟܡܗ
ܐܬܘܬܐ ܕܟܠܐ ܡܢ ܟܠܐ ܡܟܟܒܐ
ܒܢܘܟܗ ܕܝܢ ܕܘܡܗ ܒܪܝ ܡܢܗ ܡܢܝ
ܟܡܟܬ ܒܟܠܐ ܡܠܐ ܘܐܦܝܐ ܒܟܠܐ ܪܐܙܗ

5. For this is the Good One, who could have forced us to please Him,
without any trouble to Himself; but instead He toiled by every means
so that we might act pleasingly to Him of our own volition,
 that we might depict our beauty
with the colors that our own free will[2] had gathered;
whereas, if He had adorned us, then we would have resembled
a portrait that someone else had painted,
 adorning it with his own colors.

6. A person who is teaching a parrot to speak
hides behind a mirror and teaches it in this way:
when the bird turns in the direction of the voice speaking,
it finds in front of its eyes its own resemblance reflected;
it imagines that it is another parrot, conversing with itself.
[The man] puts [the bird's] image in front of it,
 so that thereby it might learn how to speak.

7. This bird is related to man,[3]
but although this relationship exists, the man beguiles and teaches
[the parrot] something alien to itself by means of itself;
 in this way he speaks with it.
The divine Being that in all things is exalted above all things
in Its love Its height bent down and
 It acquired from us our own customs;
It has labored by every means so as to turn all to Itself.

---

2. free will *(ḥeʾruta):* Lit. "freedom." Ephrem always gives great emphasis to the importance of the gift to humanity of free will.

3. related to man: That is, as a fellow creature.

8. ܕܡܦܩܬܗ ܕܫܡܫܐ ܗܝ ܟܝܢ ܐܘ ܗܝ ܕܡܥܪܒܐ
ܕܗܘ ܗܝ ܕܟܠܡܕܡ ܕܪܕܦ ܐܘ ܕܗܘ ܕܠܐ ܢܐܚ
ܕܗܘ ܗܝ ܕܟܠܡܕܡ ܕܠܐܝ ܐܘ ܕܗܘ ܕܠܐ ܠܐܐ
ܒܐܬܪ ܗܢܐ ܟܒܪ ܕܢܟܦ
ܒܒܝܬܐ ܕܫܟܝܠܐ ܐܬܦܫܛ ܘܩܡ ܒܒܝܬܗ
ܦܣܩ ܗܘܐ ܡܠܐ ܫܡܝܐ ܟܕ ܟܠ ܒܡܘܒܠܗ ܗܘ

9. ܢܦܫܗ ܫܦܝ ܒܕܘܟܐ ܘܫܦܝ ܒܟܠ ܕܘܟܐ
ܡܒܪܢ ܕܗܘܐ ܒܕܘܟܐ ܗܘ ܗܘܐ ܠܗ ܡܠܐ ܒܟܠܐ
ܐܡܪ ܕܠܝ ܢܦܫܝ ܡܢܝ ܕܠܝ ܢܥܒܕ
ܐܡܪ ܘܐܬܐ ܡܢܝ ܕܢܘܕܥ
ܐܘ ܐܡܪ ܘܠܐ ܡܢܝ ܐܡܪ ܘܡܢܟܪ ܠܟ
ܕܡܫܠܡܢ ܕܢܚܠܐ ܗܘ ܟܕ ܚܙܘ ܐܡܪ ܘܡܢܝ

8. His likeness is that of an Old Man, or of a Hero;

of Him it is written that He slept,
        or again, that He slumbers not; Ps 120 (121):3–4

of Him it is written that He was weary,
        or again, that He wearies not. Isa 40:28

By binding and loosing He has helped [us] in order to teach us:

in the case of the sapphire brick,
        He contracted Himself and stood above it, Exod 24:10

then He extended Himself and filled the heaven,
        everything being in the palm of His hand. Isa 40:12

9. He manifested Himself somewhere,
        He manifested Himself everywhere;

we imagined He was somewhere, but everything is filled with Him.

He becomes small[4] that He might make us sufficient;
        He became great in order to enrich us.

He becomes small, and then again great, in order to magnify us.

Had He become small and not become again great,
        He would have been small and abused by us,

because He would have been thought to be weak.
        Therefore He became small and then again great.

---

4. becomes small: "The Great One who became small" is a phrase to designate the incarnation that is quite frequently found in Ephrem and other Syriac poets; cf. Text 8 (*Res.* 1), stanza 22.

10. ܢܛܪܗ ܕܡܠܐ ܕܐܡܪ ܐܘܪܚ ܐܒܗܘܬܢ
ܘܐܠܐ ܗܦܟ ܥܢܕ ܐܒܪܗ ܠܛܘܒܝܬܢ
ܕܡܪܐ ܕܫܟܡܐ ܗܘ ܘܒܪܐ ܒܝܬܐ ܕܡܪܢܐ
ܐܝܟܢܐ ܗܘ ܕܒܪܒܘܬܗ ܠܐ ܣܦܩ
ܐܦܠܐ ܠܡܒܘܪܘܬܗ ܡ̈ܢܟ ܦܘܡܢ ܠܗ
ܘܐܡܪ ܠܫܒܚܢ ܠܗ ܒܟܠ ܗܘ ܒܟܠ ܒܟܡ

11. ܕܢܦܩ ܙܒܢܐ ܐܬܪܝܟ ܕܗܘ ܗܘܐ ܘܠܐ ܗܘ ܗܘܐ
ܒܟܪ ܠܗ ܐܦܐ ܒܣܘܦܗ ܕܟܣܝܘܗܝ ܒܢܘܪܐ ܠܗ
ܘܠܐ ܙܝܢ ܢܫܬܟܚ ܘܢܫܪܐ ܕܗܘܝ ܗܘ
ܡܢ ܕܡܘ ܠܒܘܫܗ ܚܝܝ ܕܢܦܩ
ܕܠܗ ܠܟܠ ܠܗ ܕܡܘܬܐ ܘܥܕ ܠܐ ܢܦܩ ܡܢܗ
ܕܙܘܬܐ ܕܐܝܡܘܬܐ ܢܦܩ ܠܗ ܒܡܘܬܒܘܬܗܘܢ

10. Let us wonder at how, when He became small,
        He made our own small state great.

Had He not reverted and become great,
        He would have made our opinion of Him small,

imagining Him to be weak—and by thus imagining,
        our conception [of God] would be diminished.

He is an Essence whose greatness we are not capable of grasping—

no, not even in His smallness.
        He grew great—when we had gone astray;

He grew small—when we had grown feeble.
        In every way did He labor over us.

11. He wished to teach us two things: that He became [flesh],
        yet He did not come into being. John 1:14

In His love He made for Himself a countenance,
        so that His servants might behold Him;

but, lest we be harmed by imagining He was really like this,

He moved from one likeness to another, to teach us

that He has no likeness. And though He did not depart

from the form of humanity, yet by His changes[5] He did depart.

◆

5. changes: For a discussion of this term in Ephrem, see McVey 1988.

TEXT 3

The Symbols Depicted by Noah in the Ark (*Fid.* 49)

This comparatively short poem provides a good example of Ephrem's imaginative use of typology. Noah is an important figure in any typological understanding of the Old Testament. Just as Christ stands at the end of the Old Testament and at the beginning of the New, so Noah stands at another key turning point in the biblical history of humanity: he alone, because of his righteousness, survives the Flood, together with his family, and thus witnesses a new beginning. The Ark, which ensures his safety, is also laden with symbols: guided by Christ, its "steersman," it travels crosslike over the surface of the earth, foretelling the Cross; at the same time the Ark serves as a type of the Church and of Faith, while the Flood too points forward to the new waters of Baptism. But, whereas the waters of the Flood brought death to sinners, those of Baptism, by contrast, will bring salvation to sinners who take refuge in the Church, the new Ark. The dove, too, which conveys an olive twig back to Noah, announcing the recession of the waters of the Flood (Gen 8:11), symbolizes the Holy Spirit who anoints with olive oil all who are baptized. Ephrem's self-deprecatory words in the final stanza are a characteristic feature of many of his poems.

A number of these themes reappear in other texts in this collection, notably Text 16 (*Virg.* 7) and Text 19 (*Nis.* 1). A more literary translation of this poem (with a discussion of the imagery of the balance) is given by Palmer (1993b, 175–82).

Meter

The *qala* is given as *sheḥreh d-Bardaisan,* the opening words of *Haer.* 56. Ephrem uses the meter in *Fid.* 49–65 and *Haer.* 14, 49–51, and 53–56. The metrical pattern consists of six pairs of five syllables. For the acrostic, see the General Introduction (p. xv).

Text

The *madrasha* is preserved in Beck's manuscripts A, B, and C (see above, on Text 2 [p. 17]).

ܥܠ ܛܠܝܐ ܕܚܣܪܘ ܕܒܪ̈ܝܬܐ

1. ܐܘ ܡܢ ܕܚܙܐ ܗܘܐ ܢܦܫ ܕܐܝܟ ܒܫܘܫܢܬܐ
ܒܦܠܓܘܗܝ ܒ̈ܢܝ ܓܢܣܗ ܫܦܝܪ ܗܘܐ ܒܡܫܬܠܬܐ
ܕܐܬܩܒܠ ܒܠܒܘܬܐ ܘܢܬܠܚܡ ܚܕܐ ܢܦܫܐ
ܠܥܝܢܐ ܕܢܦܫܬܐ ܠܚܡܗ ܗܘܐ ܒܫܘܦܪܐ
ܕܠܗ ܗܘܐ ܒܡܫܬܥܠܐ ܘܐܬܪܝܡ ܒܩܘܡܬܐ
ܢܦܫܐ ܘܩܛܝܪܐ ܗܦܟܐ ܒܕܡܝܐ ܠܗ

ܥܘܢܝܬܐ : ܐܡܟܝܢ ܒܥܘܕܪܢܟ

1. How splendid was Noah, whose example surpassed

that of all his contemporaries:
they were weighed in the scales of justice

and were found wanting; a single soul, with its armor of chastity,[1]

outbalanced [them all]. They were drowned in the Flood,

having proved too light in the scales, while in the Ark[2]

the chaste and weighty Noah was lifted up.
Glory be to [God] who took pleasure in Noah!

Refrain: Praises to Your dominion!

---

1. armor of chastity: Observing the chronological data in the biblical text, Ephrem and other Syriac writers deduce that Noah observed *qaddishuta,* or abstinence from marital intercourse, for the first five hundred years of his life. (See also Text 5 [*Nat.* 17], n. 6.)

2. Ark *(kewela):* This is the term found in Matt 24:38 (Peshitta) and in Luke 17:27 (Curetonianus and Peshitta); in Peshitta Genesis (and Sinaiticus at both Matt 24:38 and Luke 17:27) *qibota* is employed, and this is the term that Aphrahat always employs. Ephrem's use of *kewela* and its appearance in Curetonianus, however, indicate that the term had already come into use prior to the time of the Peshitta revision of the New Testament (ca. 400); perhaps the intention was to provide a distinction between Noah's Ark and the Ark of the Covenant (also *qibota,* alongside *arona*).

2. ܦܬܚ ܢܦܫ ܐܣܬܟܠܬܗ ܒܝܢܬ ܐܝܟ ܓܒ̈ܝܢ
ܘܪܕܡ ܐܝܟ ܛܘܦܢܐ ܫܒܩ ܠܗܘ ܕܒܥܐ
ܘܡܠܐ ܠܗ ܕܗܘܐ ܘܒܝܢܬ ܐܝܟ ܕܝܢ
ܡܫܚ ܐܝܟ ܐ̱ܪ̈ܝܢ ܕܐܦܢ ܠܥܒ̈ܕܝܢ
ܘܐܝܟ ܐܦ ܠܐܣܝ̈ܐ ܓܒܪܐ ܡܒܪ ܣܒܐ
ܘܢܦܫ ܒܟܢܘܫܬܐ ܐܫܡܥܝܢ ܠܥܠܡ ܕܒܝܬܗ܀

3. ܦܪܫܬ ܒܛܘܦܢܐ ܟܠܗ ܕܡܪܐ ܟܠ
ܡܢ ܡܕܢܚܐ ܢܦܩܬ ܘܠܡܥܪܒܐ ܫܡܫܬ
ܥܠ ܝܡܐ ܗܠܟܬ ܘܒܓܙܪ̈ܬܐ ܡܫܚܬ
ܦܪܫܬ ܕܟܠ ܥܡ̈ܐ ܢܣܐ ܗܘܐ ܒܥܕܬܐ
ܘܐܟܪܙ ܕܡܫܝܚܗ ܦܪܐ ܠܟܠ ܓܒ̈ܝܢ
ܘܡܠܐ ܠܟܠ ܦܢ̈ܝܢ ܐܫܡܥܝܢ ܠܦܪܘܩܗ

2. Noah extended his ministry either side [of the Flood],

depicting two types, sealing up the one that had passed,

opening up that which followed. Between these two generations

he ministered to two symbols,[3] dismissing the former,

making preparation for the latter.
He buried the generation grown old,

and nurtured the youthful one.
Praises be to the One who chose him!

3. Over the Flood the ship of the Lord of all[4] flew:

it departed from the east, it rested in the west,

it flew off to the south, and measured out the north;

its flight over the water served as a prophecy for the dry land,

preaching how its progeny would be fruitful in every quarter,

abounding in every region. Praises to its Savior!

---

3. symbols *(razaw[hy]): Raza,* of Persian origin, is capable of many senses in Syriac. In Biblical Aramaic it simply meant "secret," but in Syriac it normally means either "mysteries" (corresponding to Greek *musteria*), or (as here) "symbols," with a strong sense, in that for Ephrem (and early Christian writers in general) the symbol is understood as partaking in what it symbolizes, and is not simply just like (but essentially different from) it, as in the modern usage of the term. On Ephrem's use of this and related terms, see especially Murray 1975–76 and Beck 1982.

4. Lord of all: The title is already found in Peshitta Sir 24:8 and in Wis 6:7 and 8:3. It is very common in Ephrem, who is particularly fond of titles where the second element is *koll;* on this feature see Botha 1993.

4. ܪܡܫܐ ܒܥܘܒܗ̇   ܢܐܡ ܕܢܛܘܪܗ
ܙܡܪܗ ܕܫܦܝܪܐ   ܘܫܡܥܗ ܕܡܚܒܢܐ
ܕܐܬܐ ܡܪܒܝ ܠܟ   ܠܒܬܐ ܕܝܠܗ ܡܟܐ
ܘܒܬܪ ܠܒܢܝܬܐ   ܡܫܘܐܒ ܒܪܝܫܗ
ܘܪܘܚܐ ܣܓܕ ܗܘܐ   ܡܫܡܫܐ ܡܫܡܫܢܘܬܗ
ܘܢܘܪܐ ܕܦܘܪܩܢܗ   ܐܩܝܡ ܒܦܪܘܩܗ

5. ܬܘܕܝ ܠܐܘܪܚܐ   ܘܫܘܒܚܘܗܝ ܒܒܬܘܠܐ
ܡܘܕܝ ܚܕܐ ܠܚܕܐ   ܕܐܝܟ ܕܐܫܬܦܩܘ
ܠܥܠܡܗ ܕܒܬܘܠܐ   ܗܘܝ ܐܦ ܐܫܬܦܩܘ
ܠܡܦܩܐ ܕܒܥܠܬܐ   ܕܚܝܐ ܒܫܒܝܠܬܗ
ܐܘܪܐ ܕܢܡܘܣܐ   ܘܡܫܚ ܒܒܪܬܗ
ܠܡܦܩܐ ܕܒܬܘܠܐ   ܡܘܚܒܐ ܒܫܒܝܠܬܗ

4. [The Ark] marked out by its course the sign of its Preserver,
—the Cross of its Steersman,[5] and the Wood of its Sailor
who has come to fashion for us a Church in the waters [of baptism]:
with the threefold name He rescues those who reside in her,
and in place of the dove, the Spirit administers Her anointing[6]
and the mystery of His salvation. Praises to its Savior!

5. His symbols are in the Law,[7] His types are in the Ark,
each bears testimony to the other: just as the Ark's recesses
were emptied out, so too the types in Scripture
were emptied out; for by His coming He embraced
the symbol of the Law, and in His churches He brought to completion
the types of the Ark. Praise be to Your coming!

---

5. its Steersman *(sappaneh):* Thus also *Nis.* 1.3 (Text 19, stanza 3).

6. Her anointing: In early Syriac texts, including both Ephrem and Aphrahat, the Holy Spirit is treated grammatically as feminine, inviting the use of feminine imagery (though in Ephrem, in particular, this is by no means just confined to the Spirit). On the Holy Spirit as grammatically feminine, see Brock 1991a, and in general on female imagery in Ephrem, see McVey 2001.

7. Law *(ʾurayta):* Ephrem uses the Jewish Aramaic term here (and sometimes elsewhere) instead of the more normal Greek loanword *namosa* (from *nomos*).

6. ܪܒܝܚ ܗܘܐ ܦܘܡܐ ܕܢܦܠ ܒܡܡܘܬܗ
ܕܚܝܠܐ ܕܦܪܘܩ ܠܒܘܒܝ ܚܢܘܢ ܕܐܦ
ܛܥܡ ܒܡܡܘܬܐ ܠܐܦܘ ܘܒܡܘܬܗ
ܢܦܩܘ ܒܢܝܐ ܕܗܘܐ ܐܬܐ ܡܢ ܘܡܫܒܚܬܐ
ܠܐܦܐ ܒܢܘܚܡܬܐ ܕܗܘܐ ܠܒܢܝ ܫܒܠܐ
ܒܫܘܡܐ ܕܒܫܘܩܝ ܐܡܬܝ ܒܢܘܢܕܝ

6. My mind wanders, having fallen into the flood

of our Savior's power. Blessed is Noah who,

though his ship—the Ark—floated around over the Flood,

yet his soul was recollected. May my faith, Lord,

be a ship for my weakness, for the foolish are drowned

in the depths of their prying into You.[8]
Praises be to Him who begot You!

◆

8. prying into You: For Ephrem, the human intellect can legitimately investigate all that belongs to Creation, but he is always insistent that it is both impossible and blasphemous to try to cross over the "chasm" that lies between Creator and Creation. Since the Son lies beyond this chasm, any investigation, or prying into, his eternal generation from the Father (such as was undertaken by the neo-Arians) is utterly anathema to Ephrem. (For the important theme of the unbridgeable [except by God] "chasm" in Ephrem, see Koonammakkal 1998.)

TEXT 4

The Paradox of Mary's Birthgiving
(*Nat.* 11)

Mary features prominently in several of the *madrashe* on the Nativity, and Ephrem introduces a profusion of Old Testament symbols and types that illustrate the relationship between her and the wondrous Child she bears. In the present poem he only employs a few of these, as he ponders on the paradox of the virgin mother, the mortal being who bears the Godhead, the container who contains the Uncontainable.

Stanza 6 provides the title and words for John Tavener's "Thunder Entered Her."

Meter

The *qala* is given as *manu sapeq la-mmallalu,* a title taken from the opening words of *Eccl.* 38. The meter consists of 4+4+4 4+4+4+4 4+4+4 syllables. Ephrem employs this meter in *Nat.* 5–20, *Eccl.* 38–42 (where the *qala* title is given as *hanaw yarḥa,* the opening words of *Nat.* 5), *Fid.* 81–87, *Haer.* 41–44 and 46, and *Ieiun.* appendix 1 (for this, and for *Haer.* 46, the *qala* title is given as *hanaw yarḥa*). In later liturgical manuscripts this meter is sometimes also given the *qala* title *marganita* (based on *Fid.* 81–85, "On the Pearl").

Text

The poem is preserved complete only in Vatican Syr. 112 of 551 CE (Beck's G). Beck's edition also makes use of five later manuscripts, of the ninth to the eleventh century, but these only give select verses (thus, for example, the earliest of these, British Library Add. 14515 of 873 CE [Beck's M], has only verses 1–4 and 6).

ܥܠ ܩܠܐ ܕܡܢܗ ܢܦܩ ܒܡܡܠܠܗ

1. ܠܦܘܡܝ ܡܪܝ ܠܐ ܐܢܫ ܣܟܠ
ܐܡܢ ܢܦܪܘܫ ܒܬܘܒܬܐ ܢܦܪܘܫ
ܡܪܢ ܩܐܡ ܘܡܬܒܥܐ
ܠܐ ܐܢܫ ܢܟܠܝܘܗܝ ܘܐܦ ܗܘ ܕܐܡܪ
ܠܐ ܬܬܟܪܐ ܠܟ ܡܢ ܢܦܫܟ

ܒܥܘܬܐ : ܠܘܬ ܐܒܗܘܬܐ ܕܕܚܠܐ ܠܗ ܟܠ
ܐܝܟ ܡܪܐ ܟܠ

2. ܐܡܪ ܗܘܐ ܒܚܙ ܗܘ ܒܚܘܪܗ
ܘܚܠܝ ܒܗ ܟܠ ܗܘܬ ܠܟ ܐܝܟ
ܗܘܬ ܠܟ ܚܕܐ ܡܟܢܫܝܢ ܗܘܐ ܠܗܘܢ
ܟܕ ܢܣܒܬܐ ܒܦܠܓܝܢ ܗܘܐ
ܗܐ ܙܒܢܐ ܗܘܦܪܐ ܕܐܡܗ

1. No one quite knows, Lord, what to call

Your mother: should we call her "virgin"?

—but her giving birth is an established fact; or "married woman"?

—but no man has known her. If your mother's case

is beyond comprehension, who can hope to understand Yours?[1]

Refrain: Praise to You to whom all things are easy,[2]
for You are Lord of all.

2. She alone is Your mother,

but she is Your sister,[3] with everyone else. She became Your mother,

she became Your sister, she was Your bride too,

along with all chaste [souls].[4] You, who are Your mother's beauty,

Yourself have adorned her with everything!

---

1. There is an underlying anti-Arian polemic implied at the end of this verse.
2. Perhaps based on Matt 19:26 and parallels; similarly Text 19 (*Nis.* 1), stanza 10.
3. sister: Since the baptized have become brothers and sisters to Christ at baptism (cf. Rom 8:29) and Mary's own baptism is understood as having occurred through the presence of Christ in her womb (see Text 5 [*Nat.* 17], n. 3).
4. bride . . . along with all chaste [souls]: See Text 18 (*Fid.* 14), where the soul is the bride of Christ (with the body as the bridal chamber).

3. ܡܟܝܪܬܐ ܕܗܘܬ ܠܓܒܪ ܗܘ ܕܒܢܝܐ
ܟܕ ܠܐ ܐܢܬܬܐ ܫܡܫܬ ܗܘܬ ܕܝܢ
ܕܠܐ ܟܝܢܐ ܒܪ ܕܐܬܝܠܕ
ܐܘ ܩܕܝܫܐ ܘܒܬܘܠܬܐ ܗܘܬ
ܟܕ ܝܠܕܬ ܩܕܝܫܬܐ

4. ܡܢܐ ܒܗ ܡܪܝܡ ܚܕܬܐ ܒܥܘܠܘܗܝ
ܘܒܬܘܠܬܐ ܫܡܐ ܒܥܠܗ
ܕܠܐ ܐܘܟܠܐ ܢܚܬܐ ܒܟܪܣܗ
ܕܠܐ ܒܥܒܪܐ ܠܐܘܪܚܐ ܕܐܢܬܬܐ
ܡܟܝܪܐ ܕܫܡܥܐ ܒܒܬܘܠܗ ܥܡ ܒܥܠ

5. ܐܘ ܒܪ ܐܠܗܐ ܛܘܪ ܕܝܢܐ
ܐܟܘܠ ܦܐܪܗ ܐܘ ܒܪ ܐܟܘܠ
ܫܡܥܘܠ ܘܚܙܐ ܐܘ ܒܪ ܐܫܝܐ
ܕܒܢܝܢ ܒܬܘܠܬ ܐܘ ܒܪ ܐܒܪܗܡ
ܒܢܘܪܐ ܕܚܫܚܐ ܢܛܪܐ ܒܩܘܒܗ

3. She was betrothed [to Joseph] in a natural way
before You came; she conceived in a manner
quite beyond nature after You had come,
O Holy One, and was a virgin
when she gave birth to You in a holy fashion.

4. With You Mary underwent all that
married women undergo: conception
—but without intercourse; milk [flowed][5] in her breasts
—but against nature's pattern: You made her, the thirsty earth, Isa 53:2
all of a sudden into a fountain of milk!

5. If she could carry You, it was because You, the great mountain, Dan 2:35
had lightened Your weight; if she feeds You, it is because
You had taken on hunger; if she gives You to drink, Matt 4:2
it is because You, of Your own will, had thirsted;
if she fondles You, John 4:7
[You, who are] the fiery coal[6] of mercy,
preserved her bosom unharmed. Isa 6:7

---

5. milk [flowed]: The miraculous nature of this is again brought out in Text 7 (*Eccl.* 36), stanza 4; compare also *Odes of Solomon* 35.6.

6. fiery coal: The term, taken from Isaiah's vision (Isa 6:7), is also used of the eucharistic host in Text 17 (*Fid.* 10).

6. ܛܘܪܐ ܗܘ ܐܡܝܢ ܥܠ ܒܪܗ ܡܪܐ
ܘܗܘܐ ܥܒܕܐ ܥܠ ܡܠܟܐ
ܘܫܒܩ ܥܗܕܗ ܥܠ ܒܪܗ ܪܒܝܐ
ܘܫܠܡ ܡܠܬܗ ܥܠ ܪܒܐ ܒܟܠ
ܐܡܪܐ ܗܘܐ ܒܗ ܢܦܩ ܥܕ ܦܬܐ

7. ܛܒܫܐ ܘܦܠܛ ܒܪܫܐ ܕܐܡܝܢ
ܡܠܟ ܒܟܠܐ ܥܠ ܥܠܡܝܢܐ
ܢܦܩ ܥܕ ܡܫܡܫܝܢ ܥܠ ܒܪܗ ܪܡܐ
ܢܦܩ ܥܕ ܡܫܝܢ ܥܠ ܒܪܗ ܐܒܐ
ܘܟܠܗ ܘܢܦܩ ܥܘܠܐ ܫܡܝܐ

8. ܥܠ ܥܝܕܪܐ ܘܟܠܗ ܩܢܝܐ
ܩܡ ܥܘ ܒܪܫܐ ܥܠ ܐܝܢ ܒܟܠ
ܘܡܢܐ ܥܦܢܐ ܥܠ ܡܫܩܐ ܒܟܠ
ܘܡܢܐ ܙܘܡܐ ܥܪܬܐ ܘܫܒܚ
ܢܦܩ ܗܘܐ ܩܢܘܢ ܡܟܠܝܗ ܟܠܠ

6. Your mother is a cause for wonder: the Lord entered into her
and became a servant; He who is the Word entered
—and became silent within her; Thunder entered her cf. Ps 29:3
—and made no sound; there entered the Shepherd of all,[7]
and in her He became the Lamb, bleating as He came forth.

7. Your mother's womb has reversed the roles:
the Establisher of all entered in His richness,
but came forth poor; the Exalted One entered her,
but came forth meek; the Splendrous One entered her,
but came forth having put on a lowly hue.

8. The Mighty One entered, and put on insecurity
from within the womb; the Provisioner of all[8] entered
—and experienced hunger; He who gives drink to all entered
—and experienced thirst: naked and stripped
there came forth from her He who clothes everything![9]

◆

7. Shepherd of all: A title that is also found in *Nat.* 4.128, 18.19, and elsewhere in Ephrem.

8. Provisioner of all: This occurs as a title of Christ a number of times in Ephrem's poetry, e.g., *Virg.* 23.10, 30.4, and 36.8; it already occurs in the *Acts of Thomas* 113 (Wright 1871, 1:280), although there it refers to the Father.

9. clothes everything: That is, in the case of human beings, with the "robe of glory" at baptism; for this see Text 5 (*Nat.* 17), n. 3.

TEXT 5

Mary's Invitation to Everyone (*Nat.* 17)

In the opening four stanzas it is Mary who speaks, describing her experience as the mother of such an extraordinary child. She ends by contrasting herself with Eve, who put on "leaves of shame," whereas she has put on a "robe of glory"—an allusion to the baptism she is considered to have received by virtue of the presence of Christ in her womb (see the notes below). In stanzas 5 and 6 Ephrem addresses Christ, but the speaker reverts to Mary again in stanza 7, where she begins to address various categories of women (including slaves), telling them what her Son can offer them. Her words continue at least to the end of stanza 11, after which the voice of the poet himself seems to speak directly. In stanzas 12–18 there is a polemical undercurrent, aimed against the Marcionites, who held that the world was created by a Just God (the Demiurge) who was different from the supreme God of love with whom the incarnation was associated. Ephrem understands that the blind man healed in John 9:6 had been born without any pupils. The miracle is thus not just of healing, but constitutes an act of creation—which makes nonsense of Marcion's views.

Meter

The phrase *bar qaleh* indicates that the *qala* is the same as for the previous poem; for this see on Text 4 (*Nat.* 11).

Text

The poem is preserved complete in two sixth-century manuscripts, British Library Add. 14571 (of 519 CE; Beck's D) and Vatican Syr. 112 (of 551 CE, Beck's G). The later manuscripts used in Beck's edition again only preserve select verses.

ܒܪ ܩܠܗ

1. ܛܥܝܢ ܥܘܠܐ ܕܛܥܝܢܐ ܐܢܐ
ܐܡܪܐ ܡܪܝܡ ܘܐܪܟܢ ܟܢܦܘ̈ܗܝ
ܘܫܩܠ ܣܡܢܝ ܒܝܬ ܓܦ̈ܘܗܝ
ܘܦܪܚ ܒܐܐܪ ܘܐܫܬܘܕܝ ܠܝ
ܕܪܘܡܐ ܘܥܘܡܩܐ ܕܒܪܝ ܢܗܘܘܢ

ܥܘܢܝܬܐ : ܒܟ ܐܬܒܣܡܬ ܒܪ ܡܪܝܐ ܕܟܠ ܡܢܝܢ

2. ܚܙܬ ܓܒܪܐܝܠ ܕܡܪܝ ܩܪܐ
ܘܪܒ ܟܘܡܪ̈ܐ ܟܒܪ ܣܒܐ
ܕܐܚܕ ܠܒܪܗ ܚܙܬ ܠܡܓܘ̈ܫܐ
ܕܒ ܡܠܟ̈ܐ ܘܟܠܗܘܢ
ܕܒ ܡܠܟܘܬܐ ܕܐܬܐ ܡܟܒܐ

1. "The tiny Child I carry Himself carries me,"
said Mary; "He lowered His wings,
took me and placed me between His pinions;
He soared into the air, and promised me:
Both height and depth shall be your Son's."

Refrain: Praise to you, Son of the Creator,[1] Lover of all!

2. "I saw Gabriel, and he called Him 'Lord'; Luke 1:28
and [Simeon], chief of the priests, an aged servant, Luke 2:25–28
who carried Him in honor; I saw the Magi
—they bowed down to Him; while Herod I saw Matt 2:11
troubled, because the King had come. Matt 2:3

1. The title "Son of the Creator" given to Christ recurs in stanzas 14 and 18 and is deliberately anti-Marcionite. The same title occurs quite frequently in the cycles *On Faith* and *Against Heresies.*

3. ܐܦ ܡܫܝܚܐ   ܕܚܢܢ ܡܒ̈ܪܐ
ܕܢܐܒ ܡܘܬܐ   ܡܢܗܠܐ ܡܒ̈ܪܐ
ܕܢܚܘܬܐ ܚܝܐ   ܒܡܘܪܢܝ ܐܒܪܘܡ
ܕܐܬܐ ܒܚܘܒܗ   ܕܝܬܐ ܘܢܚܘܬܐ
ܕܒܪܢܗ   ܒܒܐ ܕܝܪܘܗ

4. ܒܡܘܟܟܗ   ܠܝܬܐ ܕܒܪܝܐ
ܒܟܡܟ ܚܘܐ   ܐܡܪ ܒܟܡܟ
ܒܡܘܟܟܗ   ܢܚܬܐ ܕܡܘܒܠܐ
ܕܒܟܠ ܫܡܝܢ   ܦܪܫܐ ܐܒܘܪܐ
ܕܦܓܪܐ ܚܘܒܟ   ܒܡܟܡܟܐ ܟܠ

3. "Satan, who slew the newborn of the Hebrews, Exod 1:16
wanting to destroy Moses, now kills the children, Matt 1:16
hoping that the Living One will die. To Egypt will I flee, Matt 1:13
as [Satan] has come to Judea to go toiling around,
trying to hunt his own Hunter.[2]

4. "In her virginity, Eve put on
leaves of shame, but your mother has put on, Gen 3:7
in her virginity, a garment of glory[3]
that encompasses all, while to Him who covers all
she gave a body as a tiny garment."

---

2. For Christ as the "Hunter" of Satan, compare *Commentary on the Diatessaron* 4.13, where he is "the Hunter of Death." Elsewhere Ephrem uses the title with a different emphasis: in *Sermo de Domino Nostro* 15 Christ is the Hunter who "hunts for the life/salvation of the lost," and in *Nat.* 4.36 and *Virg.* 32.8 he is "the Hunter for humanity" and "the Hunter for all."

3. The imagery of the Robe of Glory, deeply embedded in the Syriac tradition, is used to describe the various stages of salvation history: Adam and Eve are originally clothed in it in Paradise, but lose it at the Fall; Christ, the Divine Word who "put on the body," deposits humanity's lost Robe of Glory in the River Jordan at his baptism, and at each Christian baptism it is received in potential from the Font (often described both as the Jordan and as a womb; see Jones 2003); finally, at the Last Judgment, it becomes the clothing of the Righteous in reality (see Brock 1982 and 1999a). Since Christ's presence in the Jordan makes the Robe of Glory available again to humanity, his presence in Mary's womb is understood as constituting her baptism, thus providing her with her Robe of Glory (see Text 4 [*Nat.* 11], n. 3). Mary's giving Christ "a body as a tiny garment" and receiving in return a "Robe of Glory" is one of the ways in which Ephrem brings out the idea of exchange involved in the incarnation; this is expressed in *Fid.* 5.17 in epigrammatic form: "He gave us divinity, we gave Him humanity."

5. ܛܘܒܝܗ ܠܐܒܐ ܕܐܝܬ ܒܒܪܗ
ܘܒܪܚܡܬܗ ܚܙܝܐ ܡܚܒܐ ܗܘ
ܟܝ ܒܪ ܡܚܒܐ ܘܩܕܘܫ ܡܩܕܫܐ
ܟܝ ܗܘ ܒܦܘܫܩܐ ܠܐ ܙܕܩܐ ܠܗ
ܐܦ ܠܐ ܠܒܢܝܐ ܕܒܝܬܐ ܘܒܪܐ

6. ܗܘܐ ܠܗܘܢ ܚܕܐ ܢܦܫܐ ܘܦܓܪܐ
ܒܢܦܫܐ ܚܝܬܐ ܕܟܠܠ ܘܡܥܡܪ ܒܗ
ܡܠܬܗ ܚܝܬܐ ܗܘܬ ܠܗ ܠܚܝܐ
ܕܗܘܬ ܠܦܓܪܐ ܐܝܟ ܗܝ ܠܢܦܫܗ
ܘܐܝܟ ܗܝ ܒܢܦܫ ܘܐܫܬܠܛ ܒܘܗܝ

7. ܕܐܝܬ ܠܗ ܡܫܘܚܬܐ ܐܘ ܡܢܝܢܐ
ܗܐ ܢܬܚܘܡܘܗܝ ܕܐܝܬ ܠܗ ܟܝܠܐ
ܗܐ ܢܡܫܚܘܗܝ ܕܐܝܬ ܠܗ ܣܟܐ

5. Blessed is she, in whose heart and mind
You are: she is a royal palace[4]
—because of You, O Royal Son. She is the Holy of Holies
for You, the High Priest. She knows no worries Heb 8:1
or cares of home—or husband.

6. Eve proved the cranny—and the sepulcher—
for the accursed serpent; there entered her and dwelt in her
its evil counsel; she became its bread
since she had become dust. But You are our Bread,
You are our Bridal Chamber,[5] our Robe of Glory.

7. "Is any woman living in chastity[6] afraid?
—He shall preserve her. Has any some wrongdoing?
—He shall forgive it. Has any some evil spirit?

---

4. royal palace *(birta):* Perhaps based on Prov 9:1 (Wisdom built herself a house), though both Septuagint and Peshitta have "house." The description of Mary as a palace (based on the residence of Christ "the King" in her womb) becomes a commonplace in later Greek and Syriac liturgical poetry.

5. Bridal Chamber: Here evidently Christ's Body is meant, whereas in Text 18 (*Fid.* 14), stanza 5, it is the body of the communicant (though a variant reading identifies it, less appropriately there, as Christ's Body: see Text 18 [*Fid.* 14], n. 3).

6. chastity *(qudsha):* Lit. "sanctity." In early Syriac literature the term *qaddisha,* literally "holy," often has the technical sense of "continent," referring to married couples who refrain from sexual intercourse. The terminology is derived from Exod 19:10 (taken in conjunction with 19:15). In contemporary Judaism this was seen as a temporary ascetic practice, but in early Syriac Christianity as a permanent undertaking (see especially Aphrahat, *Dem.* 6, 7, and 18). On this topic in general, see Griffith 1995 and Brock 1992 (ch. 8).

ܗܐ ܙܪܥܗ ܘܕܐܒܗ̈ܘܗܝ
ܗܐ ܒܪܬܐ ܠܒܢ̈ܘܗܝ

8. ܕܐܦ ܠܗ ܥܒܕܐ ܢܐܬܐ ܢܗܘܐ
ܐܚܐ ܠܪ̈ܚܡܘܗܝ ܕܐܦ ܠܗ ܒܪܬܐ
ܐܘ ܒܪܐ ܠܐܡܗ ܐܬܐ ܢܗܘܐ
ܡܒܢܝܐ ܡܫܒܚ ܘܕܐܦ ܠܗ ܥܒܕܐ
ܢܥܒܕܘܗܝ ܐܬܐ ܢܥܒܕܘܢ ܡܢܗ

9. ܒܪ ܥܠܝܐ ܒܪܝ ܘܡܫܠܠ ܢܣܒܢ
ܚܕ ܗܘ ܐܒܘܗ ܘܥܒܕܐ ܕܠܗ
ܐܘܦ ܕܢܗܪܐ ܕܐܬܝ ܡܢܝ
ܕܟܠܢ ܘܕܟܠܡܕܡ ܐܬܝ ܠܗ ܠܦܘܠܝ
ܘܐܬܝ ܐܒܝ ܘܐܬܝ ܡܘܠܝ

10. ܒܪܐ ܥܠܝܐ ܒܪܝ ܐܡܟ ܗܘܝ ܠܗ
ܐܦ ܒܝ ܐܦܠܘܣ ܘܫܡܫܬܐ
ܒܝ ܒܪܐ ܥܠܝܐ ܗܘ ܒܝ ܐܬܬܒܪܐ
ܘܡܬܒܪܟܐ ܗܘ ܚܘ̈ܝܐ ܒܒܢ̈ܝܐ
ܒܒܘܟܘ ܫܦܝܪ ܐܦ ܒܝ ܐܬܢܚܡ

—He shall drive it out. For those with diseases
here is One who will bind up their fractured state.

8. "Has any woman a child? Let him come and be
brother to my Beloved. Has she a daughter or niece?
Let her come and become
the betrothed of my most precious one. Has any one a slave?
Let him release him to come to serve his Lord.

9. "My Son, the freeborn who bears Your yoke Matt 11:29
has a single reward, while the slave who carries
the double yoke of two masters,
in heaven and on earth—he shall have two blessings,
a double reward for his double burden.

10. "My Son, the freeborn girl is Your maidservant
if she serves You, whereas a girl who is in slavery
is freeborn with You: let her find comfort in You,
for she has been liberated with that hidden freedom
that is stored up in her bosom if she loves You.

11. ܐܘ ܢܟ̈ܦܬܐ ܡܦܚ ܒܗ ܒܪܚܘܡܗ
ܕܒܚܝܢ ܢܡܪܐ ܘܐܦ ܠܡܬ̈ܠܐ
ܕܢܦܩܘܢ ܐܦ ܟܬܒܐ
ܕܢܬܟܠܨܘܢ ܒܪ ܒܪܘܬܐ ܗܘ
ܘܐܬܐ ܕܢܚܒܘܢ ܥܠ ܒܬܘ̈ܠܬܐ

12. ܗܟܢܐ ܚܕܬܐ ܕܡܫܒܚܘ ܩܘܠܠܐ
ܒܟܠ ܢܘܡ̈ܝܐ ܚܕܬܐ ܠܐܘܪܚܐ
ܘܟܬܒ ܒܐܘܪ ܒܟܬܝܒܬܐ ܚܕܬܐ
ܗܘܐ ܒܪܘܡܗ ܘܒܟܠ ܗܦܟ
ܐܝܟ ܦܣܬܐ ܒܗ ܕܟܬܒܐ

13. ܠܗ ܡܫܝܚܐ ܕܠܐ ܟܬܒܐ
ܗܒܘ ܢܘܡ̈ܝܐ ܠܗ ܚܛ̈ܝܐ
ܗܒܘ ܕܛܥܝܗܘܢ ܕܥܠ ܡܫܒ̈ܚܐ
ܗܒܘ ܦܘܠܚܗܘܢ ܘܐܪܥܗ ܦܘܩܕܐ
ܦܫܘܩܐ ܢܗܘܢ ܐܦ ܐܓܪܗܘܢ

11. "Chaste women, yearn[7] for my Beloved
so that He may dwell in you; and you too who are unclean
He wishes to make holy. The churches too
He wants to adorn. Son of the Creator is He
who has come to restore all creation.

12. "He has renewed the heaven, because foolish men cf. Isa 65:17
had worshipped all kinds of stars; He has renewed the earth
which had grown old in Adam. With his spittle John 9:6
there took place a novel fashioning:
He who is capable of all things puts aright both bodies and minds.

13. "Come, all you who are blind, receive light
without payment; come, you lame, cf. Isa 55:1
receive back the use of your legs; you who are deaf and dumb,
receive back the use of your voices;
those whose hands are crippled shall also regain their use.

---

7. yearn: The manuscript has *swḥ*, but this must be a corruption for *swḥy* (imperative f. pl.), which alone fits the syntax.

14. ܟܕ ܒܪܘܬܐ ܗܘܐ ܕܡܚܝ ܟܐܘܗܝ
ܟܠ ܒܥܘܕܪܢܝ ܠܐܚܐ ܕܫܢܝܩ
ܡܢ ܒܬܘܠܬܐ ܢܐܬܐ ܙܪܘܗܝ
ܠܡܢܐ ܒܟܝ ܘܡܡܫܚܦ ܠܗ
ܒܥܙܐ ܒܟܝ ܒܬܝܐ ܡܝܘܪ

15. ܒܗܝܢܐ ܐܒܘܪܐ ܚܙܝ ܕܒܐܬܪܗ
ܒܫܠܐ ܕܣܬܘ ܢܦܩܐ ܕܩܛܝܐ
ܐܝܟ ܫܘܪܐ ܠܗ ܕܠܗ ܗܘ ܢܦܫܐ
ܢܡܠܟ ܐܢܫܐ ܒܫܘܪܐ ܐܚܪܝܐ
ܐܬܦܡܝ ܠܗ ܕܟܕ ܡܕܡܝܐ ܗܘ

16. ܒܦܘܡܗ ܠܘ ܟܬܒܐ ܘܠܐ ܒܡܠܐ
ܫܡܥ ܕܘܟܝܐ ܠܐ ܒܥܝܢ ܫܢܝܩ
ܐܝܟ ܠܫܡܥܗ ܘܡܫܬܥ ܐܒܝܢ
ܒܗܘܪܐ ܢܒܥܝ ܠܐ ܐܝܟ ܡܠܐ
ܘܠܐܡܗ ܒܢܬܐ ܒܬܫܡܫܬܗ

14. "He is the Creator's Son, whose treasure stores are filled
with every benefit. He who needs pupils,[8]
let him approach him:
He will fashion mud, and transform it, John 9:6
fashioning flesh and giving light to the eyes.

15. "With a little mud He showed how, through Him,
our dust was fashioned; the soul of the dead man, too, Gen 2:7; John 11:43 [Lazarus]
bore witness to Him how, by Him, man's breath
is breathed into him. By these latter witnesses Gen 2:7
He is to be believed to be Son [of God], the First Principle.

16. "Gather together and come, you lepers, receive cleansing
without any trouble; for there is no need,
as in Elisha's case, of dipping seven times 2 Kgs 5:10 [Namaan]
in the river [Jordan]: [Christ] does not tire men out any more
with the sprinklings as the priests of old did."

---

8. pupils: Ephrem, along with several other early commentators, understood that the man whose sight was healed in John 9 had been born without pupils, thus making it a miracle involving creation, rather than just healing.

17. ܫܡܥ ܕܐܬܝܠܕ ܒܪܐ ܕܝܢ
ܘܫܡܥ ܕܢܚ ܘܐܦܠܐ ܘܕܡܐ
ܠܘܩܒܠ ܗܘ ܕܟܠ ܠܐ ܐܝܬ ܐܬܪܐ
ܒܥܘܒܪܗ ܠܐ ܡܬܒܨܪܐ
ܒܪ ܡܪܐ ܟܠ ܡܢ ܡܪܐ ܟܠ

18. ܐܢ ܢܣܒ ܟܐܢܐ ܐܒܪ ܦܐܪܐ
ܘܐܝܬ ܡܪܝܪܐ ܒܟܠ ܦܐܪܐ
ܚܠܝܢ ܒܦܐܪܐ ܘܐܝܬ ܕܡܪܝܪܝܢ
ܐܠܐ ܒܒܥܠܝܗܘܢ ܫܘܚܠܦ ܕܐܪܓܫܬ
ܒܟܠܗܘܢ ܩܢܝܢ ܕܒܪ ܒܪܘܝܐ ܐܝܬ

17. Elisha's "seven times" symbolizes the purification
of the woman with seven spirits; while the hyssop and blood — Luke 8:2; Heb 9:19 [Lev 14:6–7]
are powerful types too. There is no place here
for thinking that [Christ] is "alien":[9]
[Christ], the Son of the Lord of all,[10]
is not alienated from the Lord of all.

18. If it was the "Just God" who made a body leprous,
while You cleanse it, then the Fashioner of the body
hated the body, while You loved it;
but as it is, You fashioned it, and the bandages
that You put on it cry out that You are the Creator's Son.

◆

9. "alien": The last two stanzas contain a polemic against the Marcionites who held that the Creator God (Demiurge, or "Just God") was different from, and inferior to, the supreme deity (the "Good God"); it was knowledge of the latter that Christ was supposed to have brought. For Ephrem, Christ's miracle in John 9, creating the pupils of the blind man out of dust and spittle, shows that Christ is the Son of the Creator, who is accordingly to be identified—against Marcion—as the same as the supreme God.

10. Son of the Lord of all *(bar mare koll):* This is found in a few other places in Ephrem (e.g., *Nat.* 4.194); Aphrahat, *Dem.* 2.19, has the fuller form, *bar marya d-koll.*

TEXT 6

Mary and Eve as the World's Two Eyes (*Eccl.* 37)

In the New Testament Paul had already introduced the Adam-Christ typology; to this was added in the second century its counterpart, Eve-Mary. In the course of time many different typological patterns were developed. In the present poem, after a brief invocation, Ephrem compares Eve and Mary to the world's two eyes. According to Ephrem's understanding of optics, the eye is enabled to see only when it is filled with light, and the more light, the more it sees. The left eye, Eve, malfunctions as a result of the Fall, and so does not let in the divine light of truth, with the consequence that the world goes astray. With Mary, however, who lets in the Light (that is, Christ in her womb), the world regained a right eye which functions as it should, thus allowing humanity to see the path to God again.

The poem contains the beginning of an alphabetic acrostic (*alaph* to *waw*); for the broken sequence in stanza 6, see the General Introduction (p. xv).

Meter

The *qala* title is given as *ʾaynaw d-naggira ruḥeh,* the opening words of *Eccl.* 2. The meter consists of 5+5 5+5 5+5 5+5 syllables and is used quite frequently by Ephrem: *Eccl.* 2–5, 10, 35–37, 43–44, 49–50; *Azym.* 1–2; *Fid.* 32–33; *Haer.* 29; *Ieiun.* appendix 3; *Nis.* 5–7, 25–33; and *Virg.* 11. For some of these, different *qala* titles are given, thus: *ʾurhay d-bet nahrin* (*Ieiun.* appendix 3), *malka shmayyana shayyen shigishuteh* (*Nis.* 25–33), and *ʿanak ḥnigaʾit* (*Haer.* 29, *Nis.* 5–7, and *Virg.* 11).

Text

This *madrasha* is preserved complete only in Vatican Syr. 111 (of 522 CE; Beck's B), though parts of it are also preserved in British Library Add. 14574 (of fifth or sixth century; Beck's F), to which a fragment in the Egyptology Department of the Metropolitan Museum of Art, New York, belongs (21.148.11; see Brock 1997, 491 n. 2).

ܥܠ ܩܠܐ ܕܐܡܗ ܕܡܫܝܚܐ ܕܘܢܚܗ

1. ܐܝܟܘ ܒܥܘܒܟܝ ܩܠܗ ܕܐܡܘܪܐ
ܘܐܕܢܗ ܕܫܡܥܬܐ ܒܪܐܐ ܕܒܥܠܬܐ
ܬܠܬܗܘܢ ܐܕܢܐ ܕܐܫܬܡܥܘ ܩܠܐ ܗܘ

ܒܥܘܬܐ : ܒܟ ܐܬܚܒܒ ܢܘܗܪܐ

2. ܒܟܠܠܗ ܕܚܝܐ ܚܙܝ ܒܬܫܡܫܬܐ ܘܬܘܕܝܬܗܘܢ
ܗܘܝ ܒܟܝܢܝܗܘܢ ܡܦܩ ܒܦܘܪܬܗܘܢ
ܡܪܟܠ ܒܟܠ ܐܬܠܗܘܢ ܘܢܚܣ ܒܬܘܕܝܗܘܢ

3. ܟܠܢܐ ܗܝ ܕܡܪܝܡ ܗܝ ܐܘܟܠܗ ܕܢܘܗܪܐ
ܕܒܟܠܠܗ ܐܝܟܘ ܟܠܡܐ ܘܟܡܘܬܗܘܢ
ܕܚܝܠ ܒܝܬ ܚܝܐ ܟܠܡܐ ܕܟܠ ܟܬܝܡ

1. Illumine with Your teaching the voice of the speaker
and the ear of the hearer: like the pupils of the eye
let the ears be illumined, for the voice provides their rays of light.

Refrain: Praises to You, O Light!

2. It is through the eye that the body, with its members,
is light in its different parts, is fair in all its conduct,
is adorned in all its senses, is glorious in its various limbs.

3. It is clear that Mary is the land[1] that receives the source of light;
through her it has illumined the whole world, with its inhabitants,
which had grown dark through Eve, the source of all misfortunes.

1. land: This carries as a resonance Mary as the "thirsty land" (Isa 53:2), for which see Text 8 (*Res.* 1), stanza 3.

4. ܕܟܝܢ ܒܐܪ̈ܙܘܗܝ   ܠܚܘܫܒܐ ܕܚܕܐ ܟܠܗ
ܫܡܝܐ ܘܫܡܘܫܐ   ܘܟܠܗ ܐܚܪ̈ܬܐ ܬܘܒ
ܫܡܫܐ ܘܢܘܗܪܐ   ܟܕ ܡܚܘܪܐ ܒܟܠܐ

5. ܗܐ ܟܘܟܒܐ ܐܬܪ̈ܝܢ   ܒܬܪ̈ܝܢ ܡܬܒܥܐ ܒܗ
ܚܙܐ ܗܘܐ ܟܠܗ   ܫܡܫܐ ܕܫܡܝܐ
ܟܠܗ ܕܡܫܝܚܐ   ܢܘܗܪܐ ܡܕܢܚ

6. ܒܟܝܢܐ ܕܫܡܫܐ ܗܘܐ   ܚܙܝ ܟܘܟܒܐ ܒܗ
ܘܟܕ ܡܣܬܟܠ ܐܢܐ   ܒܗܠܠ ܠܐܘܟܠܬܐ ܕܐܣܒܪܗ
ܣܒܪܗ ܗܘܐ ܕܟܠܗܐ ܗܘ   ܒܐܪܥܐ ܡܢܗ ܡܦܩܬܐ

7. ܘܟܕ ܢܦܩ ܡܢ ܝܡܐ   ܘܢܦܘܩܐ ܣܓܝܐܐ
ܕܡܪܐ ܟܠܗ ܒܦܘܩܕܢܗ   ܘܦܬܚ ܐܬܪ̈ܘܗܝ ܕܚܠܗ
ܕܡܫܝܚܬܐ ܕܐܣܒܪܗ   ܐܝܬܐ ܗܘ ܕܢܚܬܘܗ̇)

4. [Mary and Eve] in their symbols resemble a body, one of whose eyes
is blind and darkened, while the other is
clear and bright, providing light for the whole.

5. The world, you see, has two eyes fixed in it:
Eve was its left eye, blind,
while the right eye, illumined, is Mary.

6. Through the eye that was darkened the whole world was darkened,
and people groped and thought that every stone
they stumbled upon was a god, calling falsehood truth.

7. But when it was illumined by the other eye and the heavenly Light
that resided in its midst, humanity became reconciled once again,
realizing that the discovery they had made
was destroying their very life.

◆

TEXT 7

Christ as Light in Mary and in the Jordan (*Eccl.* 36)

In this *madrasha* Ephrem reflects on light as a symbol of Christ. The poem is elaborately constructed and falls into three sections: 1–5, 6–11, and 12–15. In each of these the stanzas go together in pairs, with each pair linked to the next by a common theme (stanza 5, however, is an exception, since it summarizes the previous two pairs). Thus, for example, in stanzas 1–4 we find the following pattern of relationships:

1–2	eye:	light
	Mary:	Christ
3–4	Jordan:	Christ
	Mary:	Christ

In the next section, stanzas 6–11, Moses and the sun, serving as representatives of Scripture and Nature, provide analogies: in Moses' case the radiance with which his face shone on Sinai came from outside, whereas in the case of both Mary and the Jordan the presence of Christ the Light is interior. The sun, which is the source of its own light, offers an illustration of the state of the righteous at the resurrection, when they will serve as the source of their own light, since they have allowed Christ the Light to shine within themselves. Ephrem will certainly have expected his readers to see Isa 60:19 as the background to what he is saying.

In the final section Ephrem, with the resurrection in mind, prays to be saved from the fate of the wicked who, instead of being robed in splendor, will "put on the garment of all their sins." (There is an earlier translation in Brock 1976a.)

Meter

For the *qala* and the meter, see on the previous Text 6 (*Eccl.* 37). In several cases a line has 6+5 syllables, rather than 5+5 (thus, for example, stanza 4, line 1a; stanza 6, lines 1a and 2a).

Text

The poem is preserved solely in Vatican Syr. 111 (of 522 CE; Beck's B).

ܒܪ ܩܠܗ

1. ܟܣܝܐ ܒܢܘܗܪܐ   ܡܬܕܡܝܐ ܒܢܦܫܗ
ܘܡܬܚܙܝܐ ܒܐܝܕܗ   ܘܡܬܡܫܫܐ ܒܕܝܢܗ
ܘܡܬܕܘܫܐ ܒܐܝܩܗ   ܘܡܬܓܫܫܐ ܒܡܦܪܘ

ܥܘܢܝܬܐ : ܒܪܝܟ ܒܪܘܝܗ ܕܢܘܗܪܐ

2. ܡܪܝܡ ܒܪܐ ܟܣܝܐ   ܢܘܗܪܐ ܫܪܐ ܒܓܘܗ
ܘܡܪܗ ܒܐܪܥܝܬܗ   ܘܡܚܐ ܒܡܚܘܬܗ
ܕܫ ܒܡܪܢܝܬܗ   ܘܙܠ ܒܡܘܒܠܬܗ

3. ܢܘܪܐ ܕܒܥܝ ܗܘܐ ܠܗ   ܒܪܬܐ ܘܩܦ ܠܫܡܗ
ܒܟܠ ܪܚܝܐ ܕܡܬܐ   ܠܫܡܗ ܕܒܫܘܬܐ
ܘܡܚܕ ܒܥܘܠܬܐ   ܘܐܬܩܘ ܒܡܬܒܘܚܬܐ

1. When it is associated with [a source of] light an eye becomes pure,

   it shines with [the light that] provisions it,
   it gleams with its brightness,

   it becomes glorious with its splendor, adorned by its beauty.

   Refrain: Blessed is the Creator[1] of light!

2. As though on an eye the Light settled in Mary;

   It polished[2] her mind, clarified her thought

   and made pure her understanding, causing her virginity to shine.

3. The river in which He was baptized
   conceived Him again symbolically;

   the moist womb[3] of the water conceived Him in purity,

   bore Him in chastity, made Him ascend in glory.

---

1. Creator: The manuscript has *baryeh,* but for metrical reasons this needs to be corrected to *baroyeh.*

2. polished *(mraq):* The verb is often used in connection with the polishing of mirrors (which were of metal in antiquity and so needed to be kept in a high state of polish in order to be effective).

3. womb: Elsewhere Ephrem speaks of the three wombs that Christ entered: Mary's, that of the Jordan, and that of Sheol; compare also Text 8 (*Res.* 1), stanza 7, where Ephrem also speaks of the Father's womb. This imagery is preserved in several of the Syriac baptismal services where the font is described as a womb that gives birth to spiritual children.

4. ܒܥܘܒܐ ܕܒܝܐ ܕܢܘܗܪܐ ܐܝܟ ܒܒܪܬܐ ܐܢܫܝܐ
ܕܒܗܢܬ ܕܠܐ ܒܪܐ ܘܡܒܪܬܐ ܕܠܐ ܐܘܒܠܐ
ܕܒܢܬ ܒܡܘܗܒܬܐ ܒܡܪܢܘ ܕܡܘܗܒܬܐ

5. ܕܢܚܐ ܒܗ ܢܘܗܪܗ ܙܡܚܐ ܒܗ ܡܒܪܗ
ܐܬܠܝ ܒܪܫ ܛܘܪܐ ܘܕܢܚ ܒܗ ܒܪܫܐ
ܘܐܦܝ ܒܒܠܒܘܫܗ ܘܐܢܗܪ ܒܫܘܒܚܗ

6. ܐܝܐ ܕܠܒܫ ܫܡܫܐ ܡܢ ܒܪ [illegible] ܗܘܐ ܠܗ
ܢܘܪܐ ܕܒܥܒܕ ܗܘܐ ܠܗ ܡܢ ܒܗ ܒܠܒܫ ܢܘܗܪܐ
ܦܐܪܐ ܕܫܦܝܪܐ ܒܦܘܗ ܡܢ ܒܗ ܐܬܝܠܕ ܗܘܐ

7. ܘܐܡܟ ܕܐܬܝܠܕ ܫܡܫܐ ܒܬܫܒܘܚܬܐ
ܕܗܘܦܐ ܚܕܐ ܡܟܠܐ ܒܥܠܐ [illegible] ܐܬܝܠܕ
ܦܐܪܐ ܕܫܦܝܪܐ ܗܘܐ ܠܗ ܘܢܘܪܐ ܕܒܥܒܕ ܗܘܐ ܠܗ

4. In the pure womb of the river
you should recognize the Daughter of man

who conceived without any man, who gave birth without intercourse,

who brought up, through a gift,[4] the Lord of that gift.

5. As the Daystar in His river, the Bright One in His tomb, Luke 1:78

He shone forth on the mountain top[5]
and gave brightness too in the womb;

He dazzled[6] as He went up [from the river],
gave illumination at His ascension.[7]

6. The brightness which Moses put on was wrapped on him from without, Exod 34:29ff.

the river in which Christ was baptized put on Light from within,

[Mary's] body, in which He resided, was made gleaming from within.

7. Just as Moses gleamed with the [divine] glory

because he saw the splendor[8] briefly, how much more should the body

wherein [Christ] resided gleam, and the river in which He was baptized?

---

4. gift: Probably Ephrem has in mind the gift of milk flowing in the breasts of Mary, a virgin (as in *Nat.* 11.4 [Text 4]). The wording is reminiscent of *Odes of Solomon* 35.5–6: "Like a child carried by its mother, He gave me milk, the dew of the Lord, and I was brought up by His gift, and found rest in His perfection." It seems unlikely, however, that Ephrem knew the *Odes of Solomon*.

5. mountain top: It is (perhaps deliberately) unclear whether this refers to the Transfiguration or to the Ascension.

6. dazzled: Ephrem probably has in mind the early tradition that at Christ's baptism there appeared above or in the Jordan either light (so some Old Latin manuscripts of the Gospels) or fire (so first in Justin Martyr). In Syriac tradition it is fire that is more commonly referred to, and this is depicted visually in the famous illuminated Rabbula Gospels, dated 586 CE. For a discussion of this tradition going back to the Diatessaron, see Petersen 1994, 14–20.

7. ascension: This could, alternatively, be taken as referring to Christ's "going up" from the Jordan after his baptism.

8. splendor: Lit. "exaltation."

8. ܐܝܟܐ ܕܒܥܝܢ ܡܘܬܐ ܦܐܝܐ ܠܗܘܢ ܕܒܪܐ
ܠܐ ܝܗܒ ܒܚܘܣܝܐ ܕܢܣܒ ܠܗܘܢ ܕܡܢܗ
ܕܢܗܘܐ ܕܡܢ ܐܦܝܗܘܢ ܫܡܫܐ ܡܢܢ ܕܟܠܗܘܢ

9. ܒܪܝܐ ܕܟܬܒܐ ܘܠܐ ܡܫܬܒܚܐ ܢܗܘܐ
ܐܚܪܢܐ ܒܟܬܒܘܗܝ ܕܬܬܟܬܒܘܗܝ ܢܗܘܐ
ܡܬܕܡܝ ܘܐܟܣܢܝܐ ܒܩܫܝܐ ܕܐܬܒܘܣܡܐ

10. ܐܢ ܓܝܪ ܐܦ ܫܡܫܐ ܠܐ ܗܘܐ ܡܬܚܙܐ ܢܗܘܐ
ܕܘܪܩ ܒܚܘܣܝܐ ܠܐ ܓܝܪ ܡܨܐ ܫܡܫܐ
ܢܗܘܐ ܟܠ ܢܘܗܪܐ ܕܥܝܢܐ ܗܝ ܕܐܟܣܢܝܐ

11. ܗܘܝ ܒܢܘܚܡܐ ܢܘܪܐ ܐܦ ܐܪܙܐ
ܕܒܘܚܡܘܗܝ ܕܚܝܐ ܘܒܚܘܫܘܗܝ ܐܝܟܐ
ܗܢܘܢ ܒܗܘܢ ܗܘܝ ܢܗܘܐ ܒܢܘܗܪܐ

12. ܐܚܝܕ ܒܗܘ ܝܘܡܐ ܗܐ ܕܒܟܠܗܝ ܒܢܝܐ
ܒܘܡܐ ܕܟܠ ܝܘܡܝܢ ܒܟܝܢܐ ܕܟܠ ܒܘܠܝܢ
ܕܝܠܗܘܢ ܒܗܘܢ ܢܟܠ ܫܡܫܐ ܘܣܘܢܩܐ

8. The brightness that the stammering Moses
put on in the wilderness Exod 4:10
did not allow the darkness to darken the inside of his dwelling,
for the light from his face served as a sun[9] that went before his feet,

9. like the supernal beings whose eyes need
no other light, since their pupils
flow with light, and they are clothed in rays of glory.

10. For if the sun chases out darkness without using light
apart from its own—for the sun needs
no luminary for light, seeing it is the source of [its own] rays—

11. so too at the Resurrection the righteous are light,
for their clothing is splendor, their garments brightness:
they become their own light through the [source of] light.

12. Save me, Lord, on that day when the wicked put on
the garment of all [their] sins, clothing full of stains,
whence spring up for them darkness and torment,

---

9. served as a sun *(shammesh):* The double translation is intended to bring out the double entendre.

13. ܐܝܟ ܕܐܦ ܡܢܗ ܕܫܡܫܐ ܒܒܘܪܘܢܐ
ܢܒܥܘܢ ܒܥܪܘܬܐ ܬܢܢܐ ܘܐܛܠܐ
ܦܐܪܐ ܕܫܒܒܘܬܗ ܘܫܒܝܐ ܕܥܪܕܘܬܗ

14. ܛܒܐ ܕܛܥܢ ܠܟ ܫܡܫܐ ܒܐܣܝܐ
ܘܥܠܝܐ ܫܘܪܐ ܘܟܝܢ ܒܩܒܠܐ ܫܪܝܐ
ܢܬܛܫܐ ܒܛܫܝܘܬܟ ܐܘܪܐ ܕܒܘܢܟ

15. ܐܘܪܗ ܒܪܘܚܗ ܕܢܘܗܪܐ ܕܒܗ ܗܘ ܙܪܥ
ܢܘܗܪܐ ܡܫܝܚܐ ܡܫܚܗ ܒܒܥܘܬܗ
ܕܢܘܗܪܐ ܕܙܪܥܗ ܗܘ ܕܢܘܗܪܗ ܕܦܪܘܩ

13. just as from the body in times of sickness
there spring up bitter pain,[10] suffering, and fever,
as fetters for its wrongdoing and a rod to chastise it.

14. O Good One, who has prepared for us the sun by day
and by night the moon with the candelabra of the stars,
may Your glorious comfort reach me through Your grace.

15. Give thanks to the Creator of light because in it is depicted
the heavenly Light; give praise to the Maker
of light because it is a symbol of the Light of our Savior!

◆

10. bitter pain *(mraruta):* This form is not attested in the dictionaries; probably the text should be corrected to *mrarta* (ANP).

TEXT 8

The Paradoxes of the Incarnation
(*Res.* 1)

In this poem, the first part of which contains an acrostic with Ephrem's own name, the poet explores various aspects of the paradoxes that are involved in the incarnation. For the acrostic with Ephrem's name, see the General Introduction (p. xv).

Meter

The *qala* title is lost. The meter, which consists of 7 4+4 4+4 4+4 syllables, is elsewhere given the *qala* title *ʾo bar ḥire/ḥayya* (*Fid.* 36–38; *Nat.* 27).

Text

The poem is preserved complete solely in British Library Add. 14627 (sixth or seventh century; Beck's B). In this manuscript the opening of the first stanza is lost, but the text can fortunately be supplied from excerpts from the *madrasha* in the Mosul Fenqitho (6.162–64; see Slim 1967; Brock 1997, 504). In fact excerpts from this *madrasha* are to be found in two different places in the Mosul Fenqitho: 6.107 (stanzas 7–9, 12–13, 16) and 6.162–64 (stanzas 1, 6, 17, interspersed with stanzas of unknown origin).

1. ܐܬܐ ܠܝ ܐܡܪܐ ܡܢ ܥܢܗ ܕܕܘܝܕ
ܓܕܝܐ ܘܒܘܟܪܐ ܡܢ ܐܒܪܗܡ
ܗܘܐ ܠܝ ܐܡܪܐ ܗܘܐ ܠܝ ܒܘܟܪܐ
ܦܨܝܗ ܒܕܒܚܐ ܕܡܗ ܠܒܪܗ
ܒܪܝܟ ܫܘܡܠܝܗ

ܥܘܢܝܬܐ : ܒܪܝܟ ܒܘܟܪܟ

2. ܦܪܚ ܘܢܚܬ ܗܘ ܡܪܐ ܟܠ
ܘܠܒܫܗ ܠܠܒܘܫ ܒܣܪܐ ܕܡܝܬܐ
ܟܠ ܦܘܩ̈ܕܗ ܢܡܘܣܗ ܘܫܠܡ
ܗܘܐ ܡܕܒܚܐ ܠܡܪܐ ܟܠܐ
ܒܪܝܟ ܕܒܚܗ

1. The Lamb has come for us from the House of David, Matt 1:1
the Priest and Pontiff from Abraham; Heb 9:11
He became for us both Lamb and Pontiff,
giving His body for sacrifice, His blood for sprinkling. Exod 12:6–7
Blessed is His perfecting!

Refrain: Blessed is Your rising up!

2. The Shepherd of all flew down
in search of Adam, the sheep that had strayed; Luke 15:4–5
on His shoulders He carried him, taking him up:
he was an offering for the Lord of the flock.
Blessed is His descent![1]

1. His descent *(ruḥḥapeh):* Lit. "hovering." The term (derived from Gen 1:2, for which see Text 16 [*Virg.* 7], n. 7) is normally used in connection with the Holy Spirit.

3. ܕܫܡܥ ܛܠܝܐ ܘܡܒܪܐ ܚܝܐ
ܟܠ ܗܘ ܡܪܝܡ ܐܘܟܝܬ ܙܥܘܪܬܐ
ܐܝܟ ܫܡܫܐ ܢܦܠ ܠܗܘܢ ܒܡܫܘܠ
ܫܡܥ ܐܝܟ ܟܦܐ ܘܟܣܝܐ ܚܕܬܐ
ܒܪܝܟ ܩܘܪܒܢܗ

4. ܡܕܒܪܢܗ ܕܪܩܡܗ ܠܫܘܒܚܢ
ܡܢ ܐܢܫܘܬܐ ܕܐܟܪܐ ܗܘܐ
ܠܗܐ ܒܗ ܒܢܝܐ ܘܐܬܪܘܕ ܒܗ
ܒܒܝܬܐ ܢܫܟܚ ܟܠ ܢܩܦܬܐ
ܒܪܝܟ ܡܫܒܚܗ

5. ܡܢ ܪܘܡܐ ܚܝܠܐ ܢܚܬ ܠܗ
ܘܡܢ ܒܗ ܟܪܣܐ ܫܦܪܐ ܢܨܚ ܠܗ
ܡܢ ܥܒܪܐ ܬܢܢܐ ܕܢܚܘ ܠܗ
ܘܟܠ ܡܫܝܚܐ ܡܠܟܐ ܣܓܕ ܠܗ
ܒܪܝܟ ܐܝܩܪܗ

3. He sprinkled dew and life-giving rain
on Mary, the thirsty earth. Isa 53:2
Like a seed of wheat He fell again to Sheol John 12:24
to spring up as a sheaf, as the new Bread. Lev 23:11; John 6:36
Blessed is His offering!

4. Knowledge of Him chased error away
from humanity that had become lost;
the Evil One was led astray by Him and was confounded.
[Knowledge of Him] poured out all kinds of wisdom upon the peoples.
Blessed is His fountain!

5. From on high did Power[2] descend to us, Luke 1:35
from within a womb did Hope shine out for us,
from the grave has Salvation[3] appeared for us,
and on the right hand the King for us is seated. Ps 110:1
Blessed is His glory![4]

---

2. Power *(ḥayla):* The "Power of the Most High" in Luke 1:35 was usually interpreted by Syriac writers as referring to the divine Word rather than to the Holy Spirit.

3. Salvation: *Ḥayye* in early Syriac texts means "salvation" as well as "life"; thus the Greek *sōtēria* is always rendered by *ḥayye* in the Old Syriac Gospels.

4. His glory *(iqareh):* Based on Ezek 3:12; cf. stanza 22 and *Nis.* 41.14 (Text 13). The phrase is occasionally found in later literature, e.g., the Syriac translation of the *Life of Antony* §12, 84 (Draguet 1980, T. 29, 134). In normal Syriac usage *iqara* has the sense of "honor" rather than "glory."

6. ܡܢ ܪܘܡܐ ܕܢܚ ܐܝܟ ܢܘܗܪܐ
ܘܡܢܗ ܕܡܪܝܡ ܐܝܟ ܒܣܪܐ
ܡܢ ܩܝܣܐ ܢܚܬ ܐܝܟ ܦܐܪܐ
ܣܠܩ ܠܫܡܝܐ ܐܝܟ ܪܫܝܬܐ
ܒܪܝܟ ܙܟܘܬܗ

7. ܡܠܬܗ ܕܐܒܐ ܐܬܬ ܡܢ ܥܘܒܗ
ܘܠܒܫܬ ܦܓܪܐ ܒܥܘܒܐ ܐܚܪܢܐ
ܡܢ ܥܘܒܐ ܠܥܘܒܐ ܢܦܩܬ
ܘܡܠܝܢ ܡܢܗ ܥܘܒܐ ܢܟܦܐ
ܒܪܝܟ ܕܫܪܐ ܒܢ

8. ܡܢ ܪܘܡܐ ܢܚܬ ܐܝܟ ܡܪܐ
ܘܡܢ ܟܪܣܐ ܢܦܩ ܐܝܟ ܥܒܕܐ
ܘܒܪܟ ܡܘܬܐ ܩܕܡܘܗܝ ܒܫܝܘܠ
ܘܒܩܝܡܬܗ ܚܝܐ ܣܓܕܘ ܠܗ
ܒܪܝܟ ܢܨܚܢܗ

6. From on high He flowed like a river,

from Mary He [stemmed] as from a root, Isa 11:1; Luke 3:32; Rom 15:12

from the Cross He descended as fruit,

as the firstfruit He ascended to heaven. Col 1:18

Blessed is His will!

7. The Word came forth from the Father's womb,[5] John 1:18

He put on the body in another womb;

from one womb to another did He proceed,

and chaste wombs are filled with Him.

Blessed is He who has resided in us![6] John 1:14

8. From on high He came down as Lord,

from within the womb He came forth as a servant;

Death knelt before Him in Sheol,

and Life worshipped Him at His resurrection.

Blessed is His victory!

---

5. The Word . . . the Father's womb *(ʿubbeh):* The word used in John 1:18 can mean both "bosom" (so the Greek) and "womb," and it is in the latter sense that Ephrem takes it, providing a parallel with the womb of Mary. In this line the Word *(mellta)* is treated grammatically as feminine, as sometimes elsewhere in early Syriac texts; normally, however, the masculine is preferred.

6. resided in us *(shra ban):* It is very likely that Ephrem has in mind John 1:14, even though all the known Syriac versions (Syriac Diatessaron, Peshitta, Harklean) have a different verb *(aggen)* here. References to (as opposed to citations of) both Luke 1:35 and John 1:14 in early Syriac writers regularly employ the verb *shra,* rather than *aggen;* possibly this usage may go back to the first oral kerygma in Syriac (see Brock 1989a and 1993).

9. ܡܪܝܡ ܛܥܢܬܗ ܐܝܟ ܕܒܬܘܠܐ
ܒܗܝܢܐ ܛܥܢܬܗ ܐܝܟ ܡܪܒܝܢܐ
ܙܥܘܪܐ ܛܥܢܬܗ ܐܝܟ ܥܠܝܡܬܐ
ܫܦܝܐ ܛܥܢܘܗܝ ܐܝܟ ܠܐܒܘܐ
ܫܘܒܚܐ ܠܐܒܘܗܝ

10. ܡܢ ܟܠ ܒܢܝܢ ܐܘܠܕܬ ܘܡܘܗܒ
ܐܦ ܚܘܒܫܐ ܟܡ ܡܫܒܚܐ
ܘܗܘ ܡܒܐ ܐܝܟ ܚܘܒܫܗܘܢ
ܘܗܘ ܦܪܘܫܐ ܐܝܟ ܬܫܒܚܬܗܘܢ
ܒܪܝܟ ܡܘܠܕܗ

11. ܡܢ ܦܘܡ ܢܦܩܐ ܐܘܠܕܬܐ ܡܘܒ ܗܘܐ
ܛܒܐ ܕܐܒܢܐ ܘܢܦܫܐ ܕܒܟܝ
ܡܢ ܦܘܡܗ ܛܒܐ ܚܕܬܐ
ܕܢܚܬܐ ܚܕܬܐ ܡܘܒ ܠܝ
ܒܪܝܟ ܡܘܗܒܗ

9. Mary carried Him as a child,
the priest [Simeon] carried Him as an offering, Luke 2:28
the Cross carried Him as one slain,
heaven carried Him as God.
Praise to His Father!

10. From every side He stretched out and gave
healing and promises:
children ran to His healings,
the discerning ran to His promises.
Blessed is His revelation!

11. From the fish's mouth He gave a coin Matt 17:27
whose imprint was temporal, whose currency passing; cf. Matt 22:21
from His own mouth He gave a new imprint,
giving us the New Covenant.
Blessed is its Giver!

12. ܡܢ ܥܠܝܐ ܥܠܝܘܬܗ
ܘܡܢ ܡܪܘܡܐ ܐܦ ܪܡܘܬܗ
ܡܢ ܡܬܟܠܐܕܡ ܐܦ ܒܥܡܪܘܬܗ
ܘܡܢ ܟܠ ܕܪܝܡ ܐܦ ܡܟܝܟܘܬܗ
ܒܪܝܟ ܫܘܒܚܗ

13. ܡܢ ܕܟܝܢܐ ܗܘܐ ܒܚܒܠܬܐ
ܘܡܢ ܪܘܚܐ ܒܟܝ ܢܫܡܬܐ
ܡܢ ܡܕܘܪܐ ܗܘܐ ܒܠܒܘܬܐ
ܘܡܟܠܝܐ ܗܘܐ ܒܟܝܢ ܡܕܝܢܐ
ܒܪܝܟ ܬܘܠܕܗ

14. ܡܢ ܫܡܝܐ ܠܐ ܪܚܩ ܗܘܐ
ܘܡܢ ܬܚܬܝܐ ܠܐ ܥܒܪ ܗܘܐ
ܠܬܫܡܫܬܐ ܐܦ ܚܕܐ ܗܘܐ
ܘܠܡܫܡܫܢܘܬܐ ܐܦ ܫܡܫ ܗܘܐ
ܒܪܝܟ ܡܘܠܕܗ

12. From God is His divinity,
from mortals His humanity,
from Melkizedek His priesthood, Heb 5:6
from David's line His kingship. cf. Matt 1:6, Luke 1:32
Blessed is His combining them!

13. He was one of the guests at the Wedding Feast, John 2:1–11
He was one of the fasters in the Temptation, Matt 4:1–11
He was one of the watchful in the Agony, Matt 26:26–36
He was a teacher in the Temple. Mark 12:35
Blessed is His instruction!

14. He did not shrink from the unclean,
He did not turn away from sinners;
in the sincere He greatly delighted,
for the simple He greatly longed.
Blessed is His teaching!

15. ܡܢ ܡܕ̈ܒܪܐ ܠܐ ܚܣ ܕܢܓܠܘܢܝ
ܐܦ ܠܐ ܢܓܠܘܢܝ ܡܢ ܩܘܪ̈ܝܬܐ
ܦܩܕ ܡܫܠܡܘ ܙܝܢ ܐܢ̈ܫܐ
ܘܐܦ ܡܫܡܫܘ ܙܝܢ ܢܒ̈ܝܐ
ܒܪܝܟ ܡܘܠܕܗ

16. ܡܘܠܕܗ ܠܝ ܕܘܟܝܐ ܗܘ
ܘܐܦ ܒܡܠܕܗ ܠܝ ܣܘܟܝܐ ܗܘ
ܐܦ ܡܚܝܠܘܬܗ ܠܝ ܚܝܠܐ ܗܝ
ܐܦ ܫܘܒܚܗ ܠܝ ܙܘܡܪܐ ܗܘ
ܒܡܐ ܢܘܕܐ ܠܗ

17. ܡܢ ܐܡܗܬܐ ܣܡܟ ܐܒܐ
ܘܡܢ ܡܕܒ̈ܪܐ ܐܝܢ ܟܠܐ
ܡܢ ܙܘܓܐ ܣܡܟ ܥܠܡܐ
ܘܡܢ ܦܬܘ̈ܩܐ ܡܫܩܐ ܟܠܐ
ܒܪܝܟ ܦܘܪܩܢܗ

15. He did not hold back His footsteps from the sick
or His words from the simple;
He extended His descent to the lowly,
and His ascension to the highest.
Blessed is His Sender!

16. His birth gives us purification,
His baptism gives us forgiveness,
His death is life to us,
His ascension is our exaltation.
How we should thank Him!

17. By the greedy He was considered a glutton, Matt 11:19
but by those who know, the Provider of all;
by drunkards He was considered a drinker, Matt 11:19
but by the discerning, the One who gives everyone to drink.
Blessed is His foresight!

18. ܒܥܘܒܐ ܛܥܝܢܐ ܗܘܐ ܒܛܢܗ
ܘܒܓܪܡܝܗܘܢ ܡܫܝܚ ܩܘܒܠܗ
ܙܒܢ ܟܦܘܪܐ ܒܥܝܢ ܡܘܠܟܗ
ܘܒܠܒܥܝܪܐ ܐܦܝܗ ܒܘܠܒܗ
ܒܪܝܟ ܦܘܪܩܢܗ

19. ܙܒܢ ܡܘܠܕܗ ܡܬܪܝ ܩܠܕܗ
ܘܒܒܪܘܢܐ ܓܒܝܢ ܩܘܠܕܗ
ܒܒܥܒܐ ܡܘܬܠܐ ܗܘ ܡܦܢܐ
ܘܒܠܬܢܬܐ ܕܪܡܐ ܘܦܘܢܐ
ܫܠܝܡ ܒܘܪܟܗ

20. ܟܢ ܒܝܢܐ ܐܬܢܦܫ ܗܘܐ
ܘܟܢ ܗܘ ܒܢܐ ܐܬܠܐܠ ܗܘܐ
ܟܢ ܗܪܘܪܗ ܩܠܒܢܒ ܗܘܐ
ܒܫܠܝܐ ܒܥܪܗ ܕܪܒܐ ܕܢܒܪܗܘܢ
ܒܪܝܟ ܡܘܠܕܗ

18. To Caiaphas His conception was a scandal, Matt 26:63–65
but to Gabriel His birth was glorious; Luke 1:31–35
to the unbeliever His ascension is a source of difficulty,
but to His disciples His exaltation is a source of wonder. Acts 1:9–10
Blessed is His discernment![7]

19. With His Begetter His birth is certain,
but to the investigator it is fraught with difficulty;
to supernal beings its truth is crystal clear,
but to those below, a subject of enquiry and hesitation
—yet one which cannot be investigated!

20. By the Evil One He was tempted, Matt 4:1–11 and par.
by the [Jewish] people He was questioned, Matt 26:57ff.
by Herod He was interrogated:
He spurned him with silence when he wished to probe Him. Luke 23:9
Blessed is His Begetter!

7. discernment *(purshaneh):* The word could also be translated "separation," thus alluding to Luke 24:51, "he was separated *(etpresh)* from them" (sc. his disciples); if this is correct, then Ephrem will already have known the Peshitta reading there (the one surviving Old Syriac manuscript, the Sinaiticus, has "was raised").

21. ܡܢ ܒܢ̈ܬܐ ܒܢܘܗܪܐ ܫܒܚܘܗܝ
ܐܦ ܡܢ ܕܡ̈ܝܬܐ ܒܫܡܝܐ ܡܢܠܐܘܗܝ
ܐܝܟ ܕܠܡܫܠܡܐ ܒܫܡܝܐ ܠܐܠܗܘܗܝ
ܐܝܟ ܠܡܠܟܐ ܒܡܒܪܐ ܫܡܫܘܗܝ
ܒܪܝܟ ܡܘܠܕܗ

22. ܡܢܘ ܠܝ ܡܪܝ ܕܐܒܘܬܟ
ܗܘܐ ܕܐܡܪ ܠܒܪܐ ܕܝܗܒܟ
ܕܒܐ ܕܒܥܐ ܫܡܐ ܕܒܪܐ
ܡܒܥܐ ܕܝܠܝ ܕܫܡܥ ܒܗܠܠ
ܒܪܝܟ ܐܡܪܟ

21. They thought He was one of those baptized in the river [Jordan],
they accounted Him amongst those that sleep while at sea, Matt 8:24
they hung Him like a slain man on the Cross,
they laid Him like a corpse in the grave.
Blessed is His humiliation!

22. Whom have we, Lord, like You—
the Great One who became small, the Wakeful who slept,
the Pure One who was baptized, the Living One who died,
the King who bore disgrace to ensure honor for all!
Blessed is Your honor!

◆

TEXT 9

On the Fall (*Ieiun.* 3)

Ephrem here takes up the theme of the Fall and the immensity of God's compassion in sending "a robe of glory to cover Adam's naked state" (stanza 2)—where Adam is understood as the representative of the human race as a whole, and the "robe of glory" represents the new possibility of restoration and salvation provided by the incarnation. In stanza 3, he points out that the Tree of Knowledge has the potential to be either beneficial or harmful: it is beneficial to those who use it rightly, in obedience to God, but harmful to those who snatch at its fruit out of selfish presumption. In other words, knowledge in itself is neutral, neither good nor bad; it is only made good or bad by the way in which it is approached and by the uses to which human beings put it. Ephrem then applies this to the Lenten Fast (stanza 5): as examples in the Old Testament show, a fast that is accompanied by backbiting is abhorrent to God. The final verse expresses wonder at God's great love for humanity and his rigorous respect for human free will: it would have been easy for him to rescue fallen humanity by mere divine decree, but out of respect for the free will with which he has endowed human beings, God himself chose to "put on humanity" at the incarnation in order to invite humanity back to himself.

Unusually, there is no refrain given in the manuscripts.

Meter

The *qala* title for *Ieiun.* 1–5 is given as *hanaw nisan brika;* the same meter is used for *Res.* 4–5 where, however, it has the *qala* title *hanaw ṣawmeh d-bukra,* the opening words of *Ieiun.* 1. The meter itself is highly complex and has been variously analyzed, notably: (a) Douayhi (Hage 1987, 38a; no. 69) gives 6+5+5 5+5+5 4+4+5 4+7+7 6+4+6; (b) Lamy

(1902, 4:492; no. 48) has 6+5+5 5+5+6 8+5 5+7+5 6+10; (c) according to ANP it should be 6+5+5 5+5+6 4+4 5+5 7+5 (or 5+7) 4+4+4. (Beck simply describes the meter as "unklar.")

Text

The poem is preserved complete only in British Library Add. 14438 (sixth century; Beck's C), though stanzas 1, 3, 5, and 6 also occur in British Library Add. 14627 (of sixth or seventh century; Beck's B). Of the two rather later manuscripts which Beck employs, British Library Add. 14506 has only stanzas 1–2, and British Library Add. 14512 only stanza 5.

ܥܠ ܛܠܐ ܕܗܘܐ ܢܦܩ ܒܪܡܫܐ

1. ܡܢ ܕܝܢ ܐܪܡܫ ܚܙܐ ܗܘܐ ܠܐܪܥ ܘܒܟܝܬܐ
ܘܒܟܝܬܐ ܙܢܝܬܐ ܟܕ ܢܦܠܐ ܒܟܠܗ ܥܠܡܐ ܒܫܡܫܘܬܗ
ܘܫܠܛܬ ܘܡܫܬܒܠܐ ܐܪܥ ܡܥܠ ܘܫܘܐ ܒܪܝܬܐ
ܐܝܟܢܐ ܡܬܥܒܕ ܘܩܐܡܐ ܡܦܢܝ ܗܘܐ
ܡܥܒܕܘܬܐ ܪܒܐ ܘܟܢܘܫܬܐ ܐܘܡܐ ܘܟܢܫܐ
ܒܪܝܟ ܗܘ ܕܡܥܠ ܫܡܫܐ
ܕܢܘܗܪܐ ܒܪܝܬܗ ܟܠܗ ܘܡܢ ܢܘܗܪܐ

2. ܡܛܠ ܡܛܪܐ ܗܘܐ ܕܢܚܬܐ ܐܘܪܚܐ ܕܫܡܝܐ ܕܐܬܦܪܫܘ ܡܢ ܥܠܡ
ܐܦ ܟܝܢܐ ܗܘܐ ܠܗ ܚܙܝܐ ܦܪܝܫܐ ܚܙܝܢ. ܠܟܐ ܘܢܗܪܘ ܠܗ
ܡܛܠ ܡܛܪܐ ܗܘܐ ܕܠܐ ܢܚܬܐ ܗܘܐ
ܟܕ ܚܙܐ ܠܐܪܥ ܪܒܐ ܕܐܫܬܦܠ
ܘܢܚܬܐ ܕܡܪܝܡ ܠܦܪܐ ܠܫܡܫܐ ܕܙܒܢܗ
ܒܪܝܟ ܗܘ ܕܫܠܗ ܠܫܪܒܘܗܝ
ܘܡܛܪ ܐܫܬܠ ܡܕܒܪܐ ܠܟܠܒܢܘܬܗ

1. Who has peered back to see Adam and Eve,

and the crafty serpent, with cunning in his heart but peace on his lips,

stretching out as he beguiles Adam [who] is childlike[1]
and Eve who is simple? Gen 3:1–6

The Tree is blossoming, its fruit glistens,

the fault is great, while Justice remains resplendent and mighty.

Blessed is He who mixed with His just sentence

a flood of mercy when He showed pity on the guilty.

2. Who would be able to look upon that honored pair
who were stripped naked all of a sudden?

The Evil One stood there, a happy onlooker,
while the Good One saw him and watched him.

Who could fail to weep

seeing the great Adam thus brought low,

the chaste man covering his shame with leaves? Gen 3:7

Blessed is He who had pity on him in his leaves

and sent a robe of glory[2] to cover his naked state.

---

1. childlike: Similarly in stanza 6 and in *Par.* 7.6 and 15.12, 14. In his *Commentary on Genesis* (2.14) Ephrem rejects the idea that Adam and Eve were childlike in the sense that they were inexperienced (and so less to blame).
2. robe of glory: See Text 5 (*Nat.* 17), n. 3.

3. ܡܢܘ ܢܫܡܥ ܡܬܪܝܢ ܥܠ ܗܘ ܐܡܝܢܐ ܕܐܫܘܝ. ܠܒܥܘܬܐ
ܢܣܝܐ ܗܘ ܓܝܪ ܚܝܠܐ ܕܒܥܐ ܡܢ ܒܢܝܐ ܗܘܐ ܥܠܬܐ ܠܒܥܝܬܐ
ܐܦ ܕܡܬܒܥܝܐ ܗܘ ܘܠܐ ܡܬܒܥܝܐ ܗܘ
ܘܒܟܠ ܡܬܒܥܝܐ ܗܘ ܕܒܗ ܡܬܒܥܐ ܐܢܫ
ܡܢܐ ܗܝ ܡܬܘܒܥܬܐ ܕܐܒܐ ܘܡܪܕܘܬܐ ܕܒܟܠ
ܒܪܝܟ ܗܘ ܦܐܪܐ ܕܡܥܠܝ ܡܬܒܥܬܗ
ܕܐܟܠ ܟܠܢܐ ܠܗ ܡܢܘܬܐ

4. ܐܝܟ ܝܘܡܐ ܚܙܐ ܗܘܐ ܝܘܢܐ ܒܡܪܓܢܝܬܐ ܕܒܗ ܠܗ
ܗܦܟ ܢܦܩܘ ܠܝܘܡܐ ܗܘ ܕܪܡܫܐ ܗܘ
ܕܒܠܝܐ ܦܬܗ ܠܡ ܦܬܗ ܗܘܐ ܠܗ ܡܢܗ ܕܐܗܘܐ ܡܢܗ
ܘܠܒܫ ܗܘܐ ܓܘܢܗ ܕܐܠܒܫ ܦܫܝܛܘܬܗ
ܪܡܙ ܗܘܐ ܠܗ ܟܠܐ ܦܪܝܫܐ ܕܐܝܬܘܗܝ ܒܐܘܟܝܬܐ
ܒܪܝܟ ܗܘ ܡܠܟܐ ܕܐܒܐ ܕܝܠܗ
ܟܠܐ ܘܐܒܪ ܐܒܘܗ ܕܐܝܟ

3. Who is there who can expound concerning that Tree
   which caused those who sought it to go astray?

   It is an invisible target, hidden from the eyes,
   which wearies those who shoot at it.

   It is both the Tree of Knowledge, and of ignorance:

   it is the cause of knowledge, for by it a person knows

   what is the gift that was lost, and the punishment that took place.

   Blessed is that Fruit[3] which has mingled a knowledge

   of the Tree of Life into mortals.

4. The serpent peered out and saw that the dove in paradise was hungry;

   the Pernicious One turned himself into a dove.

   He who is utterly accursed became like her,
   so that she might become his;

   he put on her colors, so that she might put on his ugliness,

   he sung to her a pleasant song, so that she might fly off amid laments.

   Blessed is that voice of the Father which came down

   to give comfort and to remove our mother's woe.

---

3. Fruit: I.e., Christ.

5. ܠܐ ܢܗܘܐ ܠܗ ܠܟܝܢܐ ܙܘܥ ܒܩܘܫܬܐ ܕܢܦܩܬ ܚܒܪܝܢ
ܙܘܥܐ ܓܝܪ ܠܐܘ ܗܘܐ ܘܦܘܪܫܢܗܝ ܠܒܝܫܬܐ
ܒܫܡ ܟܝܢܐ ܒܪܘܚܢܘܬܗ ܐܘ ܪܚܡܬܐ ܕܫܠܦ ܠܟܝܢܐ
ܐܟܠܗ ܒܣܪܐ ܕܐܝܟܐ ܒܪܘܚܐ ܕܗܐ ܠܒܗ ܗܘܐ
ܘܐܟܠܗ ܒܣܪܐ ܕܐܝܟܢܐ ܗܘܐ ܐܘܟܠܐ ܒܟܠܒܐ
ܒܪܝܟ ܗܘ ܕܝܗܒ ܦܓܪܗ
ܠܒܢܝ ܦܓܪܐ ܕܢܟܠܘܢ ܡܢ ܢܘܟܠܬܐ

6. ܐܝܟ ܚܝܠܐ ܚܙܐ ܗܘܐ ܢܦܫܐ ܒܓܘܗ ܗܘܬܐ ܘܐܬܦܪܫ ܘܕܒܪܗ
ܟܕ ܙܡܢܗ ܡܪܐ ܗܘܐ ܦܪܫ ܠܗ
ܙܟ ܚܘܒܗ ܠܟܠ ܠܡܠܟܗ ܠܟܘܢ ܐܢܫܘܬܐ
ܡܐ ܡܒܪܘܬܗ ܕܢܬܡܗ ܠܡܕܒܪܢܘܬܗ ܐܡܪ ܠܗ ܒܒܢܘܗܝ
ܒܝܬ ܡܠܟܘܗܝ ܡܬܚܡܠܐ ܕܐܬܐ ܒܪܘܡܪܡܐ
ܐܡܫܗ ܐܡܫܗ ܠܪܘܡܐ
ܕܢܫܡܥܘܢ ܬܟܒܪܗ ܕܚܙܐ ܒܗܐ ܬܟܒܬܐ

5. Let not our fast provide delight for the Evil One
as we use backbiting on our friends;

for of old they proclaimed a fast—and stoned Naboth to death: 1 Kgs 21:12–13

the Evil One was delighted with their fasts!

O fasters, who instead of bread devoured the flesh of a man;
during the fast they lapped up blood.

Because they devoured human flesh, they became food for the dogs. 1 Kgs 21:24

Blessed is He who gives His own Body

to our crazed mouths, so that we might cease from backbiting!

6. Mercy peered out, saw a soul in the pit, and devised how to draw it up.

Through His mere nod He could have saved that soul,

yet He girded up His love in readiness
for His labor and put on humanity.[4]

He acquired its childlike state so as to bring it to [true] knowledge;

He sung to it with His lyre lowly songs, inviting it to be raised up.

His Cross lifted Him up to the heights

so that Eve's children might likewise rise up [to join] the beings on high.

◆

4. put on humanity: Although "put on a body" is the most frequent metaphor for the incarnation in early Syriac literature, many other variations are found; for the present one, see also *Haer.* 35.7 and *Commentary on the Diatessaron* 2.14, and compare "he put on our humanity," found in the *Acts of Thomas* 80, 113 (Wright 1871, 250, 281); Aphrahat, *Dem.* 3.16; and the *Anaphora of Addai and Mari* (Gelston 1992, 50 [D24]). For this usage in general, see Brock 1982; also Text 16 (*Virg.* 7), n. 17.

TEXT 10

Eyes that are Blind and Eyes that are Opened (*Ieiun.* 6)

The abundant biblical lections during Lent offer to their hearers an infinite number of treasures. All too often, however, through the misuse of free will, human beings have blinded their own interior eye, so that they are no longer able to perceive these riches set before them in the biblical text. To remedy the situation, Ephrem begs Jesus to repeat the healing miracles he performed for the blind in the Gospels; in doing so Ephrem exploits the contrasted situations in a highly striking and imaginative way.

It will be noticed that the poem contains an acrostic, giving the author's name, ᵓPRYM. Again there is no refrain given, though here the last line of each stanza serves as one. An interesting study of this *madrasha* is given by Botha 2000.

Meter

The *qala* title is given as *a(n)t mar(y) aktebtah,* the opening words of Text 17 (*Fid.* 10), which, however, has a different *qala* title, namely *izgadda haddaya.* The meter consists of the following syllabic pattern: 5+6 7+4 4+4 4+5 5+6. In the present poem it will be noticed that there are a number of irregularities. Ephrem uses the meter elsewhere for *Fid.* 10–25, *Eccl.* 29–30, and *Nis.* 50.

Text

Unlike the previous text from this cycle, the present poem is only found in British Library Add. 14571 (of 519 CE; Beck's D).

ܥܠ ܛܠܐ ܕܐܝܟ ܡܪܝ ܐܒܪܗܡ

1. ܐܬܒܢܝܬ ܗܘܝܬ ܐܬܪܐ ܒܝܬ ܪܘܡܐ
ܩܛܠܐ ܚܙܝ ܒܟ ܟܪܐ ܐܝܟ ܕܠܒܘܫܬܐ
ܘܬܐܡܢܝ ܛܠܐ ܗܘ ܡܕܝܢܐ
ܗܐ ܡܬܦܠܓܝܢ ܦܘܪܫܢ ܡܫܒܘܚܐ
ܒܪܝ ܡܠܟܐ ܕܦܠܚ ܒܟ ܬܪܘܢ ܠܡܫܝܚܗ

2. ܐܝܟ ܒܗܘܢ ܢܟܬܐ ܠܒܫܝܢܐ ܕܡܫܬܐ
ܐܝܟ ܒܗܘܢ ܫܡܐ ܘܪܡܚܐ ܒܟܠ ܐܬܪܐ
ܐܝܟ ܕܗܘ ܒܝܬܗܘܢ ܐܬܪ ܐܡܐ
ܐܘ ܠܐܬܚܙܝܬ ܡܢܝ ܐܢܘܢ ܒܟܠ ܒܐܬܪܝ
ܒܪܝ ܕܗܘ ܕܒܟܠܗ ܠܒܝ ܒܟܠ ܒܕܘܪܝ

1. In the midst of the Fast gather together and become merchants,

for the scriptures are a treasure house of divinity.

With that holy voice as the key

they are opened up before those who listen.

Blessed is that King who opened up His treasury to His people in need.

2. Here are to be found garments
for those invited to the wedding feast, Matt 22:11

here too are sackcloth and tears for all kinds of penitents,

here in their midst is One to sustain[1] athletes too:

with every kind of riches are they filled.

Blessed is He who has prepared for everyone every kind of succor.

1. One to sustain: The meter requires *zayyana,* rather than *zayna,* "armor" (ANP). This form is attested in Audo 1897.

3. ܦܬܚܘ ܗܘܟܠ ܐܒ̈ܗܝ ܘܫܡܥܘ ܡ̈ܢܗ ܒܣܘܪܗܒܐ
ܕܩܡ ܒܪܐ ܗܘܐ ܕܝܠܕܐ ܗܘ ܟܬ̈ܒܐ ܐܢܫܐ
ܗܐ ܐܚܝܕ ܟܠ ܐܢܫ ܐܦ ܡܟܬܒܗ
ܐܝܟ ܒܪܬܐ ܡܢܗ ܕܠܐ ܢܒܛܪ
ܒܪܝܟ ܗܘ ܕܗܕܐ ܐܬܝ ܒܫܠܡܗ ܕܡܫܝܚܐ

4. ܪܒܐ ܗܘ ܡܘܠܕܐ ܕܡܪܢܐ ܡܢܝܢ ܗܘܝܬܐ
ܟܕ ܛܥܢܝܢ ܛܥܢܝܢ ܒܢ̈ܝܢ ܐܝܟ ܒܥܘܠܝ
ܕܒܢ̈ܝܐ ܐܢܘܢ ܕܚܙܐܘܗ ܗܘܘ
ܠܗ ܒܡܘܠܕܐ ܕܡܪܢܐ ܗܘ ܘܕܝܢ ܗܘ
ܚܘܝ ܡܪܢ ܒܒܘܟܪܐ ܕܪܘܚܐ ܗܘ ܒܒܝܬܗ ܫܠܡ

5. ܢܦܩܘ ܕܦܬܚ ܒܒܝܬܗ ܕܒܪ ܛܝܒܘ
ܦܬܚܬ ܐܒ̈ܝ ܕܐܬܚܙܝ ܥܘܗܝ ܟܕ ܠܐ ܙܒܢܐ
ܦܬܚ ܡܪܢ ܒܢ̈ܝܐ ܕܟܬܒܘ ܐܒ̈ܝ
ܟܕ ܙܒܢܝ ܚܝܐ ܕܐܬܪܒ ܛܝܒܘܬܝ
ܛܝܒܘ ܡܪܢ ܟܠܗ ܕܐܝܬ ܒܪ ܒܥܘܠܝ

3. Open up then, my brethren, and take from it with discernment,
for this treasure house is the common property of everyone,
and each person, as if he were treasurer, possesses his own key;
who can now fail to get rich?
Blessed is He who has removed the causes of our low estate.

4. Great is the gift which is cast[2] before our blind eyes: cf. Matt 7:6
for even though we all have a pair of eyes each,
few are those who have perceived that gift,
[who are aware of] what it is and from whom it comes.
Have mercy, Lord, on the blind, for all they can see is gold!

5. O Jesus who opened the eyes of Bartimaeus, Mark 10:46
You opened his eyes that had become blind against his will;
open, Lord, the eyes that of our own will
we have rendered blind; thus shall Your grace abound.
The mud [that You made then], Lord,
tells us that You are the Son of our Maker. John 9:6

---

2. cast: Compare Matt 7:6, though the Old Syriac (Curetonianus), Peshitta, and Ephrem (*Commentary on the Diatessaron* 6.21b) all have a different verb (*rma,* "throw"). The *Liber Graduum,* however, quotes the verse using *shda,* the verb found in this stanza (Kmosko 1926, col. 888, ln. 22).

6. ܡܢܘ ܐܟܘܬܟ ܐܘ ܡܡܟܟ ܦܪܨܘܦܟ
ܒܐܘܪܚܐ ܗܘ ܪܗܛ ܘܠܐ ܗܘܐ ܒܐ̈ܦܐ ܕܐܘܪܒ ܪܒܘܬܟ
ܠܟ ܕܝܢ ܡܪܢ ܪܗܛ ܠܟ ܒܐ̈ܦܝ
ܘܦܬܚ ܟܬ̈ܒܐ ܕܐܚܝܕܐ ܚܐܘܗܬܢ
ܒܪܡ ܗܘ ܕܡܗܝܢ ܟܬܒܐ ܕܗܘܢܐ ܗܘ ܕܟܬܘܪܢܗ

7. ܡܢܘ ܕܠܐ ܢܬܡܗ ܒܐܝܟ ܘܟܦܐܠܬܗ
ܠܐܝܟ ܒܪ ܡܟܝܟ ܡܟܟ ܦܬܚ ܟܬ̈ܒܘܗܝ
ܠܟ ܕܝܢ ܡܪܢ ܡܟܝܟ ܟܒܪ
ܦܬܚ ܟܬ̈ܒܐ ܕܚܬܝܡܐ ܐܝܟ ܚܟܝܡܐ
ܒܪܡ ܕܐܚܕ ܘܦܬܚ ܟܬ̈ܒܐ ܕܚܒܪ ܗܘܐ

8. ܡܢܘ ܕܠܐ ܢܫܘܬܗ ܟܡܝܢܐ ܕܡܡܟܟ ܠܟ
ܒܟܠ ܘܦܬܚ ܟܬ̈ܒܝܢ ܐܝܟ ܘܚܕܐ ܪܒܢܘ
ܠܟ ܕܝܢ ܡܒܪܟ ܗܘܐ ܗܘ ܟܬ̈ܒܐ
ܕܟܡܐ ܢܫܐܠܘܢ ܠܡܦܫܩܘ ܪܒܐ
ܠܡܠܟܘܗܝ ܡܪܝ ܡܢ ܟܠ ܕܐܝܬ ܡܢ ܒܟܠ ܐܬܒܪܝ

6. Who is there like You, who gave such honor to our faces?

For it was upon the ground that You spat, and not upon his face, John 9:6;
thus holding our image in honor. Gen 1:26

But with us, please spit on our faces, Lord,

and open the eyes which our own free will has closed.

Blessed is He who gave the mind's eye—
which we have managed to blind.

7. Who can fail to wonder at Adam, and how his eyes were opened: Gen 3:7

in Adam's case their opening proved harmful,

but we, Lord, are greatly benefited by the opening of our eyes,

seeing that it was the Evil One who closed them.

Blessed is He who gave succor and both closed and opened up eyes.

8. Who can fail to curse that Thorn[3] which betrayed us,

who by cunning opened up Adam's eyes
so that he beheld his own shame;

he has beguiled us too and smeared over our eyes

so that we might not see the enormity of our naked state.

Curse him, Lord, at the hand of all, so that You may be blessed by all.

◆

3. Thorn *(shpaya):* Based on 2 Cor 12:7. In the Peshitta the same word is also used in 1 Sam 29:4.

TEXT 11

The Two Lambs Compared
(*Azym.* 3)

Ephrem here explores the typological relationships between the Passover lamb of Exod 12 and Christ, the new Passover Lamb. This "True Lamb" is seen as the fulfillment of the Passover lamb on two different planes: in the world of space and time he leads the "Peoples," or Gentiles, out of the error of paganism, while in the domain of Sheol, outside normal time and space, he leads out the dead, beginning at the very moment of the crucifixion (Matt 27:52).

This double Exodus brought about by the True Lamb is reflected in the very structure of the poem, as can be seen by the following diagram (based on Brock 1975–76):

Passover Lamb		*True Lamb*		
Egypt = A		Error = B	+	Sheol = C
Pharaoh = A′		Satan = B′	+	Death = C′
				Grave = C″

X represents the Passover Lamb (leading the Israelites out of Egypt)
Y represents the True Lamb (leading the Gentiles out of Error)
Z represents the Living Lamb (leading the dead out of Sheol)

STANZA				
	1	Resemblance		
	2	Comparison of		
	3	Achievements,		
	4	Differences (shadow: fulfillment)		
	5	Old = single, New = double		
	6	Jewish Exodus from Egypt	A	X
	7	Gentile Exodus from Error	B	Y
	8	Exodus of Dead from Sheol	C	Z

Stanza	Content	
9	Egypt as symbol for Sheol and Error	A: C + B
10	Egypt hands back the Hebrews	A X
11	Sheol disgorges the Dead	C Z
12	Error casts up the Gentiles	B Y
13	Pharaoh returns the Hebrews	A′ X
14	Death returns the righteous	C′ Z
15	Error returns the Gentiles	B′ Y
16	Pharaoh is symbol for Death and Satan	A′: C′ + B′
17	Egypt breached	A X
18	Satan foiled	B′ Y
19	Grave emptied	C″ Z

For some other examples of Ephrem's artistry, see Palmer 1993a.

Meter

The *qala* title is given as *ʾetkannash(w) neʿbed b-iraḥ nisan,* which has some resemblance to the opening words of *Azym.* 13. The meter, which consists of 5+4 5+4 syllables, is used by Ephrem for *Azym.* 3–6, 8–21 (7 is lost) and *Nat.* 4. In later liturgical tradition the opening words of *Azym.* 3 are normally given as the *qala* title for this meter. In all the later excerpts from this poem (see below, under Text), the opening line begins *ha qṭil (h)u,* thus removing the need to take the vocalic *shwa* in *qṭil* as a full vowel metrically.

Text

Although the poem is preserved complete only in British Library Add. 14627 (sixth or seventh century; Beck's B), excerpts from it are found, not only at several places in the Mosul Fenqitho, but also in the East Syriac Ḥudra. The stanzas found are as follows:

1–4, 6–7	= Ḥudra 2.463
1–4, 9–10	= Mosul Fenqitho 5.158
1–4, 17–18	= Mosul Fenqitho 5.45
1	= Mosul Fenqitho 6.286 (the poem consists of *Azym.* 3.1, 5.1–2, 6.1)
11–12, 18–19	= Mosul Fenqitho 6.143 (the poem consists of *Azym.* 16.5–6, 2–3; 3.11–12; 4.2–7; 13.30–31; 3.18–19!)
18–19	= Mosul Fenqitho 6.167 (the poem is again built up from diverse sources)

ܥܰܠ ܛܠܳܐ ܕܶܐܬܩܰܛܰܠ ܒܝܰܕ ܓܰܝܳܣ ܢܳܫܘܡ

1. ܗܳܐ ܡܛܰܠ ܒܰܥܒܪܶܗ ܐܳܡܰܪ ܦܰܪܚܳܐ
ܘܰܢܦܰܫ ܒܢܰܦܫܶܗ ܐܳܡܰܪ ܡܰܫܡܥܬܳܐ

ܒܥܳܝܬܳܐ : ܐܰܫܒܰܚܬܳܐ ܠܒܰܪܳܐ ܡܳܪܳܐ ܕܳܪܳܐ
ܕܰܡܠܶܟ ܥܰܠ ܐܶܕܳܫܶܐ ܠܰܡܫܰܒܚܳܘ

2. ܠܰܬܪܰܥܘܗ̱ܝ ܐܰܒܳܐ ܚܙܳܐ ܐܰܢܬ
ܢܚܳܐ ܕܐܳܦ ܕܺܝܢ ܐܰܘ ܢܦܰܩܢܝ

3. ܢܰܦܫܳܐ ܘܰܢܦܰܩ ܢܦܰܩܬܶܗ
ܕܗܽܘ ܐܳܡܰܪ ܐܶܬܳܐ ܘܐܳܡܰܪ ܡܫܡܥܬܳܐ

4. ܢܚܳܬܘܢ ܠܐܶܬܳܐ ܐܰܝܟ ܛܰܠܠܳܐ
ܢܚܳܬܘܢ ܠܡܫܡܥܬܳܐ ܐܰܝܟ ܡܫܡܥܢܳܐ

1. In Egypt the Passover lamb was slain, Exod 12

 in Sion the True Lamb was slaughtered.

 Refrain: Praise to the Son, the Lord of symbols
 who fulfilled every symbol at His crucifixion!

2. My brethren, let us consider the two lambs,

 let us see where they bear resemblance and where they differ.

3. Let us weigh and compare their achievements

 —of the lamb that was the symbol,
 and of the Lamb that is the Truth.

4. Let us look upon the symbol as a shadow,

 let us look upon the Truth as the fulfillment.

5. ܫܡܥܘ ܐܕܢܐ ܫܡܝܢܝܬܐ ܟܠܠ ܗܘ ܦܪܚܐ
ܘܚܙ ܠܐܘܪܚ ܬܪܝܨܬܐ ܟܠܠ ܗܘ ܦܪܚܝ

6. ܗܘܬ ܗܘܬ ܡܢ ܡܕܢܚ ܒܐܕܪ ܦܪܚܐ
ܡܫܡܫܬܐ ܒܒܝܬܐ ܘܠܐ ܡܟܠܬܐ

7. ܗܘܬ ܠܗܘܢ ܡܢ ܠܡܥܪܒ ܒܐܕܪ ܡܫܡܫܬܐ
ܡܫܡܫܬܐ ܒܒܝܬܐ ܘܠܐ ܡܟܠܬܐ

8. ܡܢܘ ܠܗܘܢ ܕܢܫܘܒ ܒܐܕܪ ܬܝܡܢܐ
ܡܫܡܫܬܐ ܒܬܝܡܢܐ ܐܝܟ ܡܢ ܡܕܢܚ

9. ܒܡܕܢܚ ܙܒܢ ܗܘܘ ܐܘܪܚܐ ܕܐܕܪܐ
ܟܡܘܠ ܘܒܠܘܒܢ ܗܘܬ ܡܚܝܬܐ

10. ܡܢܘܬܗ ܕܡܕܢܚ ܒܐܕܪ ܦܪܚܐ
ܢܒܥܐ ܕܐܦܝܐ ܕܠܐ ܟܒܝܪܗ

5. Listen to the simple symbols that concern that Passover,
   and to the double achievements of this our Passover.

6. With the Passover lamb there took place for the People[1]
   an Exodus from Egypt, and not an entry.

7. So with the True Lamb there took place for the Peoples
   an Exodus from error, and not an entry.

8. With the Living Lamb there was a further Exodus, too,
   for the dead from Sheol, as from Egypt;

9. for in Egypt a pair of symbols are depicted,
   since it reflects both Sheol and Error.

10. With the Passover lamb, Egypt's greed
    learnt to give back, against its wont;

1. People: The singular normally stands for the Jewish People in Ephrem, though sometimes (not of course here) it represents the Christian "People from the Peoples." On this theme in Ephrem, see Murray 2004, 41–68.

11. ܟܫܘܒܐܘ ܕܫܘܒܠ ܒܐܡܪ ܛܠܝܐ
ܐܬܡܟܟ ܠܘܬܟ ܕܠܐ ܟܦܢܐ

12. ܠܘܒܝ ܒܟܒܬܐ ܒܐܡܪ ܡܘܫܬܐ
ܥܡܗ ܦܠܚܬ ܘܫܒܪܐ ܟܠܝܠܐ ܕܝܠܗ

13. ܒܗܘ ܐܡܪ ܦܪܚܐ ܦܐܝ ܦܪܚܘܗܝ
ܟܦܐ ܕܐܝܟ ܡܛܪܐ ܗܘ ܒܠܚܘܕܘܗܝ

14. ܒܗܘ ܐܡܪ ܛܠܝܐ ܦܐܝ ܡܛܪܐ
ܐܘܪܥܐ ܕܢܫܩܗ ܡܢ ܡܒܘܥܘܗܝ

15. ܒܗܘ ܐܡܪ ܡܘܫܬܐ ܛܘܒ ܫܦܝܪܐ
ܟܠܝܠܐ ܕܐܝܟ ܦܪܚܘܗܝ ܗܘ ܒܠܚܘܕܘܗܝ

16. ܒܦܪܚܘܗܝ ܙܡܝܪ ܗܘܐ ܐܘܟܠ ܕܠܦܘܫܐ
ܒܡܛܪܐ ܘܫܦܝܪܐ ܗܘܐ ܐܣܘܡܬܐ

11. with the Living Lamb, Sheol's hunger
disgorged and gave up the dead, against its nature.

12. With the True Lamb, greedy Error
threw up, ejected, and cast out the Peoples who were saved.

13. With that Passover lamb, Pharaoh returned the People
whom, like Death, he had held back.

14. With the Living Lamb, Death has returned
the just, who left their graves. Matt 17:52

15. With the True Lamb, Satan gave up the Peoples
whom, like Pharaoh, he had held back.

16. In Pharaoh a pair of types were depicted:
he was a pointer to both Death and Satan.

17. ܐܬܬܪܥܬ ܡܨܪܝܢ ܒܐܡܪ ܦܨܚܐ
ܘܦܬܚ ܒܝ̈ܡܐ ܐܘܪܚܐ ܦܫܝܛܬ

18. ܒܗܘ ܐܡܪ ܡܫܘܚܬܐ ܐܘܪܚܐ ܕܡܫܘܚܬܐ
ܦܢܐ ܫܡܫܐ ܕܫܢ ܐܘܪܚܬܐ

19. ܗܘ ܐܡܪ ܝܡܐ ܕܘܫ ܠܥܡ̈ܡܐ
ܐܘܪܚܐ ܡܢ ܡܥܒܪܐ ܒܫܠܐ ܕܝܡܐ

17. With the Passover lamb, Egypt was breached

and a path stretched out before the Hebrews.

18. With the True Lamb, Satan, having fenced off all paths,

left free the path that leads to Truth.

19. That Living Lamb has trodden out,[2]
with that cry which He uttered, Matt 27:50

the path from the grave for those who lie buried.

◆

2. trodden out *(drash):* The phrase *drash ʾurḥa,* of Christ's action, is frequently found in early Syriac writers, but the phrase does not occur in the Syriac Bible and its source is unknown. The present passage probably reflects its original context, namely treading out (i.e., initiating) the path from death to life. A discussion of the phrase is given in Murray 2004, 299–301.

TEXT 12

Christ, the New Passover Lamb (*Cruc.* 2)

This *madrasha* develops the theme of Christ as the True Lamb in a different way, bringing out a whole series of paradoxes. It was the preexistent True Lamb, that is, the divine Word, which gave Moses instructions for the slaughter of the Passover lamb. The True Lamb was at the same time a Shepherd to Moses, the shepherd of Israel (stanza 1). Thus it was that the True Lamb gave instructions about his own sacrifice to Moses, and so paradoxically the Sacrifice was the giver of instructions to the sacrificer (stanza 2).

All the details in Exod 12 concerning the Passover lamb turn out to be typologically significant: the roasting on a spit, the bitter herbs, the unleavened bread, and the consumption of the lamb without being seated (stanzas 2–6)—to which Ephrem adds a feature derived from Isa 61:1 (compare Luke 4:18).

Two further paradoxical symbols are introduced: Isaac the lamb (Gen 22:8) rescued by the ram (Gen 22:13), where both lamb and ram serve as symbols of Christ (stanza 7); and Abel, the shepherd who both offers a lamb as a sacrifice and is himself sacrificed (Gen 4; stanzas 8–9).

Meter

The *qala* title is given as *etqaṭṭal(w) (h)waw yallude,* the opening words of *Nat.* 24. The syllabic pattern consists of five pairs of 7+7 syllables. The refrain in effect constitutes the final unit of 7 syllables in stanza 1. Ephrem elsewhere uses this meter for *Res.* 2 (Text 15) and 3; *Haer.* 22–24, 48; *Nis.* 17–21 (all of which have the same *qala* title); and *Nat.* 23–24, where the *qala* title varies in different witnesses, the other titles being *bak mar(y) metpaṣṣaḥ* and *manu kay kad mayota* (the opening words of *Nat.* 23).

Text

Like all the other poems in the Paschal cycle, this is preserved complete only in British Library Add. 14627 (sixth or seventh century; Beck's B), though the first three stanzas are also to be found in the East Syriac Ḥudra (2.477).

ܥܠ ܩܠܐ ܕܐܬܩܛܠ ܗܘܐ ܒܟܘܪܐ

1. ܐܘ ܐܡܪܐ ܟܗܢܐ ܕܢܟܣ   ܐܡܪܐ ܠܦܨܚܐ ܒܗ ܩܪܒ
ܗܘ ܡܕܝܢ ܗܘܐ ܫܠܝܛܐ ܒܦܨܚܐ   ܕܢܪܥܐ ܒܗ ܦܨܚܐ ܗܢܐ
ܕܒܚܐ ܗܢܐ ܦܨܚܐ ܗܢܐ   ܘܕܒܚܐ ܐܡܪܐ ܠܡܫܝܚܗ
ܐܡܪܐ ܕܒܚܐ ܘܡܕܒܚܐ ܗܘܐ   ܗܘ ܕܒܚܐ ܘܟܗܢܘܬܗ
ܕܪܥܠܘܗܝ ܘܕܒܚܐ ܐܢܗ

ܒܥܘܬܐ : ܒܪܝܟ ܐܡܪܐ ܕܕܒܚܐ ܦܨܚܢ

2. ܢܟܣ ܗܘܐ ܡܘܫܐ ܒܡܨܪܝܢ   ܬܘܪܐ ܘܐܡܪܐ ܣܓܝܐܐ
ܘܟܕ ܠܗ ܢܟܣ ܠܐ ܐܕܪܟ   ܕܐܡܪ ܢܟܣ ܚܕ ܕܒܚܐ
ܐܡܪܐ ܗܘ ܡܢܟܣ ܗܘܐ ܠܗ   ܘܐܡܪܐ ܚܕܘ ܕܒܚܐ
ܟܠܗ ܕܒܚܐ ܒܦܨܚܐ   ܘܐܡܪ ܢܟܣܐ ܐܘ ܢܟܣܐ
ܘܐܡܪ ܢܟܣ ܐܘ ܢܟܣ   ܒܪܝܟ ܗܘ ܕܟܠܗ ܠܐܦܝܩܘܗܝ

1. O Hidden Lamb[1] who slaughtered
the visible lamb in the midst of Egypt, Exod 12:6

who gave the staff to Moses
with which the aged man might shepherd the flock; Exod 4:2

the aged [Moses] shepherded that aged flock,
but the Lamb shepherded them both.

The Lamb was both shepherded, and saw to the shepherding:
He shepherds His shepherds,[2]

for they shepherded Him, and He shepherds them.

Refrain: Blessed is the Lamb which shepherds His own flocks!

2. In the house of Jethro Moses slaughtered
sheep and lambs many times over; Exod 3:1

though he had learnt, he did not [yet] grasp
how he could slaughter but one sacrificial beast.

It was our Lamb who was teaching him
how he might depict His own symbol.

The Sacrifice instructed the sacrificer
how he should roast, and how he should eat, Exod 12:8

how to slaughter, and how to sprinkle [the blood].
Blessed is He who instructed those who were to consume Him! Exod 12:7, 22

---

1. Hidden Lamb: Ephrem frequently uses the term *kasya,* "hidden," in connection with symbols and types of Christ.
2. His shepherds: I.e., bishops (cf. Murray 2004, 187–91).

3. ܐܡܪܐ ܚܕܬܐ ܥܐܠ ܗܘܐ   ܒܪܚܡܐ ܕܗܠܟ ܥܠܬܐ
ܕܐܡܟܐ ܢܩܘܡ ܙܪܥܗ   ܒܐܡܪ ܟܠܐ ܕܝ ܠܦܘܩܗ
ܡܪܐ ܦܩܕ ܠܗ ܘܟܒܫ ܗܘܐ   ܕܐܒܠܗ ܢܦܪܘܫ ܒܐܒܘܟܘܢ
ܐܦ ܐܡܪܐ ܢܒܥܘܢܗ   ܕܒܥܠ ܒܪܩܐ ܢܐܟܘܠ ܒܗ
ܕܗܘܐ ܒܪܟ ܟܠܡܝܢܐ   ܐܘܦ ܠܡܪܐ ܒܪܟ ܟܠ

4. ܐܡܪܐ ܠܡܫܘܚܐ ܡܠܟ ܗܘܐ   ܕܡܫܝܚܐ ܠܐ ܢܬܟܠܠ
ܕܡܥܒܪܐ ܗܘ ܢܝܫܐ ܕܩܝܡܬܗ   ܘܛܘܦܐ ܠܦܘܫܐ ܕܟܝܢܗ
ܠܐܒܘܟܘܢ ܐܦ ܦܩܕ ܗܘܐ   ܕܩܕܡ ܩܝܢܗ ܠܐ ܢܬܐܙ
ܕܒܟܠܐ ܢܬܟܠܐ ܐܝܟ ܐܘܟܠܐ   ܗܢܐ ܡܫܝܚܐ ܘܒܟܘܪܐ
ܕܗܘܐ ܗܘܐ ܐܝܟ ܩܡ ܬܝܢܐ   ܒܪܝܢ ܐܡܪܐ ܕܐܘܦ ܐܙܪܗ

3. The New Lamb[3] instructed
   that shepherd [Moses] who had grown old with [his] flock

how he might mark out His symbol[4]
   in a lamb taken from the sheep, [serving as] His type.[5] Exod 12:5

He gave orders for bitter herbs, gathering them
   so that mourning for it/Him might be present[6] Exod 12:8;
      in those who consumed it. Num 9:11

The Lamb admonished its slaughterer Exod 12:46; Num
   that no bone should be broken within it, 9:12; John 19:36

for He Himself would bind up the broken.[7] Isa 61:1;
   Thanks be the Lord who binds up all![8] Luke 4:18

4. The Lamb gave Moses instructions that it be not cooked in water, Exod 12:9

for the spit is a sign of His Cross,
   and [an open fire for] roasting the symbol of His bread.

He bade those who ate it, too, to leave nothing over from it, Exod 12:10;
Num 9:12

so that it should not be despised as ordinary food that passes away,

for it has become resplendent, being the very Medicine of Life.[9]
   Blessed is the Lamb who has made resplendent His symbol!

---

3. New Lamb: Compare *Nat.* 4.123 where Christ is described as *emra sharwaya,* "initial Lamb."

4. His symbol *(rzh, razeh):* The term for "symbol" or "mystery" is variously spelled in early manuscripts. The later West Syriac norm is *r'z'*, and in East Syriac, *'rz'*.

5. His type *(bar ṭupseh): Bar* often has the sense of "sharing in." The Greek loanword *ṭupsa (<tupos)* is common in Ephrem.

6. be present: Lit. "fly."

7. bind up *(ʿaṣeb)* the broken: Thus the Peshitta at Isa 61:1, but in the Gospel quotation of the verse in Luke 4:18 the Peshitta has "heal" (with Septuagint and Greek New Testament); the one surviving Old Syriac manuscript here (Sinaiticus) omits the phrase. A study of healing imagery in Ephrem can be found in Shemunkasho 2002.

8. who binds up all *(ʿaṣeb koll):* Ephrem is very fond of titles consisting of a participle + *koll,* and several other examples will be noticed in this selection of texts.

9. being the very Medicine of Life *('a[y]k sam ḥayye):* The particle *'a(y)k,* like Greek *hōs,* can mean either "like" (but different from), or "in its role as" (the case here, as with the same phrase in *Nat.* 13.2) (Beck 1980). Medicine of Life is quite a common designation of Christ in Ephrem; for its Mesopotamian antecedents, see Widengren 1946, 129–38.

5. ܐܡܪܐ ܦܩܕ ܟܠܐ ܙܢܗ ܕܢܐܟܠܘܢܝܗܝ ܥܡ ܦܨܚܐ
ܟܣܝܐ ܚܕܐ ܘܓܠܝܐ ܚܕܐ ܕܢܦܩ ܗܘܐ ܕܚܕܬܘܬܗ
ܘܦܪܫ ܗܘܐ ܚܡܝܪܐ ܕܚܛܝܐ ܗܘ ܒܠܫܢܐ ܘܐܟܠܘܗ ܠܐ
ܡܐܢ ܗܘܐ ܒܗ ܠܐ ܘܒܚܕ ܥܘܠܐ ܥܡ ܦܨܚܐ ܕܫܒܬܐ ܥܘܠܐ
ܥܘܠܐ ܒܗ ܚܡܝܪܐ ܡܟܠܗ ܠܐ ܒܪܡ ܗܘ ܟܣܝܐ ܕܫܒܬܐ ܠܐ

6. ܡܪܟܐ ܠܗܘܢ ܕܦܘܩܕܢܐ ܦܩܕ ܗܘܐ ܐܡܪ ܡܫܡܠܝܐ
ܟܠ ܙܢܗ ܕܐܡܪ ܐܚܪܐ ܘܠܐ ܐܢܫ ܢܐܟܠܘܗܝ ܒܪ ܥܡܡܐ
ܙܢܗ ܕܦܨܚܐ ܡܨܪܝܐ ܕܡܢܘ ܢܐܟܠܘܢܝܗܝ ܒܪ ܥܡܡܐ
ܕܡܫܬܐ ܙܘܥܝܢ ܡܘܕܝܢܘܗܝ ܘܐܦܣܘܗ ܡܦܩܝܢ ܡܢܗ
ܕܢܚܘܢ ܘܐܬܡܢܘ ܢܘܩܝܐ ܒܪܡ ܕܟܠܗ ܙܪܐ ܐܝܡܐ

5. The Lamb gave orders concerning His symbol Exod 12:8;
   that they should eat it with unleavened bread— Num 9:11

new bread and new flesh to depict a symbol of His newness,

for gone was the old leaven of Eve which made all stale with age.

Everything had grown old and everything had wasted away,
   but through the unleavened bread that renovates all

the leaven that ages all is made useless.
   Blessed is that Bread who has made everything new! 1 Cor 5:7

6. The remainder of the instructions did the True Lamb give

concerning His symbol, the temporary lamb:
   no one was to eat it sitting down, Exod 12:11

for it is a symbol of the Holy Body.
   For who would consume sitting down

Him before whom the Seraphim tremble,
   covering their faces from Him? Isa 6:2

Those who receive Him are in awe and are made holy.
   Blessed is He who gave instructions concerning
      the resplendent symbol!

7. ܠܐ ܚܙܐ ܐܡܪܐ ܚܝܐ ܕܦܨܚܐ ܒܗ ܕܟܘܠܗ̇
ܘܦܨܚܐ ܒܗ ܐܦ ܢܩܘܫܐ ܕܐܘܪܚ ܠܐܒܪܗܡ ܩܕܡܝܐ
ܕܒܪܝܬܐ ܗ̱ܘܐ ܢܡܘܣܐ ܛܠܠܐ ܗ̱ܘܐ ܘܦܪܩ ܐܢܘܢ
ܦܪܩ ܐܡܪܐ ܘܛܠܠܐ ܕܒܪܐ ܒܪܗ ܗ̱ܘܐ ܦܪܩ ܗܘܐ
ܕܢܗܘܐ ܗܘ ܦܨܚܐ ܕܚܝܐ ܒܪܝܟ ܕܐܬܐ ܘܦܨܚ ܚܝܐ

8. ܗܢܐ ܐܡܪܐ ܩܕܝܫܐ ܦܨܚܐ ܒܗ ܕܒܪܐ ܩܕܝܫܐ
ܥܒܪܐ ܠܥܡܡܝܢܐ ܘܢܦܩ ܒܗ ܡܢ ܕܡܘܬܗ
ܘܛܒܥ ܒܗ ܡܢ ܪܘܚܗ ܦܪܩ ܒܒܠܗܘܢ ܩܠܐ ܡܠܬܗ
ܕܚܝܐ ܗܘ ܗܝܡܢܐ ܐܦ ܕܚܝܐ ܪܙ ܒܗ ܕܚܝܐ ܐܦ ܕܚܝܐ
ܕܚܝܘܬܗ ܘܕܚܝܘܬܗ ܠܝ ܒܦܓܪܐ ܪܐܙ ܐܪܙܘܗܝ

7. Come and behold the Living Lamb
who has chosen shepherds for Himself,

choosing, too, slaughterers
—who made Abraham hold the knife Gen 22:10

to kill His symbol, the sheep.
He both killed and delivered His symbol—

He saved [Isaac] the lamb, but slew the ram:
by His symbol He delivered His symbol,[10] Gen 22:12–13

so that He might become the summation of all symbols.
Blessed is He who came and summed up all symbols!

8. This primordial Lamb
chose for Himself [Abel] the first shepherd; Gen 4:4

the firstborn[11] [then chose] the firstling,
and He poured into him something of His likenesses,

imprinting in him something to portray Him,
spreading over him a parable of His own slaughter;

For Abel was both shepherd and sacrifice,
and so our Shepherd and our Sacrifice has depicted in him

His own role as both Shepherd and Sacrifice.
Praise be to You, Depicter of symbols![12]

---

10. He both killed and delivered His symbol: Early Syriac writers gave several different typological interpretations of Isaac and the ram in Gen 22, and two of these are used by Ephrem: (a) Isaac represents humanity, rescued by Christ the True Lamb (thus *Nat.* 18.30); (b) Isaac and the ram are both types of Christ, with Isaac representing Christ's divinity and the ram his humanity, or flesh. This is Ephrem's understanding here. It is earlier found in Origen and is taken up in many later Greek and (dyophysite) Syriac writers. On this subject in general see Daniélou 1947, and, for some later Syriac treatments, Brock 1986, 76–80.

11. the firstborn *(bkrʾ, bukra):* Such defective spellings are not uncommon in fifth- and sixth-century manuscripts, but are very rarely found later.

12. Depicter of symbols: Ephrem employs some other divine titles with the element *ṣaʾar,* notably *ṣaʾar ʿule,* "Depicter, Fashioner of infants" (in the womb) (*Nat.* 4.161, 170), taken up later especially by Jacob of Serugh.

9. ܒܗܝܟܠ ܐܡܪܢ ܟܠܗ ܗܘܐ ܕܢܩܕܡ ܢܦܫܗ ܒܩܕܡ
ܘܐܡܪܐ ܠܐܡܪܐ ܢܩܪܒ ܗܘܐ ܘܢܩܪܒ ܒܩܕܡ ܢܦܫܗ
ܘܟܢ ܢܩܪܒ ܐܦ ܠܐܝܣܚܩ ܪܒ ܬܗܪܐ ܕܗܘܐ ܬܡܢ
ܘܐܡܪܐ ܗܘܐ ܗܘ ܕܡܩܪܒ ܘܐܡܪܐ ܗܘܐ ܗܘ ܕܐܬܩܪܒ
ܘܐܡܪܐ ܗܘܐ ܗܘ ܕܡܩܒܠ ܬܘܕܝ ܠܐܡܪܗ ܕܐܠܗܐ

10. ܒܟܠ ܕܪ ܒܘܟܪܐ ܡܚܝܠܐ ܗܘܐ ܒܪ̈ܐ ܩܛܝܠܐ ܕܐܘܡܩܘܗܝ
ܐܡܪܐ ܗܘܐ ܒܒܘܟܪܘܬܐ ܐܝܟ ܒܪܬܐ ܕܩܪܝܒܘܗܝ
ܩܕܡ ܕܢܬܝܠܕ ܒܡܘܠܕܐ ܐܦ ܟܕ ܢܣܝܒ ܩܪܒܢܐ ܗܘ
ܩܪܒܘ ܒܟܪ̈ܝܗܘܢ ܐܬܟܬܫܘ ܡܫܝܚܐ ܕܟܠܗ ܡܒܟܪܘܗܝ
ܘܢܦܪܘܢ ܕܗܐ ܒܡܫܚܘܗܝ ܒܪܝ ܕܐܒܪܗܡ ܢܚܘܬܐ

9. Our Lamb instructed Abel
to keep himself innocent first of all,

so that [as a] lamb he might offer up a lamb,
offering up first himself

and only then offering up the other.
Great is the wonder that took place there,

for it was a lamb who was making the offering
and a lamb that was being offered—

and it was the Lamb, too, who received it.
Thanksgiving be to the Lamb of God! John 1:29

10. In every generation the firstborn was killed,
acting as slain symbols of His righteous ones.

The lamb served in prophecy
as herald of the readings about Him:[13]

what was still to happen
became close, though still far off.

His servants clothed themselves first of all
with [His] names, and after [them] with His deeds,

so that [successive] generations might read of His names.
Blessed is He whom prophecy has proclaimed!

◆

13. readings about Him: Lit. "His readings/lections."

TEXT 13

Satan's Complaint (*Nis.* 41)

The second half of the cycle of *madrashe* entitled "of the Nisibenes" (also "of Nisibis") contains a series of poems where Ephrem treats the subject of the Descent of Christ into Sheol in a highly dramatic and lively fashion, with Satan and Death personified. In the present poem Satan is the speaker for the first nine stanzas: he has his suspicions that, although Jesus has successfully been crucified, He might somehow or other still wreck his own plans—despite all the care that Satan has taken ever since the time of Adam to ensnare the human race. In stanza 10 Satan's minions try to reassure him, using the example of Elisha, who like Jesus, raised someone from the dead, but nevertheless himself died. Satan, however, is quick to point out that Elisha also brought a dead person back to life *after* he himself had died. In stanza 13 Death appears on the scene, gloating over the crucifixion of Jesus, whom he addresses insultingly as "son of Mary" (implying he is illegitimate). In stanza 15 Satan comes along, wanting to take a look at Jesus, now in Sheol; it is now his turn to try and comfort Death, since Death is "all gloomy," having lost a whole lot of dead people who had risen from the dead at the moment of Jesus's own death (Matt 27:52). Satan requests Death to open up the gate of Sheol so that they can jeer at Jesus lying dead there. Death duly does so—"and out shone the radiance of our Lord's face!"

Ephrem neatly combines humor with serious theological issues when he puts into Satan's own mouth refutations of various erroneous views of Christ; a good example of this is provided in stanza 11, where Satan rebukes his underlings for supposing Jesus was just a prophet.

Meter

The *qala* title for *Nis.* 35–42 is *qarna w-shipura.* The metrical structure is a complicated one, with each stanza consisting of 4+4 4+4 9 7+7 7+7 4+7 7 10 syllables.

Text

The poem is preserved complete only in British Library Add. 14572 (sixth century; Beck's R), though stanzas 9 (end) through 16 also occur in British Library Add. 17141 (eighth or ninth century), and just stanza 13 in the Mosul Fenqitho (6.450).

ܥܠ ܛܠܐ ܕܡܪܝܐ ܘܫܡܥܘܢ

1. ܐܡܪ ܟܗܢܐ ܕܩܒܠܗ ܡܢܗ
ܕܢܫܩܘܠ ܕܥܠܡܐ ܢܗܒ ܙܘܗܝ
ܗܐ ܟܡܪ ܒܪ ܠܛܒܐ ܐܢܐ ܕܫܢܝܐ
ܘܠܐ ܡܛܠܘܡ ܗܘܐ ܠܝ ܒܛܠܝܐ ܠܐ ܚܙܝܬ ܩܕܡ ܒܝ ܡܛܠܡ
ܘܐܘܡܝܬ ܡܢܗ ܘܐܘܪܟܬܗ ܐܠܐ ܠܗ ܡܫܒܚ ܐܒܘܢܐ
ܐܠܐ ܗܘ ܡܫܝܚܐ ܕܫܠܛ ܠܗ ܒܟܠ ܗܐ ܕܒܝܬ
ܗܫܐ ܠܟܠܟܝ ܠܡ ܠܘܒܟܝ
ܕܟܘܠܗ ܒܟܠܗ ܒܪܝܬܐ ܒܟܠ ܟܝܢ

ܒܥܘܬܐ : ܒܪܝܟ ܕܐܬܐ ܘܦܪܩ ܢܟܠܗܘܢ ܕܙܢܝܐ

1. The Evil One said, "I am afraid

of this Jesus, in case he wreck my plans.

Here I am, thousands of years old

and I have never had a moment free from activity:
I have not seen anything in existence

that I have neglected or let go.
And now along comes someone
who makes the debauched chaste,

causing me to lament from now on
because he is destroying all I have built up.

My labors have been many, along with my instructing,

for I have enshrouded the whole of creation in all kinds of evil."

Refrain: Blessed is He who has come and laid bare
the wiles of the Crafty One.

2. ܦܫܛܬ ܪܘܚܗ ܥܡ ܩܛܝܠܐ
ܘܒܬܪܗ ܐܒܘܗ̱ܝ ܡܬܟܠܒܐ ܗ̱ܘܬ
ܪܘܚܐ ܕܩܛܝܠܐ ܐܡܝܢܐ ܗ̱ܘܐ ܠܗ
ܒܪܘܚܐ ܕܒܥܝܐ ܚܙܐ ܗ̱ܘܬ ܕܢܦܩ ܗ̱ܘܐ ܐܬܪܐ ܡܫܬܠܠ
ܕܡܫܐ ܗ̱ܘ ܚܙܝܐ ܕܩܛܝܠܐ ܒܚܝܠܐ ܕܩܛܝܠܐ ܠܗܘܢ
ܪܒܐ ܐܠܦܬ ܡܠܬܐ ܠܒܢܝܢܐ ܡܬܚܬܐ
ܐ̱ܝ ܠܡ ܪܘܚܐ ܐܬܒܣܡܘ
ܒܥܝܐ ܢܐܒܘܗ̱ܝ ܠܐܝܬܐ ܕܐܬܪܒܐ ܗ̱ܘ ܐܬܒܣܡܘ

3. ܠܥܠܘ ܕܐܒܐ ܘܠܡ ܒܥܘܕܪܢܗ
ܡܬܚܫܒ ܐ̱ܢܐ ܦܪܘܫܘܬܐ
ܫܬܩ ܗ̱ܘܐ ܠܥܝܐ ܕܡܠܬܐ ܚܕ ܗ̱ܘ
ܒܠܒ ܠܗ ܫܘܠܐ ܕܡܠܬܐ ܘܓܙܐ ܠܒܪܗ ܕܡܠܬܐ
ܪܡܐ ܠܗ ܙܩ ܚܕ ܡܠܬܐ ܕܐܝܟ ܡܘܪܐ ܠܗ ܒܠܡܠܬܐ
ܗܘܐ ܒܦܩ ܠܗ ܘܐܝܟ ܠܛܠܝ ܢܒܪܘܟ ܡܢܗ
ܕܒܟܠ ܐܒܢܝ ܦܪܘܫܘܬܐ
ܢܬܠܒܫܘܢ ܕܠܐ ܠܒܗ ܐܬܠܒܫܘܢ

2. "I have matched my course with the swift

and outstripped them; I engaged in battle,

and the multitudinous throng served as my armor;

I rejoiced in the throng of the populace
for they gave me a little opportunity,

seeing that the impact of numbers is powerful:
with a huge army

I raised up a great mountain of a tower,
stretching it up to heaven. Gen 11:4

If they could wage war with the height

how much more will they defeat this man who fights on earth!

3. "Using whatever opportunity time offers

I wage war with discretion.

The People[1] heard that God was one, Deut 6:4

but they made themselves a multitude of gods;
but when they saw the son of God, Jer 2:28

they rushed back to the one God,
so that on the pretext of confessing God

they deny [his son];
pretending to show their zeal, they will run away from him.

Because they are perverse on every occasion,

they will be found to be godless.

1. People: I.e., the Jews. For Ephrem's polemic against the Jews, see especially McVey 1990 and Shepardson 2001.

4. ܗܐ ܒܪ ܢܘܟܪܝܐ ܐܢܐ ܕܫܒܝܐ
ܘܟܠ ܡܟܕܪܐ ܠܐ ܒܣܝܡ ܡܢ ܡܕܡ
ܠܚܡܐ ܗܘ ܕܡܟܠܬܐ ܡܫܟܚ ܗܘܐ
ܕܒܢܝܐ ܕܠܐ ܡܫܬܝܢ ܐܡܝܐ ܐܢܘܢ ܡܢ ܡܥܕܪܐ
ܘܢܪܒܘܢ ܒܥܡܗܘܢ ܡܥܡܪܗܘܢ ܐܝܟ ܕܝܢ ܐܒܗ̈ܬܐ ܦܓܠܐ
ܘܠܐ ܡܬܒܝܢ ܠܗ ܒܐܘܪܚܐ ܕܐܘܪܟ ܒܚܝܝܗܘܢ
ܘܐܝܟ ܕܐܝܬ ܐܒ̈ܗܐ ܠܒܢ̈ܐ
ܒܥܘܗ ܡܩܡܐ ܡܢ ܐܘܪܚܐ ܕܡܒܝܬܗܘܢ

5. ܚܠܦ ܡܡܠܠܐ ܒܡܐܢܘܬܐ
ܦܓܪܐ ܐܝܟܐ ܘܒܠܥܗ ܘܡܢܗ
ܢܚܬܐ ܕܒܫܘܬܗܘܢ ܡܢ ܟܠ ܓܒܝܢ
ܒܚܝܝܗܘܢ ܡܢ ܦܪܝܫܐ ܦܘܫܩܗܘܢ ܡܢ ܗܝܟܠܐ
ܡܥܒܕܗܘܢ ܡܢ ܢܒܝܐ ܒܟܬܒܐ ܚܕ̈ܬܐ ܘܥܬܝ̈ܩܬܐ
ܡܐ ܒܡܬܝܢ ܒܡܫܠܐ ܡܫܡܐ ܠܡܒܣܡ
ܐܢ ܢܦܠܬ ܡܠܟ ܚܝܐ
ܐܘ ܕܚܝܘܢ ܐܘ ܡܝܐ ܡܠܝܐ ܡܢ ܙܪܥܗ

4. "I've had a great many years' experience,
and no child have I ever disdained—
indeed, I have been most attentive to children,
making sure that they acquired bad habits from the very start,
so that their faults might grow as they grew up.
There are some stupid fathers
who do not cause harm to the seed which I have sown in their sons,
while others, like good farmers,
have uprooted these faults from the minds of their children.

5. "Instead of using a chain, I have bound men
with sloth, and they have sat down idle.
Thus have I deprived their senses from doing anything good:
their eyes from reading, their mouths from singing praise,
their minds from learning. How keen they are
for barren and useless tales; at empty talk they excel,
but should the word of life be mentioned in their presence,
either they will drive it out, or get up and go.

6. ܒܗܐ ܦܘܪ̈ܫܢܐ ܠܗܘ ܒܪܢܫܐ
ܘܟܠ ܕܗܟܢ ܥܒܕܗ ܠܐ ܟܠ ܐ̱ܢܫ
ܗܐ ܠܒܪ ܫܡܥܬܗ ܕܒܪܢܫܐ ܐܬܡܗ
ܫܦܝܪܐ ܕܢܚܘܬ ܗܘܐ ܠܗ ܕܒܪ̈ܝܬܐ ܡܬܒܪܝܢ
ܕܡܫܬܢܝܢ ܐܢ ܡܬܐܡܪܝܢ ܟܠ ܫܡܝܐ ܕܝܢ ܐܢ ܢܬܡܠܘܢ
ܟܠ ܐܕ̈ܫܐ ܠܐ ܡܬܥܒܪܐ ܡܢ ܐܬܪܗ
ܣܓܝ ܫܦܝܪܐ ܦܪܘܫܐ
ܒܓܠܝܐ ܓܢܝܐ ܘܫܟܝܚܐ ܗܘܐ ܟܠ ܐ̱ܢܫ

7. ܒܗܘ ܐܘܦܐ ܥܡ ܒܪܬܐ
ܕܒܬܘܠܬܐ ܡܥܒܕ ܥܒܕܘܗܝ
ܐܦܪܬܐ ܕܟܠܗܘܢ ܡܢܗ ܡܫܪܝܐ
ܕܟܠܗ ܟܠܗܘܢ ܠܐ ܡܢܗ ܫܡܝܐ ܒܫܡܝܐ ܐܝܟ ܐܘܦܝܣ
ܗܐ ܕܢܫܟܚ ܒܗ ܐܝܣܝ ܗܐ ܕܝܠܕ ܙܪܥܐ ܠܐܦܪܬܐ
ܒܐܘܪܫܠܡ ܡܫܝܚܗ ܠܥܒܕܗ ܒܫܡܝܐ
ܡܛܠ ܕܚܝܐ ܒܥܘܢܝܬܗ
ܡܠܟ ܒܥܠܡܐ ܘܗܢܐ ܕܝܠ ܒܥܘܢܝܬܗ

6. “How many satans there are in a person,

but it is I alone whom everyone curses.

A person’s anger is [like]

a devil which harasses him daily. Other demons are like travelers

who only move on if they are forced to, but as for anger,

even if all the righteous adjure it,
it will not be rooted out from its place.

Instead of hating destructive envy,

everyone hates some weak and wretched devil!

7. “The snake-charmer is put to shame along with the enchanter

who daily brings snakes into submission;

the viper which is inside him defies him,

for he fails to subdue the lust within him:
hidden sin is like a snake:

when it breathes on him, he gets burnt right up.
Even when he has succeeded in catching the viper,

using his skill, delusion strikes him secretly:

he lulls the serpent with his incantations,

but by these same incantations he arouses against himself great wrath.

8. ܫܡܫܬ ܒܟܘܟܒܐ ܘܡܠܟܬ ܥܡܬ
ܡܢܗ ܕܐܘܪܡ ܕܒܢܘܗܝ ܥܡ ܟܠ
[...]
ܪܒ ܢܛܪ ܕܗܘܐ ܡܠܟܬ ܘܕܪܝ ܡܢ ܕܪܝ ܐܡܬܗ
ܕܢܐܬܐ ܒܡܘܬܗ ܕܒܢܝܐ ܠܐܝܢܐ ܕܒܗܘ ܡܢ ܚܘܒܐ
ܬܒܪܐ ܟܡܡܘܗܝ ܒܣܟܠ ܣܟܠ ܕܪܚܡܬܗ
ܒܪܡܐ ܕܗܘܐ ܠܐܚܝܬ ܢܡܪܐ
ܕܟܠ ܘܐܟܝܢ ܘܐܦ ܠܐ ܕܢܦܘܩ ܙܒܠ ܗܘܐ

9. ܪܒܝܬ ܘܚܠܦܬ ܕܢܛܪ ܗܘܐ
ܗܘܘ ܡܡܠܟ ܕܢܟܝܡ ܟܠ
ܒܐܒܢܐ ܕܐܒܬܗ ܠܐܘܪܡ ܚܕ ܗܘܐ
ܐܘܩܬܗ ܟܕ ܗܘܐ ܡܘܠܕ ܘܒܥܠܬ ܟܕ ܒܒܪܐ ܐܣܪܐ
ܘܠܐ ܢܬܟܡ ܟܕ ܒܬܚܢܐ ܚܠܐ ܕܡܥܐ ܡܢܐ ܗܘܬ
ܕܗܘܐ ܐܡܪ ܒܗ ܘܕܒܟܝܐ ܒܗܘܕܝ ܐܝ ܡܦܩ
ܟܢܬܝ ܐܝܡܐ ܗܐ ܕܡܫܝܚ
ܟܕ ܠܐ ܢܦܩܘ ܒܦܩܝܕܐ ܒܦܘܡ ܐܒܘܝ

8. "I set my stings, and sat and waited.

Who else has so stretched out his patience with everyone?

[a line is lost]

I sat beside the long-suffering and gradually bewitched him

until he was reduced to despair.
As for the person who shrinks from sin,

habit subdued him: little by little I wore him down

until he too came under [my] yoke;

once he had come and got used to it he did not want to leave it.

9. "I perceived and saw that the long-suffering person

is someone who can subdue everything.

When I conquered him, Adam was only one,

so I left him until he had fathered children
and I looked for some other work: Gen 4:1–2

so that idleness might not have experience of me
I started counting the sand of the sea, cf. Sir 1:2

to make myself patient and to test my memory,
to see if I could cope

with humanity once they had multiplied.

Before they had done so I had tried them in many things."

10. ܕܪܫܡܘ ܦܓܪܝܗܘܢ ܕܡܫܚܐ ܒܫܡܗ
ܘܢܛܪ ܢܦܫܗܘܢ ܒܬܘܩܢܬܐ
ܕܗܐ ܠܟܘܢ ܡܫܝܚܐ ܐܝܟ ܡܠܟܐ
ܘܐܬܐ ܒܫܘܠܡܐ ܒܒܢܝܬܐ ܘܐܝܟ ܠܒܪܗ ܕܐܪܡܠܬܐ
ܗܐ ܡܫܡܫ ܗܘܐ ܠܡܫܝܚܐ ܘܪܒܐ ܗܘܐ ܕܝܢ ܡܫܡܫܢܘܗܝ
ܕܡܫܚܐ ܦܫܝܛ ܒܡܫܡܫܢܘܗܝ ܗܪܐ ܡܫܡܫܢܘܗܝ
ܘܐܚܕܐ ܐܚܝ ܡܫܝܚܐ
ܕܗܐ ܠܡܫܝܚܐ ܐܝܟ ܡܠܟܐ ܒܝܕ ܟܗܢܘܗܝ

11. ܐܢ ܡܫܝܚܐ ܕܐܬܒܪܝ ܗܘܐ
ܪܒ ܗܘܐ ܫܠܝܛܗ ܒܟܠܗ ܕܡܫܝܚܐ
ܘܐܢ ܗܘ ܕܒܪܐ ܡܠܟܐ ܐܝܟ ܕܗܘܐ ܒܗ
ܒܡܠܐ ܒܗ ܦܠܚܝܢ ܡܠܐܟܐ ܒܗ ܡܘܗܒܬܗ ܕܡܫܝܚܐ ܠܡܠܐܟܐ
ܡܢܗ ܕܗܘܐ ܐܠܗܘܬܐ ܕܒܪܐ ܗܘ ܒܗ ܪܒ ܗܘܐ ܡܫܝܚܐ
ܡܢ ܥܒܕܐ ܕܗܘܐ ܒܪܝܬܐ ܐܠܗܘܬܗ
ܘܠܐ ܫܦܝܪܘܬܗ ܠܫܘܒܚܗ
ܪܒܘܬܗ ܕܦܫܝܛܘܬܗܘܢ ܠܒܪܝܬܐ

10. The servants of the Evil One disputed with him,

refuting his words with their rejoinders:

"Look at Elisha who brought a dead person back to life,

who overcame Death in the upper room, reviving the widow's son; 2 Kgs 4:10, 34–35

he is now subdued in Sheol."
Because the Evil One was very quick-witted

he refuted their words by means of their own words:

"How can Elisha be defeated, seeing that he has,

in Sheol itself, brought the dead back to life by means of his bones? 2 Kgs 13:21

11. "If Elisha, who was insignificant,

had such great power in Sheol,

if he could raise up one dead man there,

how many dead will the death of the mighty Jesus raise?

You should learn from this, my companions, how much greater

this Jesus is than us, seeing that he has cunningly deceived you

and you failed to take in his greatness,

comparing him merely to the prophets.

12. ܐܒܘܗܝ ܐܒܘܢ ܒܘܠܕܗܘܢ
ܐܡܪ ܫܡܥܐ ܠܒܢܝ ܐܠܗܘ
ܗܘ ܥܒܪ ܕܐܚܝ ܠܥܒܘܪ ܟܕ ܫܡܥ
ܐܝܟ ܣܦܩ ܠܗ ܡܘܬܐ ܘܐܢ ܕܝܢ ܐܬܐ ܠܗ ܡܘܬܐ
ܗܘܝܘ ܙܒܢܐ ܕܢܬܡܠܟ ܠܗ ܘܐܢ ܗܘ ܙܒܢܐ ܕܢܬܡܠܟ
ܐܝܟܢ ܕܚܕܐ ܕܠܐ ܡܬܐ ܠܗܠܝܢ
ܒܢܝܐ ܗܘ ܙܒܢܐ ܕܒܪ ܟܝ
ܕܒܪ ܡܬܐ ܠܐܕܡ ܒܬܠ ܒܡܫܚܗ

13. ܐܪܝܡ ܡܘܬܐ ܩܠܗ ܢܒܟܐ
ܘܬܘܗ ܕܚܙܐ ܒܡܪܢ ܕܐܡܪ
ܘܐܡܪ ܐܘ ܡܚܝܠ ܡܝܬܐ ܐܝܟܐ ܐܝܟ
ܐܝܟ ܬܘܗܐ ܠܝ ܡܬܒܘܣܬܐ ܚܠܦ ܒܢܝܢܐ ܟܠܗ
ܕܗܐ ܢܟܝܘ ܒܕܝܠܗ ܒܒܘܣܝ ܟܕ ܐ ܡܬܐܪܝܢ ܬܐܬܐ ܬܚܬܐ
ܗܘܐ ܐܝܟܢ ܒܪܗ ܕܐܪܡܠܬܐ ܚܬܪ ܟܝ
ܡܢܐ ܙܪܗ ܠܝ ܠܐܕܡ
ܒܪܝ ܗܘ ܙܒܢܐ ܕܙܪܗ ܠܝ ܒܒܪ ܕܗܝ

12. "Your consolations are of little help,"

said the Evil One to his followers,

"How can Death contain

the man who has raised up dead Lazarus;
and if Death does conquer him John 11:44

it is because he willingly subjects himself
—and if he subjects himself to it willingly,

then you should fear[2] him all the more,
for he will not die to no purpose.

He will be the cause of great horror to us,

for when he dies he will enter in and bring Adam to life."

13. Death peered out from inside his cavern,

astonished to see our Lord crucified.

"Where are you now, O raiser of the dead?

Will you be food for me in place of the tasty Lazarus, John 11:44

whose taste I still have in my mouth?
Let Jairus's daughter come and see Luke 8:55

this cross of yours; let the widow's son gaze upon you. Luke 7:15

A tree caught Adam for me, Gen 2:17; 3:6

blessed is the cross which has caught the son of David for me!"

2. fear *(dḥalun):* The two manuscripts have *dḥal(w),* but the longer form of the imperative is required by the meter.

14. ܦܘܩܕܗ ܦܠܚ ܗܘܐ ܡܘܫܐ ܘܐܡܪ
ܠܐ ܫܡܝܥ ܗܘܐ ܠܗ ܐܘ ܒܪ ܥܡܪܡ
ܕܦܘܩܕܐ ܕܒܪܟ ܘܐܬܡܠܟܘ ܡܢ ܟܠ
ܗܘܐ ܟܠܗ ܥܒܕ ܕܟܠܗ ܐܡܝܬ ܒܘܟܪܐ ܘܦܪܩ ܒܘܟܪܐ
ܟܠܐ ܡܘܬܢܐ ܡܢ ܒܢܝܐ ܠܡܨܪܐ ܫܒܩܗ ܠܗ ܡܘܬܐ
ܘܡܢ ܐܝܟ ܠܐܝܟ ܡܘܬܗ ܠܗ ܒܪܝܟ ܐܡܪܗ
ܕܥܡܐ ܕܢܬܪܘܒ ܒܪ ܐܪܡ
ܗܘ ܠܒܪܐ ܠܟܦܪܗ ܗܘܦ ܕܡܢ ܐܘܪܚܐ ܗܘ

15. ܐܬܐ ܫܡܘܐܝܠ ܥܡ ܦܠܚܘܗܝ
ܕܢܚܬܐ ܠܒܢܝ ܕܪܘܚܐ ܠܫܡܘܐܝܠ
ܘܢܚܬ ܠܫܡܗ ܕܡܘܬܐ ܒܪ ܡܠܟܗ
ܘܐܚܝܗܝ ܗܘܐ ܕܫܡܪ ܘܐܫܟܠ ܠܟܠ ܬܡܝܗܐ ܕܫܡܠ ܒܘܟܪܐ
ܚܘ ܘܢܦܩܘ ܡܢܗ ܕܡܫܠ ܩܡ ܫܡܥܐ ܕܢܒܝܐ ܗܘܐ
ܠܡܘܬܐ ܐܚܝܢܗ ܘܠܐ ܐܘܪܒܐ ܐܝܟ ܗܝܐ ܕܐܫܟܚ
ܫܡܐ ܕܢܫܩܠ ܠܟܗ ܡܢܗ
ܠܐܝܟ ܐܬܐ ܐܘ ܕܢܚܬ ܘܕܝܢܝ

14. Death opened his mouth and further said,

"Have you never heard, son of Mary,

of Moses, how he excelled all men in his greatness,

how he became a god, performing the works of God Exod 4:16;
by slaying the [Egyptian] firstborn and saving the [Hebrew], 7:1; 12:29

how he held back the plague from the living? Num 16:48;
Yet I went up with the same Moses to the mountain Deut 32:49

and God—blessed be his honor— Ezek 3:12;
handed him over to me in person.[3] Deut 34:5

However great one of Adam's sons becomes,

he will return as dust to dust, for he comes from the earth." Gen 3:19; 2:7

15. Satan came along with his soldiers

to look at our Lord lying in Sheol

and to rejoice with Death, his fellow counselor,

but he saw him all gloomy
and bewailing the dead who, at the Firstborn's cry,

had come to life and departed from Sheol. Matt 27:50, 52
The Evil One began to comfort

Death, his relative,
"You have not lost as much as you have gained:

as long as Jesus is in your grasp

everyone who has lived and is living will come into your hands.

---

3. handed him over to me in person: Ephrem seems to refer to traditions about Moses's death and burial that underlay Jude 9 and are found in a different form in the late midrash *Petirat Moshe* (Jellinek 1967, 1.1:115–29).

16. ܦܠܚ ܠܝ ܢܣܬܘܕܝ ܐܦ ܢܦܘܠ ܒܗ
ܢܒܝܐ ܘܐܡܪ ܕܐܡܟܘ ܫܒܩܝ
ܗܐ ܓܝܪ ܡܘܬܢܐ ܠܟܠܐ ܗܘܐ ܒܗ
ܘܐܡܪ ܒܗ ܐܦ ܠܟܠܡܐ ܕܢܩܒܠܐ ܠܟܠܗܘܢ
ܐܝܟ ܐܝܠܐ ܠܡܫܘܚܝ ܦܠܚ ܡܘܬܐ ܠܐܒܝܢ ܕܚܣܘܠ
ܘܐܒܝ ܡܠܟ ܐܡܪ ܕܦܪܘܩܗ ܕܡܪܢ
ܘܐܝܟ ܡܕܘܢܬܐ ܒܠܒܗ ܗܘܐ
ܡܢܗ ܘܒܠܗ ܠܐܒܝܢ ܕܚܣܘܠ ܘܐܡܪ ܒܗ

16. "Open up, so that we can see him and jeer at him;

let us ask him, 'Where is your power?'

Three days have already passed,

so let us say to him,
'You, who are three days dead,[4]
raised up Lazarus, four days dead; John 11:39

raise yourself now!'" Death duly opened up the gates of Sheol

—and out from it shone the radiance of our Lord's face!

Like the men of Sodom, they were all smitten, Gen 19:11

they groped around looking for the gate of Sheol that had vanished.

◆

4. three days dead *(tlitaya):* See Text 19 (*Nis.* 1), n. 16.

TEXT 14

A Disputation between Death and Satan (*Nis.* 53)

Ephrem continues his imaginative treatment of the theme of the Descent of Christ into Sheol, but here he makes use of the ancient Mesopotamian literary genre of the Precedence Dispute, where two contestants dispute over their prowess. The genre (which continues to be popular in certain parts of the Middle East up to the present day) was adapted by Ephrem and later Syriac poets to biblical themes, the disputants either being personifications (as in the present poem) or characters taken from biblical narratives. The structure of the Syriac poems is fairly regular: following a short introduction, the dispute or dialogue, in alternating stanzas, takes up most of the poem, which ends with a brief conclusion or doxology; in the present poem, however, where Death and Satan are disputing which has the greater power over human beings, the conclusion is absent, and the two contestants simply end up by cursing each other. Ephrem portrays them as having an extremely good knowledge of the biblical text—no doubt putting to shame many a reader!

For the background to the genre and its use elsewhere in Syriac, see Murray 1995 and Brock 1991b and 2001.

Meter

The *qala* title given for *Nis.* 52–68 is *ᵓo mawta la teshtaᶜle,* the opening words of *Nis.* 68. The meter is a straightforward one, 7+4 7+4 syllables. The meter is not used elsewhere by Ephrem.

Text

The poem is found only in British Library Add. 14572 (sixth century).

ܥܠ ܡܛܠ ܕܐܦ ܡܘܬܐ ܠܐ ܐܣܬܟܠ

1. ܬܘ ܢܫܡܥ ܟܕ ܡܬܕܡܪܝܢ ܥܠ ܐܟܘܬܐ
ܚܝ̈ܘܬܐ ܕܠܐ ܐܟܘ ܡܢ ܡܬܕܘܡ ܐܦ ܠܐ ܐܟܡܢ

2. ܡܘܬܐ ܒܟܝܡܐ ܐܡܪ ܠܗ ܒܥܕܢܐ ܗܘ ܐܟܘܬܗ
ܕܡܘܬܐ ܗܘ ܐܚܝܕ ܫܘܠܛܢܐ ܐܝܟ ܐܒܝܐ

3. ܡܘܬܐ ܫܪܝܪܐ ܗܘܝܘ ܐܦ ܢܫܡܥ ܐܢܬ
ܕܐܫܬܡܥܘܗܝ ܠܐܢܫ ܟܕ ܚܝ ܒܬܫܒܘܚܬܐ

4. ܐܝܟܐ ܕܫܡܥܬ ܗܐ ܚܕܐ ܐܢܐ ܠܚܝ̈ܐ ܘܫܡܝ̈ܐ
ܐܘܡܢܐ ܕܫܪܝܪܘܬ ܫܡܝܐ ܟܕ ܠܐ ܫܪܝܪܘܬ

5. ܗܘܝܐ ܡܫܬܘܕܝܐ ܕܫܪܪܐ ܫܡܥ ܐܟܝܐ ܗܘ
ܠܐ ܐܫܬܟܚ ܡܘܬܐ ܕܡܘܬܐ ܐܝܬ ܕܐܝܟ ܫܟܠܐ ܐܝܬ

1. Come let us listen as they contend   for victory—
   the guilty[1] ones who have never conquered,   nor shall they ever do so!

DEATH

2. Death says to the Evil One,   Victory will finally be mine,
   for Death controls the final end   as conqueror.

SATAN

3. This would be true, O Death,   should you be able
   to bring someone to death, while still alive,   by means of the lusts.

DEATH

4. I see amongst those who have died   both the good and the bad.
   The just who spurned you, Evil One,   did not spurn me.

SATAN

5. The body's dead state   is but a sleep, lasting for a time:
   do not imagine, Death, that you are [really] death,
   for you are like a shade.

1. guilty: Or "defeated." Ephrem probably intends both senses.

6. ܒܟ ܚܣܝܐ ܕܐܒܘܟ ܟܠܬܐ ܐܦ ܐܚܝ ܒܟ
ܐܢܐ ܕܝ ܠܐܡܚܝ ܕܐܒܘܟ ܗܐ ܐܚܐ ܐܢܐ

7. ܐܦ ܟܠܬܐ ܕܨܡܚܬ ܐܝܬ ܠܗ ܕܡܟܝ ܗܘ
ܒܟܠܬ ܐܝܟ ܗܘ ܕܐܬܬ ܐܚܕܬܗ ܒܗܐ

8. ܗܐ ܫܩܠ ܡܒܐ ܫܘܬܦܐ ܘܐܬܪܬܐ
ܘܒܝܬܐ ܕܫܘܦܪܐ ܡܢܗ ܕܐܒܘܗ

9. ܗܒܝ ܢܦܫܘܗܝ ܐܘ ܡܘܬܐ ܟܝ ܗܘ ܡܢܟܝ
ܐܢܐ ܐܢܐ ܕܐܬܚܬܡܬ ܐܢܘܢ ܐܝܟ ܕܢܫܘܦܘܢ

10. ܝܘܣܦ ܕܐܒܘܟ ܐܣܟܡܗ ܐܘ ܫܡܫܐ
ܒܫܡܐ ܐܒܘܟ ܘܒܥܒܕܐ ܐܣܟܡ ܘܐܪܣܟܡܗ

DEATH

6. The upright have vanquished you, Evil One,
   and they vanquish you still,

   whereas those who have vanquished you, I myself vanquish.

SATAN

7. In the case of the Upright whom you bring to death,
   it is no merit of yours,

   for it is by reason of Adam whom I conquered
   that they have drunken the cup.

DEATH

8. Look how Sheol is filled with the men of Sodom, the Assyrians, Gen 19:24; 2 Kgs 19:35

   and the Giants from the time of the Flood. Who can rival me? Gen 6:2

SATAN

9. All these, O Death, had been slain by me:

   I am the one who caused them to sin,
   so that they should come to a bad end.

DEATH

10. That Joseph[2] who overcame you, Satan, I overcame: Gen 39:7–8

    he vanquished you in the inner room,
    but I vanquished him when I cast him into the tomb. Gen 50:26

---

2. Joseph: The name deliberately reflects the last word of the previous stanza, *nsupun* (ANP).

11. ܡܘܬܐ ܕܐܒܝ ܐܘ ܡܘܬܐ ܒܪܢܫ ܕܡܠܐ
ܐܒܝ ܒܥܕܢܝ ܘܟܠ ܟܐܦܐ ܡܢܗ ܕܐܒܘܗܝ

12. ܠܟܢܐ ܕܠܐ ܕܢܦܠ ܡܢܝ ܐܘ ܫܡܝܢܐ
ܡܢ ܩܕܡ ܐܬܐܠ ܒܪܗ ܗܘܐ ܕܒܢ ܕܢܚܬܘܗ

13. ܐܘܪܗ ܕܡܠܟ ܐܘ ܡܘܬܐ ܒܟܪܣܐ ܕܒܗܡܬܐ
ܡܢܬܐ ܕܕܘܒܐ ܢܘܒܠ ܠܗ ܘܢܬܠ ܠܗܠ

14. ܠܐܒܘܢܐ ܢܫܒܩ ܠܗ ܐܢܬ ܘܐܒܝ ܘܫܡܥ
ܐܢܐ ܕܝܢ ܡܢ ܠܒܪ ܕܐܒܝ ܒܝ ܗܘ ܐܒܘܗ

15. ܕܥܒܕ ܕܡܟܝܟܘܬܗ ܒܥܘܡܩܗ ܠܗܘ ܡܘܬܐ
ܟܠ ܐܢܫ ܐܦܝܠ ܠܗܘ ܕܐܬܐ ܠܡܥܒܪ

SATAN

11. Look at Moses who conquered you, Death,
    with the sprinkling of the blood: Exod 12:22–23

he conquered you in Egypt—but at the Rock,
    who was it who conquered him? Num 20:12

DEATH

12. Take Elijah, who had no fear of you, Satan:

he fled from Jezebel's presence, out of his fear for me. 1 Kgs 19:2

SATAN

13. Take Aaron, who held you back, Death,
    by means of the fragrant incense: Num 16:46

I gave him the earrings of gold and he forged the Calf. Exod 32:2–4

DEATH

14. You went down to the contest with Job,
    but he came up having vanquished you; Job 1:12

it was I who, after he had overcome you, then overcame him. Job 1:22; 42:17

SATAN

15. Take David, who by wearing sackcloth,
    held back that pestilence: 2 Sam 24:18

on the roof I vanquished this man who had vanquished Goliath. 2 Sam 11:2; 1 Sam 17:4

16. ܗܢܘ ܕܒܥܪ ܥܡ ܒܥܠܐ ܘܡܥܠܐ ܒܝܬܐ
ܕܢܥܒܕ ܠܡܫܥܠܐ ܠܐ ܐܫܒܚ ܒܪܐ ܡܒܥܠܝ

17. ܫܡܫܗ ܕܐܒܪܐ ܡܢ ܦܘܩܕܢ ܛܒܬܐ ܕܒܝܬܐ
ܦܠܐ ܒܒܪܬܗ ܒܫܡܥܬܗ ܠܒܠܒܬܐ

18. ܫܡܥܬܠܐ ܕܒܪܘܟܐ ܒܫܪܢ ܐܘ ܫܛܝܐ
ܐܢܐ ܐܫܬܠܗ ܒܥܘ ܐܝܬܐ ܕܐܟܐ ܫܦܪܐ

19. ܫܡܫܗ ܕܒܣܦܪܐ ܘܐܘܪܐ ܒܫܪܢ ܡܘܬܐ
ܕܒܝܠܐ ܡܪܐ ܕܒܝܠܐ ܒܪܚܐ ܕܒܝܬܗ

20. ܩܫܝܬܐ ܡܢ ܛܒܥܬܗ ܫܘܢ ܒܝܬܐ
ܟܕ ܕܝܢ ܐܦܠܐ ܒܫܡܥܬܗ ܐܫܒܚ ܫܒܝܚ

DEATH

16. Take Jehu who eradicated the Temple of Baal,
 the shrine of the Evil One: 2 Kgs 10:27

he could not eradicate Sheol, the citadel of my kingdom. 2 Kgs 10:35

SATAN

17. Take Solomon who snatched away from your mouth
 the child by his judgment: 1 Kgs 3:27

I made him in his old age a worshipper at pagan altars. 1 Kgs 11:1–8

DEATH

18. Take Samuel, who spurned you in the matter of gold, Satan: 1 Sam 12:1–4

I vanquished this victor who had won a victory against bribery. 1 Sam 25:1

SATAN

19. Take Samson who, in the case of the lion's whelp, despised you,
 O Death: Judg 14:15

by means of Delilah, a delightfully easy tool,
 I harnessed him to the millstone. Judg 16:21

DEATH

20. Josiah from his youth up despised you, O Evil One, 2 Kgs 22:1–2

yet even in his old age he could not get the better of me. 2 Kgs 23:29–30

21. ܫܠܡܐ ܫܡܥܝܢ ܡܘܬܐ ܕܐܟܠ ܒܩܒܪܐ
ܕܘܕܠܗ ܕܫܒܩ ܠܗܘܪܐ ܘܫܒܩ ܠܟܠܗܘܢ

22. ܡܫܝܚܐ ܕܐܟܝ ܚܝܡܐ ܘܫܡܥ ܘܐܬܥܒܕ
ܐܘܟܠܬܗ ܠܗܘ ܡܪܝܐ ܕܟܝ ܦܪܫ ܗܘܐ

23. ܫܒܚܝ ܐܟܝ ܕܐܢܫ ܗܘܐ ܠܡܘܬܢܘܬܐ
ܠܐܝܬܐ ܐܟܝ ܘܠܒܝ ܐܝܬܐ ܐܟܡ ܘܐܒܥܪܬܗ

24. ܡܠܟܐ ܘܢܒܝܐ ܐܚܝܕ ܠܡܘܬ ܡܘܬܐ
ܕܐܟܠ ܗܘ ܐܒܘܗܘ ܕܡܘܬܐ ܘܒܘܫܡܗ ܕܡܫܘܠܐ

25. ܠܡܢܝܢ ܟܡܘܠܐ ܣܒܥܬܝܗܝ ܟܕܒܐ ܟܝܬܐ
ܗܟܝ ܠܐܠܗܐ ܐܦ ܐܢܫܐ ܡܠܐ ܢܦܫܝ

SATAN

21. Hezekiah got the better of you, O Death,
        when he overcame his allotted span of life, Isa 38:5

but I upset him when he abandoned the due sense of awe
        and disclosed his treasures. Isa 39:4

DEATH

22. Take John, who vanquished you, O Evil One, Mark 1:4;
        by providing forgiveness and baptism: Luke 3:3

it was I who extinguished that lantern Matt 14:12;
        which had laid you bare. John 5:35

SATAN

23. Simon defeated you when he revived the blessed woman: Acts 9:40

he vanquished you with a woman—and it was with a woman
        that I vanquished him, making him deny [Christ]. Matt 26:69–72

24. Apostles and prophets alike have cursed you, O Death,

saying, "Where is Death's victory and the sting of Sheol?" Hos 13:14; 1 Cor 15:55

25. It is your own Master you have confined in Sheol,
        O accursed servant:

both God and humanity abhor you, so silence yourself!

ܙܒܢܝܢ ܗܘܐ ܕܡܫܐ ܟܠ ܚܒܫܗ ܒܫܘܬܠ 26.

ܐܝܬ ܗܘܐ ܡܢܛܪܝܢ ܒܗܘܪܐ ܕܠܐܘܡ ܐܢܫܬ

ܒܢܝܗ ܕܢܒܠ ܕܒܥܪܐ ܙܒܢ ܡܢܗ 27.

ܚܪܡ ܦܘܡܗ ܗܘܐ ܕܐܡܪ ܠܗ ܕܦܠ ܘܫܡܘܕ ܠܗ

DEATH

26. It is the will of the Life-Giver of all
that has confined Him in Sheol—

and it is you who invited Him to do this by making Adam sin.

27. O companion of Nabal who, in the wilderness,
reviled his own master, 1 Sam 25:10

accursed is your mouth which said to Him,
"Fall down and worship me." Matt 4:9

◆

TEXT 15

Joy at the Resurrection (*Res.* 2)

Unlike the first *madrasha* in this cycle (Text 8), this one focuses on the feast of the Resurrection. The feast falls in Nisan, or April, the time of year when thunderstorms are common in northern Mesopotamia. Ephrem accordingly describes how the elements of Nature join in with the Church's shouts of joy as she celebrates this feast of feasts, where everyone can join in with his or her appropriate garland of praise. The reference to devastation in the final stanza indicates that this *madrasha* was composed while Ephrem was still in Nisibis, and he will have in mind one of the various sieges of Nisibis by the Persians (see the introduction to Text 19 [*Nis.* 1] [p. 222]). There is no separate refrain, but the last line of each stanza evidently is intended to serve as one.

Meter

The *qala* title is given as *etqaṭṭal(w) (h)waw yallude,* for which see on Text 12 (*Cruc.* 2).

Text

The poem is preserved complete only in British Library Add. 14627 (sixth or seventh century; Beck's B). Select stanzas, however, can be found in both the Mosul and the Pampakuda editions of the Fenqitho, as follows:

1, 8–10, + unknown	=	Mosul Fenqitho 6.167–68
2, 7, 3, 8	=	Mosul Fenqitho 4.801
2, 4, 7, 12	=	Pampakuda Fenqitho 2.407–8

This happens to be the only madrasha in the present anthology from which stanzas can be found in the Pampakuda Fenqitho.

ܥܠ ܩܠܐ ܕܐܬܛܠܡܘ ܗܘܘ ܒܢܘܪܐ

1. ܕܒܥܐ ܗܘܐ ܠܟ ܢܚܫܘܢ   ܗܘ ܕܚܠܐ ܥܠ ܦܪܘܫܐ
ܘܡܟܝܪܐ ܗܘܐ ܠܟ ܐܫܟܚ   ܘܗܘܐ ܦܠܚܗ ܠܦܪܘܫܐ
ܡܢ ܥܠܬ ܟܪܝܗܬ ܐܪܥܬ   ܒܫܡܬ ܘܐܬܬ ܡܢ ܦܪܘܫܐ
ܘܐܢܐ ܘܚܛܝܐ ܡܠܠ   ܗܐ ܒܪܝܢ ܒܗ ܠܒܪܒܪ
ܒܡܝܢܬܐ ܥܠ ܐܢܫܘܬܐ   ܒܪܝܟ ܗܘ ܕܥܠܠ ܘܐܬܥܠܠ

2. ܗܐ ܥܕܪܐ ܦܪܝܫܐ ܕܐܬܡܘܗܝ   ܒܥܠܗ ܦܘܩܕܐ ܘܥܡܠܐ
ܢܟܦܬܐ ܘܢܟܦܐ ܗܘܐ ܠܗ   ܐܝܟ ܫܡܫܐ ܘܣܗܪܐ
ܫܒܝܬܐ ܘܫܒܝܪܐ ܗܘܐ ܠܗ   ܐܝܟ ܒܢܝܐ ܘܫܡܝܐ
ܒܪܗ ܩܠܐ ܒܩܠܐ ܘܫܡܥܘ   ܘܫܒܩ ܠܒܘܗܝ ܠܫܡܝܐ
ܢܗܘܐ ܫܘܒܚܐ ܠܒܪܐ ܫܘܒܚܐ   ܒܪܝܟ ܕܒܪܟܗ ܒܗ ܫܡܝܐ

1. Your law has been my vehicle,
            revealing to me something of Paradise,

   Your Cross has been to me the key   which opened up this Paradise.

   From the Garden of Delights[1] did I gather
            and carry back with me from Paradise

   roses and other eloquent blooms
            which are here scattered about for Your feast

   amid songs [as they flutter down] on humanity.
            Blessed is He who both gave and received the crown!

2. This joyful[2] festival is entirely made up   of tongues and voices:

   innocent young women and men   sounding like trumpets and horns,

   while infant girls and boys   resemble harps and lyres;

   their voices intertwine   as they reach up together towards heaven,

   giving glory to the Lord of glory.
            Blessed is He for whom the silent have thundered out!

---

1. Garden of Delights *(ᶜedne):* An obvious play on *Eden* (not present in the Septuagint's rendering of *gan ᶜden* by *paradeisos tēs truphēs,* "Garden of Delight" [Gen 3:23]).

2. joyful: There is a word play between *pṣiḥa,* "joyful," and *peṣḥa,* "Passover."

3. ܗܐ ܕܒܥܬ ܐܘܪܚܐ ܡܢ ܠܒܪ   ܘܫܒܝܠܐ ܡܢ ܒܒܠ ܕܒܥܬ
ܚܠܝܨ ܢܦܫ ܩܠܐ ܒܩܠܐ   ܬܒܥܝܐ ܐܦ ܐܬܒܥܝܐ
ܚܠܨܘ ܩܠܝܢ ܕܟܪܐ ܡܕܝܢܐ   ܟܕ ܕܒܥܝܢ ܕܠܐܘܬܐ
ܘܒܗ ܐܘܪܚܐ ܕܠܡܫܬܪܝܢ   ܐܠܝܨܐ ܕܒܥܐ ܚܠܝܨܝܢ
ܟܕ ܡܛܪܐ ܒܥܝܐ ܕܚܝܐ   ܘܟܕ ܕܒܥܐ ܙܘܥܐ ܕܦܪܚܐ

4. ܒܒܥܝܐ ܡܠܟܘ ܗܘܝ   ܠܐ ܩܠܝܢ ܡܢ ܠܐ ܦܘܩܝܢ
ܒܒܪ ܡܝܢܐ ܢܦܠܐ ܕܚܝܠܐ   ܘܒܥܘܢ ܩܠܐ ܕܒܥܝܐ
ܒܩܠܐ ܐܬܒܥܝ ܐܬܒܥܝ   ܒܟܠܗ ܒܗ ܐܚܝܕ ܕܒܝܬ
ܠܡܦܩܐ ܕܗܘܐ ܟܕ ܟܕ   ܕܒܗܬܐ ܘܒܗܬܟܠܐ
ܐܡܪܘ ܒܗ ܡܕܝܢܬ   ܡܦܩܐ ܠܒܪܗ ܕܒܥܝܐ

5. ܒܗܝ ܓܐܘܐ ܕܡܪܕ ܠܐ ܐܢܫ   ܢܪܫܘܢܝܗܝ ܐܝܟ ܡܕܪܫܘܢܝܗܝ
ܒܪܬ ܟܝ ܕܚܘܒ ܕܚܝܠܬ   ܕܡܫܡܫܢܝܬ ܩܐܡ ܐܢܐ
ܐܬܦܪܣ ܒܛܠܘ ܕܒܝܫ   ܘܗܘܐ ܠܗ ܢܦܫ ܕܐܬܪܝ
ܘܗܘ ܟܝ ܦܫܝܘܗܝ ܡܕܪܫܐ   ܗܐ ܒܪܟܝܢ ܟܠܟܝܢ ܟܠܟܝܢ
ܘܟܠ ܐܘܪܚܐ ܕܐܪܐ ܫܡܝܢ   ܒܪܚܐ ܒܝܢܐ ܕܫܡܥܬ ܒܝ

3. The earth thunders out below, heaven above roars with thunder:

Nisan[3] has mingled together the two sounds—
  of those above and those below.

The shouts from the holy Church
  are joined with the Divinity's thunder,

and with the bright torches lightning flashes intermingle;

with the rain came the tears of sorrow,
  with the pasturage,[4] the Paschal fast.

4. It was in a similar way that in the Ark all voices cried out:

outside [the Ark] were fearsome waves, but inside, lovely voices;

tongues, all in pairs, uttered together in chaste fashion,[5]

thus serving as a type of our festival now
  when unmarried girls and boys

together in innocence sing praise to the Lord of that Ark.

5. At this festival when each person offers his fine actions as offerings,

I lament, dear Lord,[6] that I stand here so impoverished.

But my mind grows green again with your dew:
  for it a second Nisan is come,

whose flowers serve as [my] offerings,
  garlanded in all kinds of wreaths,

placed on the door of each ear!
  Blessed is the Cloud which has distilled in me its moisture!

---

3. Nisan: I.e., April.
4. pasturage: Provided by the fresh green grass of spring.
5. in chaste fashion: Lit. "purely." Ephrem probably alludes to the tradition (of Jewish origin) that both Noah's family and the animals preserved *qaddishuta* (see Text 5 [*Nat.* 17], n. 7) and refrained from intercourse in the Ark.
6. dear Lord *(rabuli):* Ephrem uses this word, taken from John 20:16 (Mary Magdalene's recognition of the risen Christ), as a term of intimate relationship to Christ.

6. ܡܢܘ ܚܙܐ ܦܪ̈ܚܐ ܕܒܩܦܣ   ܡܢ ܫܦܪ̈ܐ ܐܝܟ ܡܢ ܠܘܬܐ
ܘܡܠܦ ܚܒܪ̈ܘܗܝ ܢܬܒܥܐ   ܒܩܠܐ ܕܐܢܫܐ ܕܒܢܝܐ
ܗܐ ܡܠܐ ܐܝܟ ܚܟܝܡܐ   ܟܠ ܬܒܝܬܐ ܦܪ̈ܚܐ ܟܒܪ
ܗܘܝܐ ܐܢܘܢ ܡܒܝܢܐ   ܒܢ̈ܝ ܡܕܡܘܢ ܡܛܠܗ ܐܢܘܢ
ܐܝܟ ܡܢܗܘܢ ܡܫܬܘܕܥܐ ܕܡܢܢ   ܒܢܝ ܕܐܬܟܠܐ ܒܦܘܡܗܘܢ

7. ܦܪ̈ܚܐ ܦܐܝܐ ܘܫܒܝܠܐ   ܒܓܘܗ ܫܒܬܐ ܡܫܘܕܥܐ ܡܠܠܐ
ܚܠܦ ܚܒܪ̈ܘܗܝ ܐܬܟܠܠ   ܐܘܪܚܐ ܚܒܪ̈ܘܗܝ ܡܠܝܐ ܗܘܐ
ܡܫܠܡܐ ܒܓܘܗ ܐܝܟ ܦܪ̈ܚܐ   ܘܡܬܒܥܐ ܐܝܟ ܡܫܡ̈ܫܢܐ
ܐܦ ܗܟܢܐ ܥܡܗ ܠܡܠܟܐ   ܒܝܬܐ ܕܫܒܬܐ ܒܓܘܗ ܠܝ ܡܪܝ
ܘܫܒܝܠܐ ܐܝܟ ܗܘܝܐ   ܒܢܝ ܕܐܬܟܠܘ ܠܒܢ̈ܝܐ

8. ܗܐ ܡܫܡܫܢ ܐܝܟ ܫܦܝܪܐ   ܡܠܝܐ ܩܠܐ ܕܡܠܘ̈ܐ
ܡܢܝܢ ܠܘܬ ܡܪܝ ܒܩܠܐ ܕܐܘܪܚܐ   ܡܬܒܥܐ ܡܢ ܢܬܒܥܐ
ܠܐ ܦܪ̈ܚܝܢ ܢܚܘܪ ܠܐ ܐܢܫ   ܘܚܘܗܝ ܢܬܠܘܫ ܡܢ ܕܡܠܗ
ܗܘܝܐ ܕܡܠܗ ܒܐܘܪܚܗ   ܕܢܘܪܐ ܚܐܝܐ ܙܒܢܐ
ܡܠܠܐ ܙܒܢܐ ܢܥܒܕܘܢ ܠܗ   ܒܢܝ ܗܘ ܕܡܪܝ ܠܡܫܒܚܘ

6. Who has ever beheld blossoms
   gathered from the Scriptures, as though it were from the hills?

   With them have chaste women
   filled the spacious bosom of the mind.

   The sound of songs, like a servant, has scattered
   blossoms all over the crowds:

   these flowers are sacred, catch them with your senses,

   just as our Lord [caught] Mary's unguent. John 12:1–3
   Blessed is he who is garlanded with his handmaids!

7. Fair and eloquent flowers
   have the children strewn before the King: Matt 21:7

   the colt was garlanded with them, the path was filled with them;

   they scattered praises like flowers, their songs [of joy] like lilies.

   Now too at this festival
   does the crowd of children scatter for You, Lord,

   halleluiahs like blossoms.
   Blessed is He who was acclaimed by young children. Matt 21:15–16

8. It is as though our hearing [has embraced]
   an armful of children's voices,

   while songs coming from chaste women, Lord,
   fill the bosoms of our ears.

   Let each of us gather up a posy of such flowers,
   and with these let each intersperse

   blossoms from his own piece of land, so that, for this great feast,

   we may plait a great garland.
   Blessed is He who invited us to plait it!

9. ܪܳܥܝܳܐ ܪܰܒܳܐ ܢܶܚܕܘܿܠ ܒܶܗ   ܠܐܘܪܥܟ݂ܘܢ ܐܰܝܟ݂ ܘܰܒܪܰܟ݂ܘܢ
ܩܰܣܝܡܳܐ ܢܶܪܫܽܘܢܳܘܗܝ   ܡܩܰܡܳܐ ܩܪܺܝܢܳܘܗܝ
ܒܪܽܘܢܳܐ ܘܩܰܠܺܝܠܳܘܗܝ   ܢܶܚܘܶܐ ܡܰܠܡܠܽܘܬܳܘܗܝ
ܢܶܦܩܽܘܢ ܡܢ ܕܽܘܡܳܝܗܽܘܢ   ܕܺܝܢܳܐ ܕܠܰܒܢܳܘܗܝ
ܘܫܰܒܩܶܐ ܕܠܰܒܢܳܘܗܝ   ܒܪܶܡ ܕܐܰܣܶܐ ܠܶܗ ܢܶܫܡܳܐ

10. ܢܰܟ݂ܦܘܿ ܢܰܦܫܳܐ ܢܫܰܡܳܐ   ܒܶܢܝܳܐ ܡܫܰܡܫܳܐ ܘܰܢܩܳܐ
ܕܐܶܬܥܰܠܰܘܗܝ ܘܰܡܒܰܪܟܽܘܗܝ   ܢܶܫܡܰܬ ܐܶܢܽܘܢ ܒܰܪܫܺܝܡܳܘܗܝ
ܘܰܡܠܰܠ ܐܶܢܽܘܢ ܘܶܙܘܺܝܢܳܘܗܝ   ܚܰܠܳܐ ܙܰܒܢܳܐ ܕܦܽܘܪܩܳܢܳܘܗܝ
ܡܢ ܒܶܝܬ ܚܰܒܪܳܐ ܒܰܓܠܳܐ   ܘܰܡܫܰܒܶܩ ܦܽܘܢܳܐ ܕܰܡܒܰܪܟܳܐ
ܒܫܽܘܠܳܐ ܒܳܐܪ ܕܰܡܢܳܐ   ܟܽܠ ܦܽܘܢܳܐ ܡܢ ܠܚܽܘܕܳܐ

11. ܬܰܠܡܺܝܕ ܡܰܠܟܳܐ ܐܶܬܡܰܕܰܒܪܽܘ   ܒܝܰܕ ܒܪܳܐ ܕܦܳܬܽܘܪܳܐ ܕܰܡܠܺܝܟ
ܕܦܰܣܠܳܐ ܒܶܗ ܕܫܰܒܬܳܐ   ܢܽܘܚܳܐ ܒܶܗ ܕܡܰܪܢܺܝܬܳܐ
ܙܳܗܝܳܐ ܒܶܗ ܡܰܡܠܟܽܘܬܳܐ   ܦܰܬܚܳܐ ܒܶܗ ܡܫܰܡܫܽܘܬܳܐ
ܢܽܘܚ ܒܶܗ ܚܰܕܽܘܬܳܐ ܕܟ݂ܳܐ   ܡܰܠܟܳܐ ܕܟ݂ܳܐ ܕܰܡܒܰܪܟܳܐ
ܗܳܐ ܒܥܳܡܰܪ ܦܽܘܢܳܘܗܝ ܕܰܡܠܺܝܟ   ܒܪܶܡ ܕܢܶܦܽܘܩ ܠܶܗ ܘܰܒܪܰܟ݂ܘܢ

9. Let the chief pastor[7] weave together his homilies like flowers,

let the priests make a garland of their ministry,
the deacons of their reading,

strong young men of their jubilant shouts, children of their psalms,

chaste women of their songs, chief citizens of their benefactions,

ordinary folk of their manner of life.
Blessed is He who gave us so many opportunities for good!

10. Let us summon and invite the saints,
the martyrs, apostles and prophets,

whose own blossoms and flowers shine out like themselves—

such a wealth of roses they have, so fragrant are their lilies:

from the Garden of Delights do they pluck them,
and they bring back fair bunches

to crown our beautiful feast.[8]
O praise to You from the [saints who are] blessed!

11. Royal crowns appear poor compared with the wealth of Your crown

into which purity is intertwined, in which faith shines out,

humility shines forth and holiness is mingled in,

and great love is resplendent. O great King of all flowers,

how perfect is the beauty of Your crown.
Blessed is He who gave it us to weave!

---

7. chief pastor: I.e., bishop.
8. Delights . . . feast (*ʿedne . . . ʿidan):* Note the word play (ANP).

12. ܡܛܠ ܡܠܟܐ ܡܦܪܢܣܐ   ܘܗܒ ܠܢ ܚܘܠܡܢܗ ܦܘܪܩܢܐ

ܗܢܝ ܐܘܟܠܐ ܕܣܢܒ   ܚܝܐ ܬܒܪܐ ܕܡܘܬ

ܕܡܠܐ ܕܗܘܐ ܗܢܝܐ ܪܒܐ   ܡܟܠܠܐ ܪܒܐ ܢܣܒܘܠ ܠܟܘܢ

ܟܕ ܐܠܗ ܡܢ ܟܠ ܢܒܥܝ   ܘܟܬܒܐ ܐܦ ܠܒܪܬܐ

ܕܢܬܩܛܠ ܡܪܐ ܗܢܝܐ   ܒܙܢ ܕܒܟܒ ܘܡܪܐ ܕܢܟܒ

12. Receive our offering, O our King, and in return grant us salvation;

give peace to the land that has been devastated,[9]
rebuild the churches that were burnt,

so that when deep peace has returned
we may plait You a great wreath,

with flowers and people to plait it, coming in from all sides

so that the Lord of peace may be crowned.
Blessed is He who has acted and is able to act!

◆

9. devastated: It is not clear to which of the sieges of Nisibis Ephrem refers.

TEXT 16

Oil and Its Symbols (*Virg.* 7)

Within the cycle entitled *On Virginity* there is a small group of four *madrashe* (4–7), "On Oil and the Olive," in which Ephrem explores the many different associations that exist between oil *(meshḥa)* and Christ *(mshiḥa)*. The last *madrasha* of this group, in particular, explores a variety of typological aspects, several of which are of considerable importance for the understanding of the prebaptismal anointing (known as the *rushma,* or "mark") that was characteristic of the early Syriac baptismal tradition.

In the opening stanzas Ephrem points out that human beings possess both a physical and a spiritual side and that they need to cultivate these two aspects equally: physical labor on the land receives its reward in October, with the ingathering of its produce and the arrival of the rain after the long hot summer months of drought; spiritual toil, however, is rewarded in April, the month of the Feast of the Resurrection—and it was on Easter eve that in many places it was the custom for baptisms to take place. Agricultural labor and spiritual toil turn out to be closely interrelated, for October provides the oil for the baptismal anointing in April.

Stanzas 3–5 make use of examples from the life of Elijah in order to illustrate how moral wrongdoing in connection with the working of the land has serious consequences which can only be rectified by the effects of oil, namely, the miraculous cruse of oil in Elijah's case (1 Kgs 17), and the baptismal oil in the context of the Christian dispensation.

Ephrem goes on in the next four stanzas to explore various different aspects of the baptismal oil: as a constituent of paint it repaints the portrait, or the divine image (Gen 1:27) in which humanity has been created, seeing that this had become disfigured at the Fall (stanza 5). In the next stanza the close links between the baptismal oil and the action of the Holy Spirit at baptism are brought out: by means of the anointing with oil the Spirit imprints the mark of Christ's ownership on the "sheep" that is entering Christ's flock. In the early Syriac Church, anointing preceded the baptism in water, and so it is only in stanza 7 that Ephrem turns to this, describing the font as a "second womb" that gives new birth to God's children. Stanza 8 provides an overall view of the baptismal rite, covering all its main constituent elements: the anointing, the sanctification of the baptismal water, with the Holy Spirit "hovering" over it (using a term taken from the Creation narrative in Gen 1:2), the baptism in water, officiated by the chief priest (or bishop) and assisted by the deacons, and culminating in Communion (seen as an integral part of the baptismal rite, as remains the case in all the Eastern Churches).

Stanzas 9 and 10 continue the significance of oil in the context of baptism. First, in order to bring out the dramatic nature of its action at baptism of "drowning" sin, Ephrem compares this to the action of the Flood, thus preparing the way for the introduction (in stanza 13) of the olive leaf that announced to Noah the end of the Flood (Gen 8:11). Whereas the Flood represents the aspect of God's justice in dealing with sin, baptismal oil depicts the aspect of his compassion, and in stanza 10 the salvific roles of oil and water are brought together. Just as a diver oils himself, so too the person being baptized is accompanied by oil as he buries himself in the water (using the imagery of Rom 6:4). Similarly, just as oil *(meshḥa)* does not sink, so Christ *(mshiḥa),* as God, cannot die, yet he "clothed himself with a mortal body" and was himself baptized, thus providing the paradigm for Christian baptism and thereby the means for raising fallen humanity. Lurking behind stanza 10 is the imagery of Christ acting like a pearl diver, where Adam/humanity is the pearl which he brings up from the depths (compare Text 20 [*Fid.* 82]).

In stanzas 11–12 Ephrem touches on the various benefits provided by oil. Playing on the double sense of *ḥawbe,* both "debts" and "sins," he introduces the miracle of 2 Kings 4:1–7, where the sale of the miraculous oil saves the widow's sons from being reduced to debt bondage, and compares this to Christ who became a slave (Phil 2:7) who was sold (Matt 26:14 and par.) in order to liberate humanity, which had become enslaved to sin.

The tightly packed poem ends with yet further links between oil and Christ (stanza 13), which become visible to the spiritual eye as it gazes on a bowl filled with oil (stanza 14). In a typically self-deprecatory final stanza, Ephrem, overwhelmed by the waves of associations caused by the interaction between oil and Christ, cries out, like Simon Peter (Matt 14:30), to Christ, asking him to rescue him from drowning.

Meter

The *qala* title (covering *Virg.* 4–7) is given as *eptaḥ pum(y) b-idaᶜta,* which is also found for *Eccl.* 7–9, 11, 22, *Haer.* 37, and *Nis.* 1. The meter has the following syllabic pattern: 7+7 7+8 7+7 7+4 7+7 7+7 7+7. In the present *madrasha* the refrain serves as the seventh line. The meter is in fact the same as that for Text 19 (*Nis.* 1), but Beck has chosen to set the two poems out differently.

Text

The poem is preserved complete only in Vatican Syr. 111 (522 CE; Beck's B). Beck also uses two later manuscripts containing just excerpts: British Library Add. 17141 (stanzas 1–4, 15) and British Library Add. 17245 (stanzas 5–7).

ܥܠ ܩܠܐ ܕܐܦܬܚ ܦܘܡܝ ܚܒܝܒܬܐ

1. ܛܘܒܬܐ ܘܫܘܦܪܬܐ ܠܗܘܢ ܒܒܥܝܢ ܡܬܒܥܝܐ
ܒܥܘܒܝ ܐܘܒܐ ܫܡܝܐ ܒܥܘܒܝܢܐ ܕܙܘܥܐ ܠܬܒܐ
ܫܡܝܐ ܓܝܪ ܠܐ ܢܒܠܥ ܒܥܘܡܩܗ ܒܢܦܫܗ ܩܐܡ ܗܘ
ܘܐܘܒܐ ܓܝܪ ܐܦ ܢܣܒ ܡܢ ܐܝܕܐ ܗܘ
ܩܠܐ ܘܢܒܝܐ ܠܒܘܫܗܝ ܠܒܫܐ ܚܕܐ ܡܢ ܩܢܘܗ
ܢܦܝܪܐ ܚܙܝ ܒܓܘܢܒܠܐ ܘܒܢܒܝܐ ܒܗܪܐ

ܒܘܥܝܬܐ : ܒܥܐ ܕܢܬܒܪ ܒܝ ܦܪܘܩܝ
ܕܒ ܗܘ ܡܥܒܪ ܡܢ ܥܠܡܝ

2. ܐܡܪ ܕܡܢܝܚ ܠܠܐܬܐ ܡܢ ܚܠܐ ܘܪܐܙܗ ܕܩܝܡܐ
ܡܢܪܗ ܡܫܝܚܐ ܘܠܗ ܩܕܝܫ ܐܦ ܠܐܬܒܐ ܘܒܦܐܪܘܗܝ
ܢܦܩ ܕܡܢܝܚ ܪܒܐ ܩܕܝܫ ܡܒܥܕ ܘܡܝܬܪ
ܩܪܒ ܪܐܙܐ ܕܚܝܬܐ ܡܢ ܢܦܫܗ
ܐܡܪ ܡܫܝܚܐ ܒܪܘ ܠܝ ܚܝܐ ܢܦܩ ܡܫܝܚܐ ܠܝ
ܒܐܡܪ ܦܐܪܐ ܡܬܡܛܦܢ ܒܢܦܩ ܚܘܒܐ ܡܬܚܣܢ

1. Repentance and diligence are requisites for both worlds:

for working the land the diligent [are needed],
for spiritual toil the repentant.

Though the diligent may not become rich,
his diligence stands by itself,

and though the penitent may be utterly guilty,
he belongs to those who have conquered,

whereas the sluggards and sinners have clothed themselves
in a name that is utterly evil:

there is reproach for the idle, and for sinners reproof.

Refrain: However great is our wonder for You, our Savior,
Your glory exceeds what our tongues [can express].

2. October gives rest to the weary
after the dust and dirt of the summer,

its rain washes, its dew anoints the trees and their fruit.

April gives rest to the fasters,
it anoints, baptizes and clothes in white;

it scours off the dirt of sin from our souls.

October presses out the oil for us, April multiplies mercies for us;

in October fruit is gathered, in April sins are forgiven.

3. ܕܫܠܡܬ ܗܘܬ ܐܬܟܠ ܗܝܡܢܘܬܐ ܫܠܡܬ ܐܘܪܚܐ ܬܠܡܝܕܘܬܗ
ܟܪܣܐ ܟܠܬܐ ܫܠܡܬܐ ܗܘܬ ܐܘܪܚܐ ܕܐܒܪܗܡ ܟܠܗ ܐܒܗ̈ܬܐ
ܫܠܡܬ ܗܝ ܐܘܪܚܐ ܠܥܡܗ ܕܫܠܡܘ ܗܝܡܢܘܬܐ ܠܡܗܝܡܢܗ
ܘܡܠܟܬܐ ܗܘܬ ܠܡܪܬܐ ܕܠܐ ܠܡܠܟܗ
ܘܗܝܡܢܬܐ ܘܡܪܢܐ ܠܡܪܬܐ ܐܡܠܟ ܘܐܬܦܪܥ ܕܠܐ ܠܡܠܟܐ
ܕܗܘ ܟܠܐ ܕܝܠܗ ܠܐܘܪܚܐ ܗܘ ܐܬܦܪܥ ܠܦܘܠܐ ܠܡܪ̈ܬܐ

4. ܪܕܐ ܗܘܐ ܕܝܢ ܥܡܐ ܒܐܘܪܚܐ ܘܥܡܗ ܕܗܒܗ ܕܐܚܝܕܘܬܐ
ܘܐܘܪܙܐ ܕܡܨܪܝܢ ܐܫܬܩܠܘ ܘܐܫܬܠܡܘ ܠܗܘܢ ܐܓܪܬܐ
ܘܟܠܗ ܥܡܐ ܘܥܡܗܐ ܐܝܟ ܗܘܐ ܐܝܢ ܕܟܢܫܐ
ܘܗܘ ܕܐܬܟܠ ܒܡܪܟܒܬܐ ܘܐܝܠ ܒܡܘܬܐ
ܐܝܠ ܒܥܡܐ ܟܠܗܝܢ ܕܐܢܝܢ ܗܘܐ ܡܢܪܐ ܠܗܘܢ ܕܗܘܝܢ
ܘܐܢܫܝܢ ܠܗ ܡܢܐ ܒܢܝܐ ܡܠܠܐ ܕܥܡܐ ܡܢ ܡܥܡܗܘܢ܀

3. Because Jezebel defrauded Truth, the earth refused its produce, 1 Kgs 21:5ff.

the womb [of the earth] held back, as a reproof,[1]
the seeds that the farmers had lent it,

it suffocated the seeds within itself,
because its inhabitants had deceitfully held back truth.

Mother [earth] became barren against her custom, 1 Kgs 17:1

while the cruse and the horn [of oil] gave birth
and bore fruit against their nature. 1 Kgs 17:16

The same prophet's voice that had deprived the earth
also caused barren wombs to be fruitful.

4. Famine took its course in the land,
and the flow [of corn] to the granaries stood still;

the [grain] stores that had been full were emptied,
the oil-cellars[2] became bare.

But Elijah joined together the flour and oil as with a yoke,

and he who was lifted up in the chariot and conquered death 2 Kgs 2:11

conquered the famine, using these two symbols.
The rain provided the limit for the course of his life 1 Kgs 18:45

when the Lord of the clouds stretched out to him
a crown of plenty from His floodwaters.

---

1. reproof *(k'ata):* Beck's suggested correction to *ki'nta* seems unnecessary.
2. oil cellars *(amdane):* Evidently a bye-form of *maddane.*

5. ܒܦܬ̈ܓܡܐ ܡܬܬܢܝ̈ܢܐ   ܡܬܐܡܪ ܙܒܢܐ ܕܡܠܟܘܬܐ
ܘܒܫܡܝܐ ܛܠܝܐ ܡܬܐܡܪ   ܙܒܢܐ ܟܐܢܐ ܕܡܠܟ ܟܐܢܐ
ܒܫܡܝܐ ܕܡܠܟܘܬܐ   ܘܡܫܟܠܠ ܠܗܘܢ ܟܠܗ ܒܟܠܗ
ܡܢ ܫܘܪܝܗ ܕܐܝܟ ܩܕܡܐ   ܗܘ ܕܐܫܬܟܠܠ
ܙܢܐ ܒܗܘܢ ܙܒܢܐ ܚܕܬܐ   ܘܫܒܬܐ ܒܗܘܢ ܒܫܘܟܠܠ ܐܠܗܐ
ܘܫܘ̈ܒܚܐ ܡܫܒܚܝܢ ܠܐܠܗܐ   ܘܐܦ ܒܪܐ ܘܪܘܚ ܩܘܕܫܐ

6. ܝܘܡܐ ܗܘ ܓܝܪ ܗܘ ܡܫܝܚܐ   ܕܪܘܚ ܩܘܕܫܐ ܘܡܫܡܫܢܗ
ܘܐܝܟ ܠܫܒܬܐ ܒܗ ܗܘܐ ܠܗ   ܕܒܗ ܢܫܒܘܩ ܟܘܬ̈ܠܐ ܘܡܫܡ̈ܫܢܐ
ܪܘܚ ܩܘܕܫܐ ܓܝܪ ܒܡܫܝܚܐ   ܐܝܟ ܕܐܘܡܢܗ ܟܠ ܒܪܝܬܗ
ܒܪܐ ܒܪܝܬܐ ܕܫܒܬܐ ܗܘ   ܐܝܟ ܠܫܒܬܗ
ܐܦ ܫܒܬܐ ܟܐܢܐ ܕܪܘܚܐ   ܒܡܫܝܚܐ ܡܬܬܠܝܐ ܟܠ ܦܪܝܫܐ
ܕܡܬܡܫܝܢ ܒܡܠܟܘܬܐ   ܘܗܘܝܢ ܕܫܒܬܐ ܟܠܢܫ

5. A royal portrait is painted with visible colors,

and with oil that all can see
    is the hidden portrait of our hidden King portrayed

on those who have been signed:
    on them baptism, that is in travail with them in its womb,

depicts the new portrait, to replace the image of the former Adam 1 Cor 15:45

who had become corrupted; it gives birth to them with triple pangs,[3]

accompanied by the three glorious names,
    of Father, Son and Holy Spirit.

6. The oil is the dear friend of the Holy Spirit, it is Her[4] minister,

following Her like a disciple.
    With it the Spirit signed priests and anointed kings;

for with the oil[5] the Holy Spirit imprints Her mark on Her sheep.

Like a signet ring which leaves its impression on wax,

so the hidden seal of the Spirit is imprinted by oil on the bodies

of those who are anointed in baptism;
    thus they are signed in the baptismal [mystery].

---

3. corrupted . . . pangs *(etḥabbal . . . ḥeble):* Note the word play (ANP).

4. Her: The Holy Spirit is treated as grammatically feminine in early Syriac writers; for this feature see Text 3 (*Fid.* 49), n. 6.

5. oil: The manuscript has *ba-mshiḥa,* but Beck is no doubt right in correcting the text to *b-meshḥa* (the *shwa* being treated metrically as a full vowel).

7. ܒܫܡܫܐ ܗܘ ܕܝܢ ܕܦܪܨܘܦܐ   ܡܬܬܡܫܝܢ ܒܚܘܦܝܐ
ܦܓܪܐ ܕܡܠܟܝܢ ܒܦܐܬܘܬܐ   ܡܬܚܘܪܝܢ ܟܕ ܠܐ ܡܬܚܣܝܢ
ܢܣܒܝܢ ܒܚܘܒܐ ܐܝܟ ܙܪܥܐ   ܘܡܘܠܕܝܢ ܕܝܢܐ ܐܝܟ ܫܒܠܐ
ܕܗܘܝܐ ܒܗܘܢ ܡܬܒܥܘܬܐ   ܟܪܣܐ ܐܚܪܬܐ
ܡܛܠ ܒܫܘܒܚܐ ܡܘܠܕܗ   ܘܐܦ ܢܘܪܐ ܠܐ ܒܥܒܕܗ
ܐܘ ܠܒܪܐ ܕܝܠܕܐ ܦܓܪܗ   ܘܠܐ ܫܪܐ ܬܒܪ ܒܬܘܠܘܬܐ

8. ܒܘܢܝܬܐ ܗܘ ܡܬܡܛܝܐ ܠܗ   ܒܗܘܐ ܕܒܪܐ ܒܡܘܠܕܗ
ܡܫܝܚܘܬܐ ܕܪܘܚܐ ܡܦܪܫܢܗ   ܪܚܡ ܡܦܪܫܐ ܡܪܝܐ ܠܟܠ ܒܢܝܢܗ
ܕܟܠ ܒܢܝܐ ܒܪܝ ܠܗ   ܕܒ ܒܢܝܐ ܒܟܝܢ ܡܥܡܕ
ܟܡܐ ܢܒܝܢ ܠܐܒܪܐ   ܕܡܬܚܬܢܝܢ ܒܗ
ܐܘ ܠܒܪܐ ܕܗܘܐ ܕܢܚܬܐ   ܗܘ ܕܒܥܐ ܐܫܘܐ ܘܡܪܟܐ
ܐܘ ܠܒܬܘܠܐ ܕܐܠܕܬ ܡܢ ܡܠܟܐ   ܚܠܦ ܚܠܠܐ ܠܚܝܐ ܠܥܠܡܐ

7. With the oil of discernment bodies are anointed for forgiveness,

bodies that were filled with stains are made white without effort:[6] Isa 1:18

they go down sordid with sin, they go up pure like infants,

for baptism is a second womb for them.

Rebirth [in the font] rejuvenates the old,
as the river rejuvenated Naaman. 2 Kgs 5:14

O womb that gives birth every day without pangs
to the children of the Kingdom!

8. It is the priesthood which ministers to this womb as it gives birth;

anointing precedes it, the Holy Spirit hovers[7] over its streams, Gen 1:2

a crown of Levites[8] surrounds it, the chief priest is its minister,

the Watchers[9] rejoice at the lost who in it are found. Luke 15:10

Once this womb has given birth,
the altar suckles and nurtures them:

her children eat straight away, not milk, but perfect Bread![10]

---

6. without effort: Ephrem has in mind the energetic beating of clothes.

7. hovers *(mraḥḥpa):* Although Ephrem disapproved of identifying the "spirit of God" which hovered *(mraḥḥpa hwat)* over the primordial waters (Gen 1:2) as the Holy Spirit, he nevertheless was happy to use the verb (clearly derived from this passage) of the Holy Spirit's action over the baptismal water. For Ephrem's views and the controversy over the identity of "the spirit of God," see Brock 1999b.

8. Levites: I.e., deacons; the terminology is commonly found.

9. Watchers *(ʿire):* Besides *malʾake* for angels, Syriac frequently employs the term Watchers, found in Daniel.

10. perfect Bread: Communion is the culminating feature of all the Eastern Christian baptismal rites.

9. ܡܫܝܚܐ ܡܒܣܡ ܒܥܘܕܪܢܐ ܒܗ̇ ܒܒܣܪܐ ܡܒܣܡ ܟܐܒܐ
ܡܫܝܚܐ ܓܝܪ ܒܢܦܫܗ ܚܘܒܐ ܐܝܟ ܡܫܘܬܐ ܕܟܠܗ ܠܟܐܒܐ
ܛܘܒܐ ܓܝܪ ܐܝܟ ܟܐܒܐ ܟܐܒܐܝܬ ܒܢܦܫܗ ܠܒܢܝܢܫܐ
ܕܠܐ ܐܝܟ ܗܘܐ ܕܥܒܕܘܗܝ ܛܥܢ ܕܐܬܬܥܝܩ ܒܗ
ܡܫܝܚܐ ܕܝܢ ܒܐܣܘܬܐ ܛܒܐ ܒܢܦܫܗ ܓܘܒܐ ܒܡܒܣܡܢܘܬܐ
ܕܗܐ ܚܠܝܐ ܚܠܝܬܐ ܒܟܐܒܐ ܠܐ ܐܝܟ ܒܪܚܝܠܬܐ

10. ܡܫܝܚܐ ܒܚܘܒܗ ܗܘܐ ܟܐܒܐ ܠܒܣܘܪܐ ܕܒܫܝܢܘܬܗ
ܢܘܗܪܗ ܫܡܝܐ ܘܢܝܫܐ ܘܟܠܗ ܡܪܝܐ ܢܦܫܗ ܡܟܪ
ܡܫܝܚܐ ܚܝܠܐ ܕܠܐ ܛܥܝ ܒܟܣܪܐ ܕܛܥܝ ܡܫܬܘܬܦ
ܘܒܗܝ ܡܫܡܫ ܡܢ ܒܘܣܡܐ ܡܬܡܟܟ ܒܚܘܪܐ
ܘܡܫܝܚܐ ܚܝܠܐ ܕܠܐ ܡܠܐ ܟܠܗ ܒܟܣܪܐ ܡܫܘܠܐ
ܒܟܝ ܘܐܫܬܘܫ ܡܢ ܢܘܚܐ ܡܬܡܟܟ ܢܝܚܐ ܕܒܗ ܐܝܟ

9. Oil, the beneficial fountain, accompanies the body, that fount of ills;

for oil wipes out sins,[11] just as the Flood wiped out the unclean; Gen 6

for the Flood, acting in justice, wiped out the wicked:

those who had not subdued their lusts drowned,[12]
having brought on the Flood through these lusts;

but oil, acting in goodness,[13] wipes out sins in baptism,

for sin is drowned[14] in the water and cannot live with all its desires.

10. Oil in its love accompanies the baptized[15] in his need,

when, despising his life, he descends and buries himself in the water;

oil by nature does not sink,
but it accompanies the body on which it imprints [its mark].[16]

Once baptized, it raises up from the deep a treasure of riches.

Christ by nature cannot die,
yet He clothed Himself with a mortal body,[17]

He was baptized, and so raised up from the water
the treasure of salvation for the race of Adam.

---

11. sins: Or "debts"; there is a double entendre here, since the sale of olive oil pays the farmer's debts.

12. drowned: Lit. "floated" (as corpses in the Flood).

13. in justice . . . in goodness: This could equally be translated "like the Upright (God) . . . like the Good (God)," balancing God's two aspects of *ki'nuta* (righteousness) and *ṭabuta* (goodness), or *ṭaybuta* (grace); this balance (which can be compared with the Rabbinic *middot,* or measures, of justice *[din]* and mercy *[raḥamayim]*) is one which Ephrem frequently exploits.

14. drowned: I.e., at baptism.

15. baptized: There is a deliberate double entendre here, for the word can also mean "diver."

16. mark: The prebaptismal anointing, or *rushma* ("mark"), is a mark of ownership, among other things; see stanza 6 and *rshime,* "marked, signed," in stanzas 5 and 6.

17. clothed Himself in a mortal body *(lbesh pagra mayota):* The phrase also features in Ephrem's *Prose Refutations* (Mitchell 1912–21, 2:146). See also Text 9 (*Ieiun.* 3), n. 4.

11. ܡܢܘ ܢܦܩܘܗ ܡܫܝܚܐ ܠܒܪܝܐ ܫܒܩ ܢܛܘܦܬܐ ܕܠܐ ܐܪܕܝ
ܘܐܝܟ ܡܘܦܬܐ ܗܘܐ ܠܒܢ̈ܝܬܐ ܕܒܠܐ ܡܚܝܪܐ ܕܟܠ ܕܢܦܫ
ܡܢ ܟܦܢܐ ܕܨܗܘܬܐ ܠܘܬ ܐܚܝ̈ ܐܝܟ ܕܒܢ̈ܝܚܐ
ܘܒܟܦܢܐ ܕܒܥܘܬܐ ܒܗܘ ܢܬܒܥ ܗܘܐ
ܦܘܪܫ ܡܫܝܚܐ ܡܟܝ ܡܛ̈ܪܐ ܕܟܠ ܚܝ̈ܠܐ ܡܟܝܢ ܗܘܐ
ܦܩܘܣ ܐܒܘܝ ܕܐܝܬܝ ܗܘܐ ܠܡܦܩܣ ܐܢܐ ܡܢ ܒܟܝܢܗ

12. ܡܫܝܚܐ ܠܢܦܫܗ ܒܪܐ ܡܫܝܚܐ ܦܪܫ ܢܘܒܠܐ ܕܠܐ ܕܡܟܘ
ܫܡܫܐ ܕܡܢܗ ܐܬܢܚܬ ܒܡܐܢܐ ܕܢܒܥܐ ܠܒܢ̈ܝܐ
ܐܝܟ ܫܡܫܐ ܕܐܬܢܚܬ ܠܘܬ ܠܒܢܝܬܐ ܠܒܝܬܐ ܕܡܢ ܐܘܪܚܐ
ܡܫܝܚܐ ܗܘܐ ܠܒܪܐ ܠܒܪܝܐ ܠܢܘܗܪ ܚܐܪܐ
ܡܫܝܚܐ ܗܘܐ ܠܒܪܐ ܠܒܪܝܐ ܠܢܘܗܪ ܠܒܪ̈ܐ ܕܚܫܘܟܐ
ܐܦ ܠܦܬܐ ܐܦ ܠܒܪܐ ܙܪܩ ܡܫܝܚܐ ܠܡܫܝܚܐ

11. The oil gave itself for sale in place of the orphans,
    to prevent their being sold; 2 Kgs 4:1–7

it acts as a guardian to the fatherless,
    having restrained the fate that had tried to sever

the two brothers, like shoots, from the stock of freedom

and graft them on to the stock of slavery. cf. Rom 11:17

The price of the oil made an end to the bonds [of debt]
    that cried out against the debtors; Col 2:14

it tore up the bonds that had come to tear away
    a mother from her son.

12. Oil in its love, like Christ, pays debts that are not its own.

The treasure that of its own accord turned up
    for the debtors in the pottery vessel

is like the Treasure that also turned up for the Peoples
    in a body made from earth.[18]

The oil became a slave for sale to free the freeborn,

and Christ became a slave for sale
    to free those who were enslaved to sin. Phil 2:7

In both name and deed[19] does the oil depict Christ.

---

18. a body made from earth: I.e., Christ's human body.

19. In both name and deed: Ephrem of course plays on the similarity between *meshḥa,* "oil," and *mshiḥa,* "Christ."

13. ܢܗܘܐ ܡܫܝܚܐ ܟܠܗ ܠܟܠܢ ܡܫܝܚܐ ܓܝܪ ܡܢܝܚ ܠܟܠ
ܡܫܚ ܠܡܫܝܚܐ ܡܫܚܐ ܒܟܠ ܒܫܡܗܐ ܘܫܘܡܗܐ ܘܠܬܪܥܐ ܙܘܥܗ
ܒܫܘܒܚܘܗܝ ܫܒܚܘܗ ܒܢܝ ܥܝܪ̈ܐ ܒܫܘܡܫܘܗܝ ܫܡܫܘܗ ܒܢܝ ܡܪܝܡ
ܒܡܪܦܗ ܐܬܐ ܒܢܝ ܥܡܡܐ ܠܒܘܫܗ ܡܫܚ
ܒܫܘܒܚܘܗܝ ܙܥ ܗܘܐ ܐܒܘܗܝ ܒܫܘܡܫܘܗܝ ܙܥ ܗܘܐ ܡܠܐܟܘܗܝ
ܒܡܪܦܗ ܙܥ ܗܘܐ ܒܗܝܟܠܐ ܘܐܦ ܡܘܬܐ ܒܫܝܘܠ ܡܙܕܠܠ

14. ܦܪ̈ܨܘܦܐ ܐܝܟܐ ܕܚܙܐ ܒܟܝܢܐ ܕܡܫܚܐ ܡܫܝܚܐ
ܙܟܐ ܢܦܫܗ ܚܙܐ ܠܗܘܢ ܘܚܙܐ ܒܗ ܒܥܝܢܗ
ܠܡܫܚܐ ܚܙܐ ܒܬܪܘܗܝ ܘܕܡܫܝܚܐ ܫܡܥ ܒܢܒ̈ܝܐ ܗܘ
ܐܦ ܐܝܟܐ ܫܡܥ ܕܪ̈ܐ ܗܘ ܘܗܘܐ ܠܗ
ܡܫܚܐ ܟܠܗ ܦܪ̈ܨܘܦܐ ܘܡܫܝܚܐ ܟܠܗ ܡܫܡܠܝܐ
ܘܥܡ ܟܠ ܒܪ ܕܐܝܬܐ ܒܗ ܒܡܫܝܚܐ ܡܫܝܚܐ ܡܕܡ ܠܝ ܥܡ ܠܗܘܢ

13. Let oil in all its forms acknowledge You
in Your entirety, for oil gives rest to all.

[The olive] served Christ, who gives life to all,
depicting Him in its abundance, its branches and its leaves:

with its branches it praised Him—through the children; John 12:13; Matt
with its abundance it anointed Him—through Mary; 21:16; John 12:3

with its leaf again, through the dove it served [Noah], His type; Gen 8:11

with its branches it depicted the symbol of His victory,
with its abundance it depicted the symbol of His dying, John 12:7

with its leaf it depicted the symbol of the resurrection
and the Flood disgorged it, as Death [disgorged Christ].

14. The face that gazes on a vessel filled with oil

sees its reflection there, but he who gazes in a hidden way

sees Christ in its symbols: and as the beauty of Christ is manifold,

so too the olive's symbols are manifold.

Christ has many facets, and the oil acts as a mirror to them all:

from whatever angle I look at the oil, Christ looks out at me from it!

15. ܡܢ ܗܘ ܟܝ ܒܫܒܝܠܐ ܥܒܪ ܢܓܝܠܐ ܐܝܟܢܐ ܫܡܪܝܐ
ܕܝܠܐ ܕܫܡܠܗ ܢܓܝܪ ܩܛܝܠܐ ܢܘܒܗ ܒܡܪܒܘܗܝ ܕܩܛܝܠܐ
ܠܐܪܥܐ ܢܓܝܪܘܗܝ ܕܩܛܝܠܐ ܘܒܪܝܐ ܩܛܝܠܐ ܢܘܒܗ
ܗܘܐ ܐܘܪܚܐ ܢܓܝܠܐ ܒܢܓܝܠܐ ܘܐܬܐ ܒܫܡܪܝܬܐ
ܐܡܪ ܐܦ ܐܢܐ ܐܝܟ ܫܡܥܘܢ ܕܒܝܫ ܗܢܐ ܐܝܟ ܕܒܫܡܥܘܢ
ܗܐ ܒܡܠܘܗܝ ܕܗܘ ܢܓܝܠܐ ܡܢܐ ܕܒܝܫ ܒܫܒܝܠܐ

15. Who has overwhelmed me in my weakness
 with these insistent waves?

For when the waves of oil lift me up,
 they hand me over to the subject of Christ,

and then the waves of Christ bear me back to the symbols of oil.

The waves meet each other, and I am in their midst:

I will say as Simon said: Draw me up, Lord, as you did Simon, Matt 14:30

for the innumerable waves have worn me out;
 O Compassionate One, draw me out who am so feeble!

◆

TEXT 17

The Mysteries of the Eucharist (*Fid.* 10)

This is probably the most important of the *madrashe* where Ephrem considers the Eucharistic Mysteries. At the outset he asks for inspiration, being all too aware of his inadequacy in the face of such a theme. If John the Baptist held even Christ's sandal straps in awe, how can he hope to approach Christ's very Body? Ephrem takes refuge in the example of the woman who gained healing just through touching Christ's garment—which in another sense is indeed his body, being the garment of his divinity. The Hidden Power that lay in Christ's garment is also present in the Bread and the Wine (stanza 8), consecrated by the fire of the Spirit. The awesome nature of this fire, which can either sanctify or destroy, is illustrated from various episodes in the Old Testament (stanzas 10–13). A quotation from Prov 30:4 provides the transition to the presence of Fire in Mary's womb, which is then linked to the womb of the River Jordan and the womb of the baptismal font (stanza 17). In the final self-deprecating stanza Ephrem draws on the reply of the Syro-Phoenician woman to Jesus (Mark 7:28). (There are earlier translations in Murray 1970 and Brock 1987.)

Meter

The *qala* (covering *Fid.* 10–25) is given as *izgadda haddaya.* The meter is the same as that for the *qala* title *a(n)t mar(y) aktebtah,* which are in fact the opening words of *Fid.* 10. The syllabic pattern is as follows: 5+6 7+4 4+4 4+5. The same meter is found for *Eccl.* 29–30, *Ieiun.* 6 (Text 10), and *Nis.* 50. The vowel on the first radical *alaph* verbs *ekal* and *eḥad* is treated as absent for metrical reasons in stanzas 12 (line 4), 13 (line 4), and 14 (line 1).

Text

The poem is preserved in four early manuscripts: British Library Add. 12176 (fifth or sixth century; Beck's A), Vatican Syr. 111 (522 CE; Beck's B), Vatican Syr. 113 (552 CE; Beck's C), and British Library Add. 14571 (519 CE; Beck's D).

ܥܠ ܡܠܐ ܕܐܬܚܙܝ ܗܘܢܐ

1. ܐܢܬ ܡܪܝ ܐܬܒܥܝܬ ܕܦܬܚ ܦܘܡܝ ܘܐܡܠܠܟ
ܗܐ ܦܬܚ ܠܝ ܦܘܡܗ ܕܥܒܕܟ ܥܡ ܕܒܝܬܗ
ܐܢܬ ܡܠܠܟ ܡܪܝ ܡܢ ܡܘܗܒܬܟ
ܕܐܦ ܒܝܢܝ ܐܡܪ ܬܫܒܘܚܬܟ

ܥܘܢܝܬܐ : ܐܫܘܝܢܝ ܕܒܚܝܠܐ ܐܡܪ ܠܟ ܒܡܘܗܒܬܟ

2. ܠܬܫܒܘܚܬܟ ܕܙܕܩܐ ܕܠܐ ܡܫܟܚ ܟܠ ܐܢܫ
ܒܙܕܩܐ ܠܚܝܠܝ ܐܡܪ ܟܕ ܡܫܪܝܢ ܐܢܐ
ܥܠܝܗ ܡܢ ܫܡܝܐ ܚܝܠ ܡܘܗܒܬܟ
ܘܐܢܬ ܦܘܡܐ ܕܢܫܪܝܢ ܢܘܡܘܣ ܒܗ

3. ܟܕ ܚܕ ܗܘ ܒܢܝ ܦܫܝܩܘܬܗ ܡܫܬܐܠܐ
ܡܢܐ ܕܡܐ ܘܡܬܪܓܡܢܐ ܐܦ ܡܬܒܥܝܢܐ
ܟܝܢܐ ܡܢܐ ܐܝܟ ܦܪܢܘܬܐ
ܐܫܘܝܢܝ ܕܐܫܩܘܠ ܢܛܪܐ ܕܫܬܩܘܬܟ

1. You have had it written, Lord,
"Open your mouth and I will fill it." Ps 81:10

Look, Your servant's mouth is open, and his mind as well;

fill it, Lord, with Your Gift,

that I may sing Your praise in accordance with Your will.

Refrain: Make me worthy to approach Your gift in awe!

2. Each, according to the level of his own measure, can tell of You;

in my boldness I approach the lowest step.

Your Birth is sealed up within silence—

what mouth then dares to meditate upon it?

3. Your nature is single, but there are many ways of explaining it;

our descriptions may be exalted, or in moderate terms, or lowly.

Make me worthy of the lowest part,
that I may gather up, as crumbs,

the gleanings from Your wisdom's [table]. Matt 15:27; Mark 7:28

4. ܫܪܟܡ ܟܠܝܠܐ ܚܙܝܐ ܗܘܐ ܐܝܟ ܡܟܘܕܡ
ܓܢܐ ܒܒܘܠܝܡ ܡܪܟܒܐ ܗܘܐ ܠܡܘܬܢܝܢ
ܙܝܢܐ ܒܒܘܙܐ ܡܪܝ ܕܦܫܝܩ
ܐܝܟ ܠܬܒܥܬܐ ܡܫܡܠܐ ܠܗܘܢ ܟܘܠܐ ܗܘ

5. ܕܐܢ ܗܘ ܕܡܫܬܢܐ ܗܘ ܙܒܐ ܡܠܟܐ ܗܘܐ
ܕܠܐ ܟܡ ܫܢܐ ܐܢܐ ܒܟܪܝܐ ܡܪܝ ܕܡܣܟܝܢ
ܐܝܟ ܚܛܝܬܐ ܒܗܘ ܠܒܠܒܗ
ܕܢܚܬܡ ܐܗܦܘܣ ܕܡܢܗ ܐܬܐ

6. ܘܐܝܟ ܗܘܝ ܕܐܬܪܘܒܬ ܘܐܬܟܒܒܬ ܕܐܬܚܒܒܬ
ܐܦܠܐ ܙܘܡܒܘܠܐ ܡܢ ܡܫܠܐ ܘܒܢ ܐܬܟܒܒ
ܡܢ ܐܝܟ ܢܚܬܡ ܐܬܚܒܠ ܠܗܘܢ
ܐܝܟ ܗܘ ܦܓܪܡ ܘܐܝܟ ܚܒܠ ܐܬܚܒܠܘܗܝ

7. ܢܚܬܡ ܡܪܝ ܐܬܚܘܝ ܡܟܘܠܐ ܕܫܡܝܢܐ
ܒܒܘܫܡ ܠܒܢܐ ܗܘܐ ܒܗ ܚܝܠܐ ܒܫܢܐ
ܙܘܟܐ ܐܒܘܪܐ ܕܡܢ ܦܘܡܡ ܠܗܘܢ
ܠܗܘܪܐ ܗܘ ܙܒܐ ܕܢܘܪܐ ܒܗ ܠܡܢܗ

4. Any elevated account of You is hidden with Your Begetter;

at Your lesser riches the angels stand amazed,

while a small trickle of words describing You, Lord,

provides a flood of homilies for [mortals] below.

5. For if the great John cried out and said,

"I am not worthy, Lord, of the straps of your sandals," Mark 1:7

then I should seek refuge, like the sinful woman, Matt 9:21; Luke 8:47

in the shadow of Your garment, and there begin.

6. And as she was affrighted,
 but took courage because she was healed,

so do You heal my fear and fright,
 and so I may take courage in You

and be conveyed from Your garment to Your own Body,

so that I may tell of it according to my ability.

7. Your garment, Lord, is a fountain of medicines:

in Your visible clothing there dwells a hidden power.

Again, a little spittle from Your mouth John 9:6

became a great miracle of light,
 for light was in the clay [it made].

8. ܒܠܚܘܕܝ ܟܡܝܢܐ ܒܗ ܪܘܚܐ ܕܠܐ ܡܬܐܟܠܐ
ܒܡܥܒܪܝ ܫܪܝܐ ܒܗ ܢܘܪܐ ܕܠܐ ܡܬܡܫܚܢܐ
ܪܘܚܐ ܒܠܚܘܕܝ ܢܘܪܐ ܒܡܥܒܪܝ
ܬܗܪܐ ܦܪܝܫܐ ܕܢܦܩ ܣܦܘܬܝ

9. ܕܡܪܐ ܢܚܬ ܗܘܐ ܒܗ ܠܛܘܪܐ ܟܕ ܡܬܬܦܝܐ
ܒܪܡܬܐ ܚܙܬܐ ܒܪܐ ܐܢܘܢ ܐܝܟ ܕܒܚܬܐ
ܕܢܘܪܐ ܘܪܘܚܐ ܒܗܘܢ ܡܠܝ ܗܘܐ
ܕܢܘܪ ܘܕܪܘܚ ܢܗܘܘܢ ܟܡܝܢܐܝܬ

10. ܫܪܦܐ ܠܓܡܘܪܬܐ ܠܐ ܩܪܒ ܠܗ ܒܨܒܥܬܗ
ܒܟܘܠܒܗ ܕܐܫܥܝܐ ܡܩܪܒ ܩܪܒܬ ܒܚܣܘܕܝ
ܠܐ ܗܘ ܐܚܕܬܗ ܘܠܐ ܗܘ ܐܟܠܬܗ
ܠܝ ܕܝܢ ܗܘܐ ܝܗܒ ܡܪܢ ܬܪܬܝܗܝܢ

11. ܒܒܬܐ ܪܘܚܬܐ ܡܬܟܘܠܬܐ ܕܦܓܪܢܐ
ܩܪܒ ܐܒܪܗܡ ܘܐܟܠܘ ܬܗܪܐ ܚܕܬܐ
ܕܡܪܢ ܢܘܪܐ ܕܠܦܓܪܢܐ
ܢܘܪܐ ܘܪܘܚܐ ܡܥܘܠܝ ܐܦ ܡܫܩܠ

8. In Your Bread there is hidden the Spirit who is not consumed,
in Your Wine there dwells the Fire that is not drunk:
the Spirit is in Your Bread, the Fire in Your Wine—
a manifest wonder, that our lips have received.

9. When the Lord came down to earth to mortal men 2 Cor 5:17; Gal 6:15
He created them again, a new creation, like the angels,
mingling within them fire and spirit,
so that in a hidden manner they might be of fire and spirit.

10. The Seraph could not touch the fire's coal with his fingers, Isa 6:6–7
the coal only just touched Isaiah's mouth:
the [Seraph] did not hold it, [Isaiah] did not consume it,
but us our Lord has allowed to do both!

11. To the angels who are spiritual Abraham brought Gen 18:8–9
food for the body, and they ate. The new miracle
is that our mighty Lord has given to bodily man
Fire and Spirit to eat and to drink.

12. ܢܘܗܪܐ ܒܚܫܘܟܐ ܒܕܘܟܐ ܢܣܒܢ ܘܐܟܠܢ
ܢܘܗܪܐ ܕܚܢܢܐ ܒܠܚܡܐ ܢܣܒܢ ܘܦܪܐ
ܚܠܦ ܗܘ ܢܘܗܪܐ ܕܐܟܠܢ ܐܢܫܐ
ܢܘܗܪܐ ܒܠܚܡܐ ܐܟܠܘܗ ܘܚܝܘܗ

13. ܒܪܚܡܘܗܝ ܕܐܠܗܐ ܢܘܗܪܐ ܢܣܒܢ ܘܐܟܠܢ
ܢܘܗܪܐ ܕܒܣܡܐ ܗܘܐ ܠܢ ܠܢ ܕܚܝܠ ܚܝܐ
ܢܘܗܪܐ ܐܟܠܢ ܒܩܘܪܒܢܐ
ܘܢܘܗܪ ܡܢܗ ܐܟܠܢܗ ܒܩܘܪܒܢܢ

14. ܪܘܚܐ ܒܩܘܪܒܢܘܗܝ ܟܠ ܡܢܗ ܐܢܫ ܠܐ ܚܙܐ
ܐܘ ܫܠܡܘܬܗ ܩܕܡ ܕܟܠܒ ܡܢܗ ܕܐܒܘܢ
ܕܢܘܗܪܐ ܘܪܘܚܐ ܕܠܐ ܒܚܝܠܗ
ܡܢܝ ܘܢܣܒ ܒܩܘܪܒܢܐ ܕܐܟܠܢܘܗܝ

15. ܡܢܗ ܙܘ ܡܢܐ ܒܩܘܪܒܢܐ ܡܩܒܠ ܗܘܐ
ܗܐ ܒܩܘܪܒܢܐ ܡܒܩܒܠ ܟܢܫܗ ܕܡܪܢ
ܩܝ ܟܠܗ ܚܝܐ ܢܘܗܪܐ ܚܝܐ
ܟܠܗ ܩܘܪܒܢܐ ܢܩܒܠ ܐܟܠܘܗܝ

12. Fire descended in wrath and consumed the sinners; Gen 19:24; 2 Kgs 1:10–14
the fire of mercy has now descended and dwelt in the Bread:
instead of that fire which consumed mankind
you have consumed Fire in the Bread—and you have come to life!

13. Fire descended and consumed Elijah's sacrifices; 1 Kgs 18:38
the Fire of mercies has become a living sacrifice for us:
fire consumed [Elijah's] oblation,
but we, Lord, have consumed Your Fire in Your oblation!

14. Who has ever held in his cupped hands the wind? Come and see, Prov 30:4
Solomon, what the Lord of your father has done: cf. Ps 110:1
against nature, He has mingled fire and spirit
and poured them out in the hands of His disciples.

15. "Who has gathered up water in a veil?" he asked. Prov 30:4
Here is a Fountain in a veil—Mary's bosom.
And Your maidservants receive, within a veil,
the drop of salvation from Salvation's cup.

16. ܗܐ ܚܝܠܐ ܟܣܝܐ   ܒܡܘܫܚܐ ܕܒܝܬ ܩܘܕܫܐ
ܚܝܠܐ ܕܐܦ ܠܐ ܐܪܥܢܝܐ   ܡܫܟܚܝܢ ܚܙܝܬܗ
ܐܪܒܥ ܣܘܟܗ   ܘܢܫܠ ܪܓܫ
ܟܠ ܡܘܫܚܐ   ܕܡܕܒܚ ܐܪܒܥܬܐ

17. ܗܐ ܢܘܪܐ ܘܪܘܚܐ   ܒܥܘܒܐ ܕܝܠܕܬܟ
ܗܐ ܢܘܪܐ ܘܪܘܚܐ ܒܢܗܪܐ   ܕܒܗ ܥܡܕܬ ܡܪܝ
ܢܘܪܐ ܘܪܘܚܐ   ܒܡܥܡܘܕܝܬܢ
ܒܠܚܡܐ ܘܟܣܐ   ܢܘܪܐ ܘܪܘܚ ܩܘܕܫܐ

18. ܟܣܝܢ ܡܠܐ ܒܗ   ܚܝܠܐ ܕܟܒܪ ܟܣܝܗ
ܟܡܝܢ ܡܘܬܒ ܒܗ ܒܡܘܬܐ   ܕܗܐ ܗܪܦ ܠܟ
ܐܟܠܝܢ ܡܢܗ   ܐܦ ܐܫܬܝܢ
ܠܐ ܗܘܐ ܕܢܦܫܢ   ܐܠܐ ܕܚܝܐ ܒܢ

19. ܒܪܡܫܗ ܕܡܫܝܚܢ   ܗܘܪܐ ܗܘ ܒܥܪܘܒܬܐ
ܟܢܫܐ ܕܡܪܕܘܬܢ ܕܚܝܠܐ ܗܘ   ܙܪܥ ܙܪܘܥܐ
ܕܢ ܫܒܠܐ   ܟܕ ܒܥܡܠܢ
ܗܐ ܡܫܝܚܐ   ܕܢܘܪܐ ܒܡܐܪܬܐ

16. There is hidden power in the sanctuary's veil,
a power that no mind has ever confined:
it brought down its love, descended and hovered
over this veil on the altar of reconciliation.

17. See, Fire and Spirit are in the womb of her who bore You,
see, Fire and Spirit are in the river[1] in which You were baptized.
Fire and Spirit are in our baptismal font,
in the Bread and Cup are Fire and Holy Spirit.

18. Your Bread slays the greedy one who had made us his bread,
Your Cup destroys death who had swallowed us up;
we have eaten You, Lord, we have drunken You
—not that we will consume You up,
but through You we shall have life.

19. The thong of Your sandal is something fearful to the discerning,
the hem of Your cloak is awesome to those who understand,
yet our foolish generation, through its prying into You,
has gone quite mad, drunk with new wine.[2]

---

1. Fire . . . in the river: For the tradition of fire appearing in the Jordan at Christ's baptism, see Text 7 (*Eccl.* 36), n. 6.

2. drunk with new wine: Ephrem is here accusing the Arians of what the disciples had falsely been accused of by the mockers at Pentecost (Acts 2:13).

20. ܛܘܪܐ ܒܩܒܠܟ ܕܟܠ ܡܢܐ ܘܥܠܝ ܗܘܝ
ܥܡܐ ܪܒܐ ܡܫܬܥܒܕ ܗܘܐ ܠܐܚܝܕ ܟܠ
ܒܢܘܪܐ ܕܟܘܪܐ ܐܦ ܗܘ ܕܗܒ
ܐܫܬܥܒܕ ܗܘܐ ܕܙܢܝ ܘܥܒܕ ܒܗ

21. ܢܘܪܐ ܕܩܛܠ ܗܘܐ ܠܟܣܕܝܐ ܕܐܘܩܕ ܒܗ
ܓܘܫܡܝܗܘܢ ܕܛܠܝܐ ܪܚܡ ܒܠܒܘܫܝܗܘܢ
ܒܢܘܪܐ ܕܟܘܪܐ ܘܟܒܪܐ ܡܚܝܠܐ
ܐܫܬܥܒܕ ܗܘܐ ܡܪܐ ܕܓܘܫܡܝܗܘܢ

22. ܗܐ ܡܫܟܚ ܡܢܢ ܒܩܝܛ ܡܢ ܢܘܪܐ ܕܦܬܟܪܝܢ
ܘܟܠܗ ܐܬܪܐ ܒܥܒܕܝ ܐܠܗܐ ܟܕ ܗܘܐ ܐܬܐ
ܟܕ ܡܘܬܒܠܐ ܘܐܝܟ ܒܥܒܕܐ
ܥܒܕܝܢ ܠܗܘܢ ܕܟܠ ܐܠܗܐ ܐܦܝܢ

20. There is wonder in Your footsteps, which walked on the water: Matt 14:25

You subjected a great sea beneath Your feet,

yet Your very head was subject to just a small river,

in that it bent down and was baptized therein.

21. The river resembled John, who baptized in it:

each reflects the other in its smallness;

yet to the small river and to the weak servant

was the Master of them both subjected!

22. Look, Lord, my lap is now filled
with the crumbs from Your [table], Matt 15:27; Mark 7:28

there is no more room in the folds [of my garment],

so stay Your Gift, as I worship [before You]:

keep it in Your treasure house in readiness
to give us on another occasion.

◆

TEXT 18

The Eucharistic Marriage Feast
(*Fid.* 14)

Ephrem considered praise to be an essential element of Christian life. He here invites Christ to a wedding feast, but since the wine of praise has run out, he asks Christ to repeat the miracle he performed at the Wedding at Cana. In the fourth stanza it emerges that the wedding feast to which Ephrem is inviting Christ is in fact the wedding feast of the Eucharist, where Christ is no guest, but the Bridegroom himself. The Bride turns out to be, not only the Church, but also, on another level, the individual soul who, at Communion, receives the Bridegroom in the bridal chamber of the body (stanza 5). At this point Ephrem recalls how Moses had prepared the former Bride, the Synagogue, at Sinai, but she had proved unfaithful "in her own bridal chamber," by worshipping the Calf instead (stanzas 6–7). Ephrem shudders with dread at the thought that he might ever himself be guilty of infidelity (stanza 9). The poem concludes with the paradox of the combination of divinity and humanity in Christ.

Meter

The *qala* is *izgadda haddaya,* for which see under Text 17 (*Fid.* 10). Vocal *shwa* is treated as a full vowel in stanza 4, line 3, and in stanza 10, line 2. For the partial alphabetic acrostic, see the General Introduction (p. xv).

Text

Like the previous one, this poem has the benefit of being preserved in four sixth-century manuscripts (see under Text 17).

ܥܠ ܩܠܐ ܕܐܬܚܙܝ ܘܗܘܢܐ

1\. ܐܡܚܠܬ ܡܪܝ ܒܚܘܒܠܐ ܕܡܕܪܫܐ
ܡܙܓ ܠܗ ܚܡܪܐ ܒܚܘܫܒܝ ܩܐܡܪ ܫܘܒܚܐ
ܐܟܝܢܐ ܕܡܠܐ ܗܘܐ ܐܢܝܐ
ܚܡܪܐ ܠܟܐ ܡܟܝ ܦܘܫ ܐܬܚܘܝܬ

ܒܥܘܬܐ : ܫܘܒܚܐ ܠܟ ܡܢ ܟܠ ܕܐܪܓܫ ܒܗ ܒܡܙܘܪ

2\. ܚܡܪܐ ܕܒܐܢܝܐ ܐܣܝܢܐ ܗܘ ܐܦ ܟܪ ܠܫܘܡܐ
ܕܗܘܐ ܚܡܪܐ ܡܟܠܐ ܕܡܘܟܒ ܫܘܒܚܐ
ܕܐܦ ܗܘ ܚܡܪܐ ܫܘܒܚܐ ܐܘܟܒ
ܡܢ ܦܓܪܢܐ ܕܚܝܘ ܐܕܡܘܬܐ

1. I have invited You, Lord, to a wedding feast of songs,
but the wine—the utterance of praise—at our feast has run out. John 2:1ff.
[You are] the guest who filled with good wine the jars;
fill my mouth with Your praise.

Refrain: Praise to You from everyone
who has perceived Your truth.[1]

2. The wine that was in the jars was akin and related to
this eloquent wine that gives birth to praise
seeing that that wine too gave birth to praise
from those who drank it and beheld the wonder.

1. A different refrain is given in two of the manuscripts: "Praise to You who have poured out Your gift upon Your servant."

3. ܛܒ ܓܐܝܐ ܕܐܝܬܘܗ̇   ܕܒܬܘܠܘܬܐ ܕܠܐ ܙܘܘܓ
ܬܡܢ ܐܒܝܢܝ ܡܟܝܟ ܒܗܘܢ   ܫܦܝܪܐ ܛܒܐ
ܒܗܢܐ ܒܬܘܠܘܬܐ   ܚܒܘ ܐܒܝܢܐ
ܙܒܘ ܐܕܝܢܝ   ܡܢ ܡܪܢ ܒܦܫܝܛܐ

4. ܢܦܫܐ ܕܐܪܡܠܬܐ   ܠܒܬܘܠܘܬܐ ܕܐܚܝܬܐ
ܗܐ ܚܒܠܬܝ ܕܟܢܐ ܘܦܐܬܐ   ܐܦܪܚ ܠܥܡܠܝ
ܕܗܐ ܫܒܩܬܝ ܡܪܝ   ܐܦ ܥܒܕܝܗ
ܠܟܠ ܡܥܒܕܝܢ   ܢܫܠܠ ܒܪܝܟ

5. ܥܠܝܢ ܗܘ ܢܦܫܐ   ܐܦ ܦܓܪܐ ܒܗܘܢ ܗܘ
ܥܒܕܝܢ ܐܝܟ ܗܘ ܡܠܟܐ   ܥܡ ܚܘܫܒܐ
ܘܐܢ ܚܕ ܦܓܪܐ   ܚܒܘܬܐ ܗܘܐ ܠܝ
ܫܡܠܝܬ ܗܘ   ܠܕܝܬܐ ܥܡ ܡܠܟܐ

6. ܠܒܬܘܠܬܐ ܫܠܡ ܗܘܐ   ܡܕܝܢܐ ܒܦܓܪ ܫܡܝܐ
ܐܦܢܝ ܦܓܪܗ ܒܬܘܠܬܐ   ܘܚܬܡ ܠܒܗ
ܒܟܝܠܐ ܓܙܪܐ   ܘܫܒܩܗ ܙܒܢܐ
ܘܐܡܪ ܒܫܝܢܐ   ܡܠܟܐ ܕܫܡܝܐ

3. You who are so just, if at a wedding feast not Your own

You filled six jars with good wine, John 2:6

do You, Lord, at this wedding feast, fill, not the jars,

but the ten thousand ears with its sweetness.

4. Jesus, You were invited to the wedding feast of others,

here is Your own pure and fair wedding feast: gladden Your worlds[2]

for Your guests too, O Lord, need

Your songs; let Your harp utter!

5. The soul is Your bride, the body[3] too is Your bridal chamber,

Your guests are the senses and the thoughts.

And if a single body is a wedding feast for You,

how great is Your banquet with the whole church!

6. The Holy One[4] took the synagogue up on Sinai:

he made her body shine with garments of white,
but her heart was dark; Exod 19:14

she played the harlot with the calf,
and so the Exalted One rejected her, Exod 32:1ff.

breaking the tablets, the book of her covenant. Exod 32:19

---

2. Your worlds: I.e., both angels and human beings; but perhaps the text should be emended from *ᶜlmyk* to *ᶜlymyk*, "Your young (people)."

3. the body: One manuscript has "Your body"; although this conforms to Text 5 (*Nat.* 17), stanza 6, it does not fit the context nearly so well here.

4. The Holy One: Ephrem deliberately reflects Jewish usage.

7. ܡܢܘ ܚܙܐ ܫܡܠܝܘܬܗ   ܠܘܚܐ ܠܘܬܗ ܣܘܦܪܐ
ܡܠܬܐ ܕܒܝܬܘܢܗ ܦܪܝܫܬ   ܒܪ ܙܘܡ ܡܠܟܗ
ܒܡܪܘܡ ܒܡܪܐ   ܡܢ ܗܘ ܢܒܥܬ
ܡܪܐܗ ܕܡܗܝܡ   ܕܡܠܟ ܒܪ ܦܪܝܫܬ

8. ܢܦܘܩܘܢ ܕܠܡܦܪܐ   ܕܢܦܪܐ ܐܦ ܕܒܝܢܐ
ܡܛܠ ܗܘܐ ܙܪܘܩܘܢ ܐܠܡܬܩܢܘܢ   ܒܡܬܐ ܫܡܝܐ
ܗܘ ܕܚܫܒ ܗܘܐ   ܠܡܗܝܡܢܐ ܕܡܠܟ
ܡܠܟܐ ܫܠܝܛ   ܡܫܪܫܢܘ ܐܚܪܢܐ

9. ܐܝܟ ܡܪܝ ܢܫܬܐ   ܒܢܝ ܡܢ ܐܫܡܥܬܝܢ
ܐܝܟ ܠܟܘܢ ܟܠ ܒܫܝܢ   ܠܡܘܫܐ
ܗܘ ܫܡܥܘ   ܠܡܘܬܐ ܐܝܟ
ܒܡܘܬܐ ܐܟܝ   ܘܪܒܝܢ ܠܡܘܫܐ ܗܘ

10. ܟܠ ܕܢܗܘܐ ܠܗ   ܐܢܫܐ ܠܐܠܗܘܬܗ
ܟܠ ܒܒܢܝܐ ܒܫܡܝܐ   ܠܐܢܫܘܬܗ
ܬܘܪ ܒܒܢܝܐ   ܕܒܫܐ ܗܘ ܐܒܪܐ
ܐܦ ܬܢܝܢܐ   ܕܒܫܐ ܐܬܪܡܪܡ

7. Who has ever seen such horror in a shameful deed—
a bride who has played false in her own bridal chamber,
raising her voice?
When she dwelt in Egypt she learnt it from
the mistress of Joseph, who cried out when she played false. Gen 39:15

8. The light of the pillar of fire and of the cloud Num 14:14
drew into itself its rays like the sun
that was eclipsed on the day that she cried out, Matt 27:45
demanding the King, a further crime. Mark 15:13

9. How can my harp, O Lord, ever rest from Your praise?
How could I ever teach my tongue infidelity?
Your love gives to my shamefacedness confidence,
—yet my will is ungrateful.

10. It is right that humanity should acknowledge Your divinity,
it is right for the supernal beings to worship Your humanity;
the supernal beings were amazed to see how small You become,
and those below to see how exalted!

◆

TEXT 19

Nisibis under Siege in Comparison with Noah's Ark (*Nis.* 1)

In this *madrasha* the personified town of Nisibis is the speaker throughout. The historical setting is the third siege of Nisibis by the Sassanian shah, Shapur II, in 350 CE, when Shapur blocked the river Mydonius, causing a flood to encircle the walls of the town. (The scene is described by the Emperor Julian in his Second Oration, 62B–D [trans. Dodgeon and Lieu 1991, 198–202].) Ephrem imaginatively has Nisibis address God, comparing herself to Noah's Ark in the Flood. In the course of the poem Nisibis adduces various parallels and contrasts between her situation and that of the Ark, as she pleads for God's protection. Reference to the olive branch of Gen 8:11 in stanza 7 serves as a starting point (thanks to the association with oil) for a number of allusions to baptism (compare Text 16 [*Virg.* 7], above): in Ephrem's time the two main elements of the baptismal rite were the prebaptismal anointing, or *rushma* ("mark," a term taken from Ezek 9:4), and, following that, immersion in water. There is an alphabetic acrostic, but missing out every other letter.

Meter

The *qala* is given as *eptaḥ pum(y) b-ida*ᶜ*ta*. The meter (set out in fourteen lines by Beck) is the following: 7 7 7 8 7 7 7 4 7 7 7 7 7 8 (or 7); there are a number of minor irregularities, some of which simply involve elision (e.g., in stanza 10 *ʾeḥadt* is treated as a monosyllable); in stanza 7 *ḥadwteh* represents the older form where the *waw* retains its consonantal value (later, *ḥaduteh*). The refrain consists of the last pair of syllabic units of the first stanza. The same meter is used elsewhere by Ephrem for *Eccl.* 7–9, 11, 22, *Virg.* 4–7, and *Haer.* 37.

It will be noticed that, although the meter is the same as for Text 16 (*Virg.* 7), Beck has set out the syllabic units in individual lines, rather than having two syllabic units to a line.

Text

Like the rest of the collection of seventy-seven *madrashe* on Nisibis, this poem is preserved complete in the single manuscript, British Library Add. 14572 (sixth century).

ܥܰܠ ܡܳܠܐ ܕܐܶܡܰܪ ܦܰܘܠܳܘܣ ܒܰܐܓܰܪܬܳܐ

1. ܥܰܠܘ ܪ̈ܰܚܡܶܐ ܕܐܳܢܶܫܬ ܒܢܰܦܫ
ܐܳܢܶܫ ܗܘܳܐ ܐܳܦ ܗܽܘ ܒܪ̈ܰܚܡܰܝ
ܡܳܪܝ ܕܒ̈ܢܳܝܳܐ ܟܽܠ ܡܫܰܘܠܳܐ
ܢܶܚܬ ܡܶܢ ܪܘ̈ܡܳܐ ܢܰܦܩ ܒܫܽܘܪܳܝܳܐ
ܒܥܽܘܒܳܐ ܘܡܰܥܢܳܐ ܕܒܢܳܐ
ܒܥܽܘܒܳܐ ܘܫܡܰܝܳܐ ܛܥܺܝܢܺܝ
ܘܐܳܬܳܐ ܕܫܡܰܝܳܐ ܡܫܰܘܠܳܐ
ܕܢܶܚܬ ܠܐܰܪܥܳܐ
ܫܡܰܝܳܐ ܒܥܽܘܒܶܗ ܡܛܰܥܝܳܢܳܐ
ܕܒܶܗ ܐܶܬܪܰܘܙ ܘܠܐܰܪܥܳܐ ܐܶܬܒܰܪܟ
ܕܡܶܬܩܰܪܝܳܐ ܐܶܡܳܐ ܫܡܰܝܳܐ
ܘܫܡܰܝܳܐ ܐܶܡܰܪ ܥܰܡ ܙܰܘܓܳܐ

1. O God of mercies[1] who gave rest to Noah,[2]
who himself gave rest to Your mercies:
by offering sacrifices he stayed the Flood, Gen 8:20
he made offerings and received a promise, Gen 8:21–22; 9:9–17
he pleased You with his prayer and incense;
You acted graciously to him by means of oaths and the rainbow. Gen 9:16–17
[As a result], where the flood threatens
to harm the earth,
the rainbow is stretched out against it
so as to chase it away and give comfort to the earth.[3]
You have sworn, may You preserve peace
and may Your bow fight against Your wrath.

---

1. God of mercies *(alah raḥme):* Modeled on Dan 2:44, *alah shmayya,* "God of heaven." Ephrem also has *alah kulla,* "God of all" (*Fid.* 46.12), particularly common in Narsai, and *alah qushta,* "God of truth" (*Nis.* 62.16; *Haer.* 40.12).

2. gave rest to Noah: A play on the etymology of Noah's name (another is in stanza 10).

3. the earth: For reasons of meter the *alaph* must be elided here (as in later West Syriac usage), i.e., *wl-arʿa* rather than *wal-ʾarʿa.*

ܒܥܘܬܐ : ܡܛܘܚ ܦܛܝܡ ܒܩܘܠܐ ܩܠܝܠܐ
ܕܗܘܐ ܐܦ ܠܐܟܬܘܢ ܒܩܘܠܐ ܗܕܝܢ

2. ܠܚܢܢܟ ܡܪܝ ܐܬܪܥܝ
ܕܕܡܐ ܡܚܝܠܐ ܕܦܪܩ ܠܢ
ܟܠܐ ܪܘܓܙܐ ܒܟܠܐ ܕܪ ܡܢ ܟܠܐ
ܒܥܐ ܟܝܬ ܚܢܢܟ ܘܡܢܗ ܕܢܚܝܢ
ܕܢܟܠܐ ܪܘܓܙܗ ܡܢܢ
ܕܗܘܐ ܒܪܬܗ ܕܗ ܡܢܗ ܚܝܠܐ
ܕܪܚܡ ܡܚܝܠܐ ܕܦܪܩ ܠܢ
ܘܟܠܐ ܪܘܓܙܐ
ܒܬܘܪܝ ܡܪܝܥܝ ܐܬܪܥܝܐ
ܘܡܟܝ ܩܢܝ ܡܢܘܬܟ ܚܝܐ
ܘܢܛܪܘܗܝ ܐܘܪܚܐ ܕܢܦܩܝ
ܟܝ ܙܟܝܬ ܘܚܢܢܝ ܦܠܛܝ
ܙܟܝܬ ܢܛܪܘܬ ܟܠܐ ܕܝܢܐ
ܦܠܛܝ ܐܟܠܐ ܡܢܘܬܟ ܡܛܪܐ

Refrain: Stretch out Your rainbow against the deluge,
for its waves are lifted up against our walls.

2. It was openly rumored,[4] Lord,

that the feeble blood which Noah sprinkled

held off from everyone in every generation the wrath [of judgment]

—how much mightier is the blood of Your only-begotten [Son],

[and able] to prevent our [present] flood by its sprinkling;

for Noah's feeble sacrifices gained their effectiveness

by being a symbol of Him,

and it was this which stayed the wrath.

Do You accept the offering of my altar

and stay the deadly[5] flood from me,

so that both Your signs preserve [intact]—

Your Cross in my case, Your rainbow in Noah's.

May Your Cross cleave the ocean of waters, cf. Ps 78:12

and Your rainbow restrain the flood of rain.

---

4. It was . . . rumored: The verb could equally be taken as 1st sg. impf. (so Beck), "I will murmur."

5. deadly: The text has "Flood of life" *(ḥayye),* perhaps in the sense of "destroying life." Other possibilities are (1) to take *ḥayye* as "living people," i.e., the Persian besiegers; or (2) to treat *mamol ḥayye* as a vocative, "Flood of Salvation," with an object such as "the wrath" understood. Beck suggests emending to *ḥashshe,* "sufferings"; another possible emendation might be *mayya,* "water."

3. ܗܐ ܡܫܡܫܝܢ ܟܠ ܡܚܫܒܬܢ
ܘܢܘܒܠ ܠܛܘܒܐ ܒܒܘܫܠܐ
ܕܒܗ ܟܠܝܠܐ ܗ̱ܘ ܒܚܝܘܗܝ ܒܙܒܢܗ
ܬܓܐ ܘܥܘܬܪܐ ܘܟܠܝܠܐ ܒܙܒܢܗ
ܗ̱ܘ ܗܘܐ ܒܗ ܫܡܫܬ ܓܒܪܐ
ܘܐܦ ܗܘܝܬ ܫܡܫܬ ܢܩܒܐ
ܗ̱ܘ ܒܚܘܒܗ ܕܝܗܒ ܟܠܝܠܐ
ܘܐܦ ܒܪܘܥܗ
ܐܠܒܫܬ ܒܢܝܗ ܥܘܬܪܐ
ܐܝܟ ܡܠܐܐ ܡܫܡܫܝܢ ܢܘܪܐ
ܡܒܝܢܘ ܕܗ̱ܘ ܒܘܫܠܐ
ܘܗ̱ܘ ܫܡܫ ܠܗ ܢܒܝܐ
ܒܗ̱ܘ ܐܝܢܐ ܒܡܫܡܫܢ ܠܛܘܪܐ
ܘܟܕ ܐܢܫ ܒܡܫܡܫܢ ܫܘܪܝ

3. In my case, all kinds of storms have troubled me,
and I count the Ark fortunate:
only waves surrounded it,
[whereas siege-]mounds and arrows [as well as] waves surround me.
[The Ark] became a store of treasures for You,
but I have become a deposit of sins.
It subdued the waves through Your love,
whereas I have been blind amidst the arrows of Your wrath.
The flood escorted [the Ark],
while me the river [Mygdonius] has troubled.
O Helmsman of that Ark,
be my pilot on dry land!
You rested [the Ark] on the haven of a mountain,[6] Gen 8:4
give rest to me too in the haven of my walls.

---

6. mountain: Qardu (in southwest Turkey), rather than Ararat, in the Peshitta (Gen 8:4) and Targum.

4. ܐܘܪܚܐ ܕܪܕܝܢ ܒܗ ܒܥܒܕ̈ܐ
ܥܡܗ ܢܚܬ ܚܝܠܐ ܢܟܝܠܐ
ܕܐܦ ܢܦܩ ܢܟܝܠܐ ܕܪܗܛܐ
ܕܢܦܠ ܗܘܐ ܒܪܘܚ ܟܬܝܒ ܫܡܗ
ܘܡܪܝ ܒܡܪܘ ܟܠܠ ܒܢܝܗ ܩܠܗ
ܒܟܝ ܕܒܘܟܪܐ ܚܪܐ ܕܢܟܝܠܐ
ܘܠܐ ܢܫܬܐܠܘܢ ܢܦܩܐ ܩܕܝܫ
ܗܘ ܒܚܝܘܬܐ
ܕܒܗ ܒܟܘܠܐ ܟܠ ܐܬܣܝܡ
ܡܠܘܟܐ ܩܕܝܫ ܐܘܟܠ
ܐܝܟܐ ܕܡܫܝܚܐ ܡܦܪܝܣ ܐܦܝ
ܒܡܪܩܗ ܐܦܪܝܣ ܦܬܘܓܡܘܗܝ
ܒܝ ܢܘܪܐ ܕܡܪܘܬ ܡܫܝܚܐ
ܗܐ ܡܪܝ ܡܟܡܪ ܒܝ ܡܫܘܚܬܗ

4. Me the just [God] has punished with overflowing waters,
while He cherished the Ark amidst the waves;
for Noah overcame the waves of lust
that drowned the children of Seth[7] in his lifetime.
Because [Noah's] flesh stood fast against Cain's daughters,
his vessel tamed the surface of the waves;
because women had not defiled him,
he made the animals continent[8]—
the animals that were in the Ark in pairs;
himself married, he made marriage continent![9]
The olive whose oil brightens the countenance
brightened their faces with its plucked leaf; Gen 8:11
as for me, the river whose irrigation once brought joy,
now, Lord, it makes me downcast with its flooding.

---

7. children of Seth: According to an interpretation of "the sons of God" in Gen 6:2, 4, which is widely current in early Christian literature, these are the descendants of Seth, who descended from higher ground and mingled with the daughters of Cain, thus producing the corrupt generation drowned by the Flood; see Ephrem, *Commentary on Genesis* 6.3. This exegesis is first attested in Christian writers in the second century CE, in Julius Africanus, but it seems already to be known to Josephus, *Antiquities* 1.69–71; it replaced the interpretation of "the sons of God" as the fallen angels (thus especially in *1 Enoch* 6); for this, see Alexander 1972 and Wickham 1974.

8. made . . . continent *(qaddesh):* See Text 5 (*Nat.* 17), n. 6.

9. made marriage continent: See previous note.

5\. ܛܠܐ ܕܢܚܬ ܚܙܐ ܒܬܘܠܐܝܬ
ܘܐܦ ܩܠܝܠ ܟܬܝܒܝܢ ܕܬܚܬܝܐ
ܟܬܝܒ ܦܬܐ ܥܒܕ ܛܒܐ
ܕܟܕ ܕܡܟ ܐܚܕ ܕܗܘܐ ܣܩܘܦܐ
ܠܗ ܕܒܗܘܢ ܐܚܕ ܬܘܟܝܢ
ܐܠܐ ܕܒܗܘܢ ܬܘܟܠ ܐܙܕܝܢ
[illegible]
[illegible]
[illegible]
[illegible]
ܡܢܐ ܡܢܝ ܕܗܘܐ ܠܚܝܘܗܝ
ܢܫܡܗ ܒܗ ܕܫܡܐ ܒܢܘܗܝ
ܒܡܢܐ ܕܫܘܦ ܐܚܝܕ ܦܐܪܐ
ܒܗܘܢ ܚܙܐ ܡܘܬܐ ܚܠܦ ܦܐܪܐ

5. You in Your righteousness have seen my sordid guilt,
and Your pure eyes abhor me;
You gathered the waters [acting] through the unclean [Shapur],
so as to effect for me the purification of my wrongdoings—
not that You will submerge and purify me through them,
but [simply] to make me afraid and to chasten me.
For waves will arouse [people] to prayer
which itself will wash away my sins;
the very sight of them—a sight that brims with repentance—
has become a [form of] baptism to me.
O Lord, may [Your] mercy drown [my] sins
in the sea that was meant to drown me:
You drowned bodies in the Sea of Reeds, Exod 14:28
drown sins instead of bodies in this one!

6. ܒܟܠ ܒܪ̈ܝܬܐ ܬܐܡܝܢ
ܕܐܝܬ ܒܗ ܟܠ ܡܫܪܪܝܢ
ܕܠܐ ܬܛܥܐ ܐܘܪܚܐ ܒܪܘܥܐ
ܠܟܠ ܚܕܘ ܐܘܪܚܐ ܕܩܢܝܐ
ܡܦܩܢ ܐܢܝܢ ܚܕܐ ܠܚܕܐ
ܦܓܥܢ ܐܢܝܢ ܚܕܐ ܒܚܕܐ
ܐܘܪܚܬܐ ܕܡܢ ܬܠܬ ܐܪ̈ܒܥ
ܡܢܗ ܘܐܫܬܦܩ
ܘܗܘܬ ܠܟܠ ܡܕܡ ܡܪܥܝܬܐ
ܕܢܩܘܡ ܣܕܪܐ ܕܦܠܚ ܒܗ
ܒܟܠ ܢܦܫܐ ܡܪܟܒܐ
ܐܢ ܒܗ ܡܢܝ ܐܘ ܒܗ ܚܛܝܐ
ܒܟܠ ܒܣܘܪܐ ܢܚܒܠ
ܠܐܘܪܚܗ ܟܠܗ ܐܠܐ ܠܒܢ̈ܝܗܘܢ

6. In Your mercy You fitted out the Ark

in order to preserve in it survivors of all kinds;

so as not to bereave the earth in [Your] anger,

Your compassion made a [substitute] earth out of wood!

You emptied them out, [pouring] one into the other,

and You [poured] them back, one into the other.

But my lands have been filled and emptied

three times over,[10]

and now the waves batter against me,

[trying] to wipe out what remnants have survived in me.

You preserved a remnant in the Ark,

preserve in me too, Lord, some leaven.

The Ark gave birth on the mountain,

may I give birth in my own lands
to those who have been enclosed within me!

10. three times over: By the Persian army in 337 (or 338), 346, and 350 CE.

7. ܡܪܝ ܚܙܐ ܒܝ ܚܛܗ̈ܝ ܣܓܝ̈ܐܐ
ܕܒܚܛܗ̈ܐ ܒܠܥܬ ܚܝܠܝ
ܫܪܝܬ ܐܣܝܐ ܒܝ ܚܘܒܐ
ܒܣܡ̈ܐ ܕܐܝܬܝܗܘܢ ܒܟܠ ܐܬܪ̈ܘܢ
ܠܟܠ ܕܡܪܥ ܟܠ ܟܐܒܘ̈ܗܝ
ܕܢܣܒܘܬܗ ܒܡܓܢ ܒܪܥܘܬܐ
ܘܠܟܢ ܐܟܠܐ ܒܒܘ̈ܬܗ
ܘܐܝܟ ܕܒ ܚܝܠܐ
ܥܒܕ ܒܥܒܥܒܐ ܟܪ̈ܘܒܐ
ܘܩܠ ܙܥܘܪܐ ܒܗ ܙܘܥܐ
ܠܗܘܢ ܟܐܒ̈ܐ ܚܙܬܐ ܕܚܝܠܐ
ܘܫܪܘܢ ܦܬܚ ܦܘܡܐ ܠܡܘܒܠܝ
ܐܝܟ ܐܝܬܐ ܒܬܟܠܐ ܠܡܪܥ
ܘܐܫܪܐ ܒܝ ܚܛܗ̈ܝ ܣܓܝ̈ܐܐ

7. Lord, give joy to those who are enclosed within my fortresses,

You who gave joy to those enclosed [in the Ark]
by means of the olive [leaf]; Gen 8:11

You sent a healing doctor by means of the dove

to those who were languishing and afflicted by all kinds of waves;

he entered and drove out all their pains,

for joy at his [coming] swallowed up [their] grief;

he dismissed sorrow by means of the comfort [he brought]

and like a captain

he gave encouragement to those afraid,

sowing a word [of courage] in a place [hitherto] deserted.

[Their] eyes tasted the sight of peace

and [their] mouths were quick to open and praise You. Ps 51:15

Preserve me, like the olive [branch], on the waves,

and make those enclosed within my walls rejoice at me.

8. ܣܒܐ ܛܠܠܐ ܘܐܬܓܪܝ ܒܡܘܬܢ
ܢܐܚܕܘܢܝ ܚܝܠܐ ܣܡܟܝ ܠܗ
ܠܐ ܢܦܠ ܐܝܟ ܒܢܝ ܚܝܠܐ
ܕܠܐ ܒܢܝܢ ܡܘܒܠܝܢ ܟܠ ܚܝܠܐ
ܣܘܒܐ ܢܘܐ ܠܝ ܡܬܐܣܝܐ
ܕܟܠ ܣܘܒܝ ܒܢܝܢ ܘܡܣܢܘܬܐ
ܡܬܐܣܝܐ ܒܣܝܡܐ ܕܐܘܟܝܢ
ܐܝܟ ܣܘܪܝ
ܢܦܠܘ ܒܢܝܢ ܣܘܪܗܘܢ ܘܐܬܪܚܩܘ
ܕܟܠ ܚܝܠܐ ܒܢܝܢ ܐܘܟܝܢܘܢ
ܒܢܐ ܡܘܡܐ ܣܘܪܐ ܒܣܡܐ
ܕܟܠ ܣܘܒܐ ܒܢܝܐ ܙܒܢܘܗܝ
ܡܬܐܣܝܐ ܕܢܦܫ ܟܠ ܣܘܒܐ
ܡܕܡܬܐ ܕܣܡܐ ܒܣܡܐ ܠܒܢܝܢ

8. The flood has surged and dashed against our walls—
may the Power that supports all hold them up!
They have not fallen like the house built on sand Matt 7:26
for I have not built my teaching on sand.
May my foundations be of rock
since I have built my faith on Your rock; Matt 16:18
may the hidden foundation of my trust
support my walls.
Jericho's walls fell Josh 6:20
because it had built its trust on sand;
Moses built a wall in the midst of the sea, Exod 14:22
since his mind was founded on rock;
Noah's foundation was on rock,
hence it bore the wooden habitation over the seas.

9\. ܦܰܚܶܡ ܢܳܡܽܘܣܳܐ ܕܰܒܢܰܘ̈ܗܝ.
ܒܢ̈ܳܬܳܐ ܕܰܒܬ̈ܽܘܠܳܬܳܐ
ܘܚܠܳܦ ܢܽܘܚ ܕܰܐܪܘܺܝ ܗ݀ܘܳܐ ܒܶܗ
ܗܳܐ ܡܢܰܙܰܪ ܕܰܐܪܘܺܝ ܘܰܡܫܰܡܶܫ
ܚܠܳܦ ܢܶܫ̈ܐ ܕܶܐܬܦܰܪܰܥ ܒܶܗ
ܗܳܐ ܒܬܽܘܠܬܳܗ̇ ܕܠܳܐ ܐܰܪܘܝ
ܚܠܳܦ ܚܳܡ ܕܢܰܦܶܩ ܗ݀ܘܳܐ ܦܰܪܗܶܣܝܳܐ
ܒܶܙܚܳܐ ܕܰܐܒܽܘܗ̱ܝ.
ܗܳܐ ܒܢ̈ܳܬܳܐ ܕܝܺܗܽܘܕ̈ܳܝܳܬܳܐ
ܕܢܶܦܩܽܘ ܘܩܰܠܶܣܘ ܠܡܫܺܝܚܳܐ
ܒܫܳܪܳܐ ܐܰܡܕܺܝܢܺܝܬ ܡܰܠܟܳܐ
ܡܳܪܝ ܠܳܐ ܐܶܬܟܰܠ ܕܐܶܙܰܠ ܒܬܰܪܟ
ܒܡܰܫܪ̈ܝܳܬܳܐ ܕܙܰܪܥܶܗ ܡܶܬܐܡܰܪ
ܫܽܘܝܳܢ ܠܝ ܐܰܝܟ ܠܰܐܢ̈ܬܳܬܳܐ ܕܫܳܒܩܝܢ ܗ݀ܘܰܘ

9. Compare the souls that are within me
with the animals in the Ark:
instead of Noah mourning in the Ark,
here Your altar is mourning and humiliated;
instead of the [married] women who lived in continence,[11]
here are my unmarried virgins;
instead of Ham who uncovered his father's shame Gen 9:22
after leaving [the Ark],
here are the givers of alms,
people who have modestly clothed the naked.
In my pain I have spoken like a madman,
do not blame me, Lord, if my words have provoked You;
You silenced the diligent[12] workers who complained; Matt 20:11
have mercy on me, as upon the "last" who kept silent.

---

11. lived in continence *(etqaddash):* See Text 5 (*Nat.* 17), n. 6. In early manuscripts (fifth/sixth century) the 3rd f. pl. of the perfect does not have the affix *-y* (as in the later West Syriac orthographical tradition, followed by many modern grammars).

12. diligent: See Text 1 (*Par.* 5), n. 7. For Ephrem's unusual interpretation of the parable, see Valavanolickal 1996, 122–31.

10. ܩܕܡ ܪܓܠܐ ܒܒܝܬܐ ܟܠܗ ܟܘܫܐ
ܘܡܪܝܗ ܗܘܘ ܒܗ ܟܠ ܠܛܘܒܬܢ
ܪܘܚ ܗܘܐ ܢܦܫ ܟܠܗ ܢܘܗܪܐ
ܕܢܚ ܡܕܢܚܗ ܐܝܟ ܒܘܟܪܗ
ܐܣܝܐ ܐܘܪܚܐ ܕܐܬܪ ܟܐܒܐ
ܦܬܚ ܬܪ̈ܥܐ ܕܐܣܦܩ ܠܛܥܝܐ
ܟܕ ܗܘܐ ܢܦܫ ܟܠܗ ܛܠܠܐ
ܕܛܠܠܐ ܕܡܢ ܒܪ
ܠܒܘܫܐ ܛܠܠܐ ܕܡܢ ܒܗ
ܐܚܘܗܝ ܒܛܠܠܐ ܡܚܘܬܗܝ ܦܘܫܐ
ܡܢܝܗ ܟܠܗ ܟܘܠܐ
ܡܦܠܛ ܡܘܕܝܢܘܗܝ ܒܪܝܐ
ܡܣܟܢ ܒܚܝܠ ܒܡܣܟܢܐ
ܕܢܒܠܒܠ ܒܗ ܡܢܗ ܢܚܠܬܐ

10. You made a place of refuge in the face of [Your] wrath,
and every kind [of living thing] withdrew into it.
Noah refreshed himself in a place of quiet,
his dwelling place giving rest in accord with his name.[13]
You closed the doors so as to preserve the righteous man, Gen 7:16
You opened the floodgates to destroy the impure. Gen 7:11
Noah stood up between the fearful waves outside
and the destructive mouths [of the wild animals] within;
the waves tossed him, the mouths disturbed him.
With him You pacified[14] those within,
You calmed those outside before him;
You quickly changed [his] troubles,
since to You [all] difficult things are easy, Lord.

13. name: A play on *Nuḥ* and *nawḥa.*
14. pacified: Or "tamed."

11. ܫܡܥ ܘܬܘܟܠ ܦܘܫܩܢ ܥܡ ܢܦܫ
ܘܕܐܙܠ ܟܐܒ ܡܢ ܕܝܠܗ
ܚܙܝ ܢܦܩܐ ܦܘܪܩܢܝ
ܕܗܐ ܡܫܡܫܝ ܬܚܒܝ ܒܕܡܘܬܗ
ܒܗ ܫܒܝܠܐ ܠܥܒ̈ܕܐ
ܫܢܝ ܡܢܝ ܟܠܗ ܠܚܘܒܐ
ܘܫܩܠ ܦܘܪܥܢ ܟܐܢ̈ܐ
ܘܐܬܐ ܐܘܪܚܐ
ܘܕܐܬܐ ܡܫܟܚ ܙܘܓܗ
ܢܐܬܐ ܚܙܘ ܠܐܒܘܗܝ
ܠܐ ܢܐܬܐ ܒܫܠܐ ܠܡܫܟܢ
ܕܐܬܐ ܘܐܬܐ ܐܝܟ ܠܒܘܟܪܗ
ܐܦܪܫ ܐܘܪܚܐ ܠܡܬܒܠ
ܕܐܬܐ ܒܗ ܡܫܒܚܐ ܠܡܬܒܠ
ܐܘ ܕܐܬܚܡ ܒܡܒܥܐ
ܠܐ ܬܬܒܠܥ ܒܗ ܒܡܒܝܥܬܐ

11. Listen and weigh up the comparison between me and Noah,
and [though] my pain is lighter than his,
may Your mercy make our deliverances the same.
You see, my children stand, like him,
between the angry [within] and the destructive [outside]:
with me, Lord, give peace to those who are within,
and bring down before me the [enemy] outside,
and so make my victory a double one.
And because my slayer[15] has tripled his fury,
may Your Three-day One[16] triple His grace.
Let not the Evil One vanquish Your mercies;
overcome him who has [attacked me] twice and three times.
May my victory fly through the world,
that it may buy praise for You in the world.
You, whose resurrection was on the third day,
do not slay me at this third danger!

◆

15. my slayer: Ms. *qṭwl,* but the sense and syntax require *qṭwly.*

16. Three-day One *(tlitaya):* This title of Christ (absent from Aphrahat) is found a number of times in Ephrem: *Nis.* 2.5, 5.14, 14.25, 41.16 (Text 13); *Fid.* 22.7, 42.5, 75.6; *Commentary on Genesis* 34.5. Besides referring to Christ's three days among the dead, it can also have the sense of "intermediary."

TEXT 20

The Pearl and Its Symbolism
(*Fid.* 82)

At the end of the cycle *On Faith* there is a group of five poems (81–85) with the title "On the Pearl," in which Ephrem discovers a whole series of symbols of the incarnation. The symbolic potentiality of the pearl was enhanced for Ephrem by his awareness of the view that pearls came into being in the mollusk when lightning struck the mollusk in the sea: from this conjunction of disparate elements, fire and water, the pearl is born. The possibilities for analogy with the birth of Christ from Mary and the Holy Spirit are obvious.

In this poem Ephrem addresses the pearl directly as he explores different facets of the pearl's symbolism. In stanza 6 the reference to the crown of the King of kings (here Christ) may be intended as a deliberate contrast to the elaborately jeweled crown of the Sassanian king of kings, Shapur II, who by now ruled over Ephrem's town of origin. Stanza 10 contains a play on words between "diver" and "baptized," and for this the translation resorts to a double rendering. A similar comparison between divers who anoint themselves with oil and the baptismal candidates who are anointed with oil before being baptized has already been found in Text 16 (*Virg.* 7), stanza 10. In the last three stanzas it turns out that the pearl even symbolizes various aspects of the Passion. An English translation of all five poems on the pearl is given in Mathews 1994.

Meter

The *qala* is given as *manu sapeq,* the opening words of *Eccl.* 38. This meter, consisting of five lines each of 4+4 syllables, is known by a variety of *qala* titles (see under Text 4 [*Nat.* 11]). In stanza 7, line 5, the *shwa* implicit in *b-taga* is treated metrically as a full vowel.

Text

The poem is preserved in three sixth-century manuscripts: Vatican Syr. 111 (of 522 CE; Beck's B), Vatican Syr. 113 (552 CE; Beck's C), and British Library Add. 12176 (fifth or sixth century; Beck's A).

ܥܰܠ ܩܳܠܳܐ ܕܡܰܢܽܘ ܣܳܦܶܩ

1. ܒܡܳܢܰܘ ܕܡܰܢܝ   ܢܺܐܡܰܪ ܡܗܰܝܡܢ
ܟܰܕ ܡܳܨܶܐ ܟܺܠ   ܒܣܽܘܦܳܐ ܡܶܒܥܳܐ
ܡܰܠܺܝܟ ܟܰܡܳܐ   ܕܐܰܝܟܳܐ ܕܡܳܨܶܐ
ܕܳܐܡܳܐ ܕܡܶܬܡܶܢ   ܐܶܙܰܠ ܡܶܠܳܐ
ܡܶܬܕܰܡܝܳܐ   ܥܰܠ ܦܳܪܽܘܩܰܢ

ܥܽܘܢܺܝܬܳܐ : ܒܪܺܝܟ ܗܽܘ ܕܡܶܬܰܠܰܢ ܒܡܰܠܟܽܘܬܳܐ ܕܗܽܘܝܳܐ ܒܡܰܪܟܰܒܬܳܐ

2. ܐܶܡܰܪ ܐܰܝܟܰܢ   ܒܡܽܘܠܳܕܶܗ ܡܳܐ
ܟܰܕ ܠܳܐ ܢܶܣܒܰܪ   ܒܒܽܘܛܢܶܗ ܢܶܦܠܶܛ
ܟܰܕ ܠܳܐ ܡܕܰܥܶܪ   ܟܰܢܺܝܫ ܢܳܘܪܶܗ
ܟܰܕ ܠܳܐ ܢܶܣܒܰܪ   ܒܡܘܗܰܒܬܳܐ
ܢܶܣܒ ܠܗܘܦܟܝܢ   ܟܰܕ ܐܰܝܟ ܟܝܢ

1. What is it you resemble? Let your silence speak
to one who listens to you; with silent mouth
speak with us, for to him who hears
the whisper of your silence
your symbol proclaims in silence our Savior.

Refrain: Blessed is He who compared
the Kingdom on high to a pearl!

2. Your mother is the virgin [bride] of the sea
—without its having married her; she fell into its bosom
—without its being aware; Your conception was in it
—though it knew her not. Your symbol
will rebuke the Jewish girls when they wear you.

3. ܐܝܟܢ ܗܘܐ ܕܐܬܚܙܝ ܡܪܐ ܠܒܢܝ̈ܗܝ
ܡܢ ܟܠ ܛܒܒܢ ܕܩܢܝܢ ܗܘܐ ܠܗ
ܒܡܠܟܬ ܪܘܚܐ ܕܡܫܝܚܐܝܬ
ܡܪܗ ܪܘܚܐ ܛܒܥܐ ܠܢܒܝ̈ܐ
ܠܐܘܪ ܒܡܠ̈ܬܐ ܒܥܝܢ̈ܐ ܕܒܢܝ

4. ܡܪܐ ܠܟܢܐ ܕܒܗܘܢܐ ܒܥܝܢܐ
ܐܘܪܐ ܪܒܐ ܒܡܢܝܢ ܥܝܢܐ
ܕܠܐ ܡܢ ܐܘܪܚܐ ܘܠܐ ܐܘܘܠܐ
ܡܪܢ ܕܒܢܐ ܗ̇ܕܠܐ ܐܢܫܐ
ܗܘ ܡܘܟܪܒ ܕܡܫܝܚܐ ܗܘ

5. ܒܪܢܫ ܐܢܫܐ ܗ̇ܕܠܐ ܐܢܫܐ ܗܘ
ܕܡܫܝܚܐ ܗܘ ܐܘ ܡܣܬܒܪܐ
ܐܘܪܐ ܪܒܐ ܕܡܫܝܚܐܝܬ
ܐܬܚܘܝ ܠܦܘܡܗܘܢ ܒܥܠܡܐ ܕܡܚܒܐ
ܐܝܟ ܒܪ ܐܢܫܐ ܐܦ ܐܢܫܘܬܐ

3. You of all gems are the only one
whose begetting[1] resembles that of the Word on high,
whom, in unique fashion,
the Most High begot, while other engraved gems
symbolically resemble the supernal beings, themselves created.

4. O visible offspring of a hidden womb!
O mighty symbol, your pure conception
required no seed; your chaste birth needed
no intercourse; you have no brothers
for your birth is unique.

5. Our Lord has brothers—and yet He has none,
for He is the Only-begotten. O solitary [pearl],
great is the mystery, for your symbol
stands all alone, yet on the royal crown
you have brethren and sisters!

1. whose begetting: I.e., by lightning striking the mollusk in the water (see the introduction to the poem [p. 246]).

6. ܛܥܢ̈ܐ ܛܒ̈ܐ ܢܗܘܘܢ ܐܚ̈ܝܟ
ܥܡ ܒܢ̈ܘܠܐ ܘܡܚ̈ܫܒܬܐ
ܐܦ ܚܒ̈ܪܝܟ ܢܗܘܐ ܕܘܒܐ
ܐܦ ܒܪ ܛܘܒܟ ܠܡܠܝ ܡܒ̈ܝܐ
ܡܟܠܐ ܢܗܘܐ ܡܢ ܚܒ̈ܝܒܝܟ

7. ܡܐ ܕܫܠܡܬ ܗܘ ܡܢ ܟܠܗ ܥܡܐ
ܡܒܪܐ ܚܝܐ ܡܚܝܬ ܗܘܐ
ܒܝܡܐ ܩܠܝܠܐ ܕܐ̈ܢܫܐ ܐܢܫܝ̈ܐ
ܘܒܢ̈ܝ ܛܘܒܐ ܫܡܥܐ ܒܟܝܢܐ
ܘܐܝܬ ܒܛܘܒܐ ܥܡ ܩܕ̈ܝܫܐ

8. ܘܒܐܝܬ ܚܘܒܠܐ ܥܡ ܡܫܩ̈ܠܬܐ
ܐܬܦܠܛܬ ܕܡܢ ܗܘ ܒܦܘܡܐ
ܒܪܘܡܐ ܩܠܝܠܐ ܒܚܝܬܐ ܛܒܝ
ܡܢܐ ܒܚܥܠܐ ܥܒ ܕܝܢ ܡܠܐܝܢ
ܙ̈ܡܐ ܕܡܚܝܐ ܟܠܗ ܡܙܒܚܬܐ

6. The fair gems shall be your brothers,
along with the beryls; and other pearls
are as your companions, while gold shall be,
as it were, your relative: the King of kings shall have
a crown constituted out of your dear friends.

7. When you came up from the depths of the sea
—the living grave—you acquired[2] this
glorious band of brethren, relatives
and kinsmen. As wheat on the stalk,
so are you on the diadem, set amongst many.

8. As a debt is justly
returned to you, so you are raised from that depth
to the glorious height. The stalk in the field
bears the wheat: you the king's head,
as though on a chariot, carries about.[3]

---

2. acquired: *qanyat(y)* is the abbreviated form of *qanya (an)t(y)*.
3. carries about: I.e., on his crown.

9. ܐܘ ܒܪܐ ܡܝܬܐ ܕܫܒܩܬ ܚܝܐ
ܕܡܟܝܪܐ ܗܘܐ ܒܚܝܐ ܫܒܩܬ
ܕܪܚܝܡܐ ܗܘܐ ܘܪܚܡܘ ܚܒܩܘܗ
ܘܐܬܢܟܠܘ ܒܗ ܐܝܟ ܗܘ ܚܒܪܐ
ܕܪܚܡܘ ܠܥܘܠܐ ܘܐܬܥܠܠܘ ܒܗ

10. ܒܙܪܐ ܘܫܘܚܠܦܐ ܕܝܢ ܠܘܬܝ
ܡܢ ܡܘܬܐ ܫܒܩܘ ܠܡܩܘܪܐ
ܘܠܒܫܘ ܚܝܐ ܒܙܪܐ ܡܫܝܚܐ
ܠܒܘܫܝ ܘܫܠܚܘ ܫܟܝܢܐ ܢܦܫܐ
ܚܙܘ ܡܢ ܦܘܡܗ ܕܝ ܡܠܡܪܡܪ

11. ܒܢܝܢ ܕܡܝܐ ܠܐܡܪ ܫܠܡܐ
ܒܫܘܫܠܬܗ ܕܐܢ ܐܢܫ ܒܠܒܗ
ܘܫܩܠ ܐܦܩܘܗ ܟܠ ܡܫܡܫܬܐ
ܐܝܟ ܒܘܒܠܬܐ ܢܛܪ ܫܒܪܐ
ܒܟܠ ܐܟܬܒܘܗܝ ܟܠ ܣܐܡܢܘܗܝ

9. O daughter of the waters, who left the sea
in which you were born, who went up to the dry land
in which you were cherished: people cherished you, seized you,
and were adorned with you: so too with the Child
whom the gentiles cherished, being crowned with Him.

10. In symbol and in truth Leviathan is trodden down Ps 74:14
by mortals: the baptized, like divers,[4] strip
and put on oil, as a symbol of Christ
they snatched you and came up: stripped,
they seized the soul[5] from his embittered mouth.[6]

11. Your nature resembles the Silent Lamb
with his gentleness: even though a man pierces it,
takes it and hangs it on his ear,
as it were on Golgotha, all the more does it throw out
all its bright rays on those who behold it!

---

4. the baptized, like divers: The Syriac text just has *ᶜamode,* which can mean either "divers" or "baptismal candidates"; Ephrem certainly intends both to be understood here. A similar double entendre is to be found in the last of the *madrashe* on the Pearl (*Fid.* 85.6), where *shliḥe ᶜmad(w)* designates simultaneously "naked (divers) dived down" and "(baptismal candidates) stripped (of their clothes) were baptized."

5. seized the soul: It is conceivable that Ephrem has in mind here the Hymn of the Pearl (in the *Acts of Thomas*), where the Royal Son goes down to Egypt to rescue the pearl (i.e., soul) from the dragon (Wright 1871, 1:274).

6. embittered mouth: Possibly this may reflect Isa 14:9 ("Sheol was embittered"), since (ironically, in view of the original context) this passage was regularly understood as illustrating the Descent of Christ into the underworld.

12. ܙܒܢ ܒܦܘܩܕܢܢ ܦܘܩܕܢܗ ܕܒܪܐ
ܕܒܫܡܝ ܚܡܐ ܢ̈ܫܐ ܒܒܪܗ ܒܗ
ܒܘܣܡܐ ܒܒܪ ܒܢ ܘܐܦ ܒܢ ܒܠܒܗ
ܐܝܟ ܕܠܐܡܬܦܪܫܝ ܘܕܚܢ ܐܡܠܟܝ
ܐܝܟ ܕܒܚܫܒܢ ܫܠܐ ܦܘܩܕܢܢ

13. ܘܐܢ ܚܣܘ ܒܟܝܢܢ ܘܐܦ ܠܐ ܢܣܒܘܢ
ܘܐܢ ܚܝܠܝ ܐܡܠܟܝ ܕܢܣܒܘܢ ܟܐܦܐ
ܚܣ ܒܠܠ ܟܐܦܐ ܘܐܝܠܐ ܕܡܚܝܢ
ܘܗܘ ܒܟܠܗ ܟܘܢ ܡܠܠ ܚܡܗ
ܕܡܝܐ ܘܒܘܣܡܐ ܙܒܢ ܦܘܩܕܢܗ

12. In your beauty is depicted the beauty of the Son
who clothed himself in suffering: nails went through Him. cf. John 20:25
Through you the awl passed, you too did they pierce,
as they did His hands. But because He suffered He reigns
—just as your beauty is increased through your suffering.

13. If they had spared you, then they would not have cherished you,
for, if you have suffered, you now reign. Simon Peter
had pity on the Rock by which all who struck it Matt 16:22; 21:42–44
were wounded. It is because of His suffering
that His beauty now adorns both height and depth.

◆

APPENDIX 1

The Main Editions and English Translations of Ephrem's Works

TITLE	CSCO	OTHER EDITIONS	ENGLISH TRANSLATIONS[1]
In Genesim et in Exodum commentarii	Tonneau 1955	Mobarak and Assemani 1732–46, vol. 4	Mathews and Amar 1994; Salvesen 1995 (Exod only)
Hymnen de Fide [87]	Beck 1955	Mobarak and Assemani 1732–46, vol. 6	Morris 1847; Russell Forthcoming 1
Hymnen contra Haereses [56]	Beck 1957a	Mobarak and Assemani 1732–46, vol. 5	
Hymnen de Paradiso [15]	Beck 1957b	Mobarak and Assemani 1732–46, vol. 6	Brock 1990b
Hymnen contra Julianum [4]	Beck 1957b	Overbeck 1865	Lieu 1989; McVey 1989
Hymnen de Nativitate [28]	Beck 1959	Mobarak and Assemani 1732–46, vol. 5; Lamy 1882–1902, vol. 2	Morris 1847; Gwynn 1898; McVey 1989

1. Selections translated into English include Brock 1983 (earlier translations of Texts 4, 8, 10, 11, 15, 16, 18, and 20) and Brock 1989b (earlier translations of Texts 2, 3, 5, 6, 9, and 13). Forthcoming English translations are promised for *Haer.*, *Ieiun.*, and the Paschal cycles. For a detailed guide to available English translations up to c. 1989, see Brock 1990a.

TITLE	CSCO	OTHER EDITIONS	ENGLISH TRANSLATIONS
Hymnen de Epiphania [13]	Beck 1959	Lamy 1882–1902, vol. 1	Gwynn 1898
Soghyatha [6]	Beck 1959		Brock 1994 (nos. 1–4)
Hymnen de Ecclesia [52]	Beck 1960b	Mobarak and Assemani 1732–46, vols. 5 and 6	
Sermones de Fide [6]	Beck 1961b	Mobarak and Assemani 1732–46, vol. 6	Morris 1847; Russell Forthcoming 2
Carmina Nisibena [77]	Beck 1961a; 1963	Bickell 1866	Gwynn 1898 (nos. 1–21, 35–43, 52–68)
Hymnen de Virginitate [52]	Beck 1962b	Lamy 1882–1902, vols. 2 and 4	McVey 1989
Hymnen de Ieiunio [10]	Beck 1964a	Lamy 1882–1902, vol. 2	
Hymnen de Azymis [21]	Beck 1964b	Lamy 1882–1902, vol. 1	
Hymnen de Crucifixione [9]	Beck 1964b	Lamy 1882–1902, vol. 1	
Hymnen de Resurrectione [5]	Beck 1964b		
Sermo de Domino Nostro	Beck 1966	Lamy 1882–1902, vol. 1	Gwynn 1898; Amar 1992
Sermones I [8]	Beck 1970a	Mobarak and Assemani 1732–46, vols. 5 and 6; Lamy 1882–1902, vol. 2	Malan 1866 (no. 7)
Sermones II [4]	Beck 1970b	Mobarak and Assemani 1732–46, vols. 5 and 6; Lamy 1882–1902, vols. 1 and 2	Burgess 1853 (no. 1); Morris 1847 (no. 3); Gwynn 1898 (no. 4)

TITLE	CSCO	OTHER EDITIONS	ENGLISH TRANSLATIONS
Sermones III [5]	Beck 1972b	Mobarak and Assemani 1732–46, vol. 5; Lamy 1882–1902, vols. 2 and 3	
Sermones IV [4]	Beck 1973	Zingerle 1869; Overbeck 1865	Miller 1984 (no. 2); Gwynn 1898 (no. 4, partial)
Hymnen de Abraham Qidunaya	Beck 1972a	Lamy 1882–1902, vol. 3	
Hymnen de Juliano Saba	Beck 1972a	Lamy 1882–1902, vol. 3	
Nachträge zu Ephraem Syrus	Beck 1975		Brock 1994 (nos. 1–2)
Sermones in Hebdomadam Sanctam	Beck 1979		
Letter to Publius		Brock 1976b	Brock 1976b; Amar 1992
Prose Refutations 1–2		Mitchell 1912–21	Mitchell 1912–21
Commentary on the Diatessaron		Leloir 1963; Leloir 1990	McCarthy 1993
Commentary on Acts (Armenian)		Akinian 1921	Conybeare 1939 (Lat. tr.)
Commentary on the Pauline Letters (Armenian)		*Srboyn Efremi* 1836, vol. 3	*S. Ephraem Syri commentarii in Epistolas* 1893 (Lat. tr.)
Mēmrē sur Nicomédie (Armenian)		Renoux 1975	Renoux 1975 (Fr. tr.)
Hymnes conservés en arménien [51]		Mariès and Mercier 1961	Mariès and Mercier 1961 (Lat. tr.)

There are also a number of recent translations of hymn cycles into other languages, e.g.:

Azym., Cruc., Res.:	In French in Rouwhorst 1989 and Cassingena-Trevédy 2006; in Italian in De Francesco 2001, with extensive introduction and notes.
Eccl.:	In French in Cerbelaud 2004.
Epiph.:	In French in Cassingena 1997; in Italian in De Francesco 2003.
Ieiun.:	In French in Cerbelaud 1997.
Nat.:	In French in Cassingena-Trevédy 2001; in Italian in De Francesco 2003.
Par.:	In French in Lavenant 1968; in Italian in De Francesco 2006.
Virg.:	In French in Cerbelaud 2006.

APPENDIX 2

Index of *Qale* Employed in the Present Collection

Note: Where text numbers are given in parentheses, the *qala* is an alternative found elsewhere.

TEXT	QALE
8	ܐܘ ܒܪ ܚܝܐ/ܚܐܘܪܐ
14	ܐܘ ܡܘܬܐ ܠܐ ܬܬܡܟܠܠ
(6)	ܐܘܪܗܝ ܕܟܠܗ ܢܗܘܪܝ
(10), 17, 18	ܐܝܟܢܐ ܗܘܝܐ
6, 7	ܐܝܟ ܕܢܟܪܝܐ ܙܘܚܗ
10, (17)	ܐܝܬ ܡܪܝ ܐܠܗܘܬܟ
(1)	ܐܫܬܡܥܘ ܟܠܠ ܡܫܝܚܐ
16, 19	ܐܦܬܚ ܦܘܡܝ ܒܪܒܬܐ
11	ܐܬܟܢܫܘ ܢܒܥ ܒܪܝܚ ܢܦܫ
12	ܐܬܡܠܟܘ ܒܗܘ ܬܒܥܘܪܐ
(1), 2	ܒܬܪ ܒܥܘܬܐ
(12)	ܒܟ ܡܪܝ ܡܫܝܚ

TEXT	QALE
1	ܕܰܚܠܳܐ ܕܡܰܪ̈ܒܥܳܬܳܐ
(11)	ܗܳܐ ܡܶܫܬܰܐܶܠ ܗ̱ܘܳܐ ܒܥܽܘܕܪܳܢ
(4)	ܗܳܢܰܘ ܝܰܪܚܳܐ
9	ܗܳܢܰܘ ܢܺܝܣܳܢ ܒܪܺܝܟܳܐ
(9)	ܗܳܢܰܘ ܨܰܘܡܶܗ ܕܒܽܘܟܪܳܐ
(6)	ܡܰܠܟܳܐ ܡܫܺܝܚܳܐ ܡܰܢܽܘ ܢܫܰܒܚܽܘܢܳܟ
(12)	ܡܰܢܽܘ ܗ̱ܘ ܟܶܝ ܡܶܢܘܳܬܳܐ
4, 5, 20	ܡܰܢܽܘ ܢܶܫܟܰܚ ܠܡܰܡܠܳܠܽܘ
(4)	ܡܳܪ ܠܢܰܒܺܝܳܐ
(6)	ܠܳܟ ܚܰܢܳܢܳܐ
(1)	ܦܰܪܕܰܝܣܳܐ
13	ܡܳܪܳܐ ܘܡܰܣܬܰܒܪܳܐ
3	ܫܡܰܥܘ ܕܰܟܪܽܘܙܺܝܢ

Bibliography

Standard Reference Works

Beck 1960a and 1962a; Leloir 1963a; Ortiz de Urbina 1965, 56–83; and Murray 1982. For Ephrem Graecus, see Hemmerdinger-Iliadou 1960, Geerard 1974–87, 2:366–468, and Geerard and Noret 1998, 227–50. Issues 1/2 (1998) and 2/1 (1999) of *Hugoye* [http://syrcom.cua.edu/Hugoye] are also largely devoted to articles on Ephrem.

Bibliographic Resources

There is now a complete bibliography on Ephrem compiled by Den Biesen (2002). Previous bibliographies on Ephrem can be found in *Parole de l'Orient* 4 (1973), supplemented by Brock 1996, 78–94, Brock 1998, 273–79, and Brock 2004, 304–11.

Works Cited

Akinian, N. 1921. *Srboyn Efremi asorvoy meknut'iwn gorcoc' arak'loc'.* Vienna: Mekhitarist Congregation.

Alexander, P. 1972. The Targumim and Early Exegesis of "Sons of God" in Gen. 6. *Journal of Jewish Studies* 23:60–71.

Amar, J. 1992. Byzantine Ascetic Monachism and Greek Bias in the Vita Tradition of Ephrem the Syrian. *Orientalia christiana periodica* 58:123–56.

———, ed. and trans. 1995. *A Metrical Homily on Holy Mar Ephrem by Mar Jacob of Sarug.* Patrologia orientalis 47.1. Turnhout: Brepols.

Audo, T. 1897. *Simtā dleshānā suryāyā/Dictionnaire de la langue chaldéenne.* 2 vols. Mosul: Imprimerie des Pères Dominicains.

Beck, E., ed. and trans. 1955. *Des heiligen Ephraem des Syrers Hymnen de Fide.* CSCO 154–55/Syr. 73–74. Louvain: Durbecq.

———, ed. and trans. 1957a. *Des heiligen Ephraem des Syrers Hymnen contra Haereses.* CSCO 169–70/Syr. 76–77. Louvain: Durbecq.

———, ed. and trans. 1957b. *Des heiligen Ephraem des Syrers Hymnen de Paradiso und Contra Julianum.* CSCO 174–75/Syr. 78–79. Louvain: Secrétariat du CorpusSCO.

———, ed. and trans. 1959. *Des heiligen Ephraem des Syrers Hymnen de Nativitate (Epiphania)*. CSCO 186–87/Syr. 82–83. Louvain: Secrétariat du CorpusSCO.

———. 1960a. Éphrem le Syrien (Saint). Pages 788–800 in vol. 4 of *Dictionnaire de spiritualité ascétique et mystique, doctrine et histoire*. Edited by M. Villier et al. 17 vols. in 24 parts. Paris: Beauchesne, 1932–95.

———, ed. and trans. 1960b. *Des heiligen Ephraem des Syrers Hymnen de Ecclesia*. CSCO 198–99/Syr. 84–85. Louvain: Secrétariat du CorpusSCO.

———, ed. and trans. 1961a. *Des heiligen Ephraem des Syrers Carmina Nisibena*. CSCO 218–19/Syr. 92–93. Louvain: Secrétariat du CorpusSCO.

———, ed. and trans. 1961b. *Des heiligen Ephraem des Syrers Sermones de Fide*. CSCO 212–13/Syr. 88–89. Louvain: Secrétariat du CorpusSCO.

———. 1962a. Ephraem Syrus. Pages 520–31 in vol. 5 of *Reallexikon für Antike und Christentum*. Edited by T. Klausner et al. 21 vols. to date. Stuttgart: Hiersemann, 1950–.

———, ed. and trans. 1962b. *Des heiligen Ephraem des Syrers Hymnen de Virginitate*. CSCO 223–34/Syr. 94–95. Louvain: Secrétariat du CorpusSCO.

———, ed. and trans. 1963. *Des heiligen Ephraem des Syrers Carmina Nisibena (Zweiter Teil)*. CSCO 240–41/Syr. 102–3. Louvain: Secrétariat du CorpusSCO.

———, ed. and trans. 1964a. *Des heiligen Ephraem des Syrers Hymnen de Ieiunio*. CSCO 246–47/Syr. 106–7. Louvain: Secrétariat du CorpusSCO.

———, ed. and trans. 1964b. *Des heiligen Ephraem des Syrers Paschahymnen (De Azymis, De Crucifixione, De Resurrectione)*. CSCO 248–49/Syr. 108–9. Louvain: Secrétariat du CorpusSCO.

———, ed. and trans. 1966. *Des heiligen Ephraem des Syrers Sermo de Domino Nostro*. CSCO 270–71/Syr. 116–17. Louvain: Secrétariat du CorpusSCO.

———, ed. and trans. 1970a. *Des heiligen Ephraem des Syrers Sermones I*. CSCO 305–6/Syr. 130–31. Louvain: Secrétariat du CorpusSCO.

———, ed. and trans. 1970b. *Des heiligen Ephraem des Syrers Sermones II*. CSCO 311–12/Syr. 134–35. Louvain: Secrétariat du CorpusSCO.

———, ed. and trans. 1972a. *Des heiligen Ephraem des Syrers Hymnen auf Abraham Kidunaya und Julianos Saba*. CSCO 322–23/Syr. 140–41. Louvain: Secrétariat du CorpusSCO.

———, ed. and trans. 1972b. *Des heiligen Ephraem des Syrers Sermones III*. CSCO 320–21/Syr. 138–39. Louvain: Secrétariat du CorpusSCO.

———, ed. and trans. 1973. *Des heiligen Ephraem des Syrers Sermones IV*. CSCO 334–35/Syr. 148–49. Louvain: Secrétariat du CorpusSCO.

———, ed. and trans. 1975. *Nachträge zu Ephraem Syrus*. CSCO 363–64/Syr. 159–60. Louvain: Secrétariat du CorpusSCO.

———, ed. and trans. 1979. *Sermones in Hebdomadam Sanctam*. CSCO 412–13/Syr. 181–82. Louvain: Secrétariat du CorpusSCO.

———. 1980. Die Vergleichspartikel *ʾyk* in der Sprache Ephräms. Pages 15–41 in *Studien aus Arabistik und Semitistik: Anton Spitaler zum 70. Geburtstag von seinen Schülern überreicht*. Edited by W. Diem and S. Wild. Wiesbaden: Harrassowitz.

———. 1982. Zur Terminologie von Ephräms Bildtheologie. Pages 329–77 in *Typus, Symbol, Allegorie bei den östlichen Vätern und ihren Parallelen im Mittelalter*. Edited by M. Schmidt and C. F. Geyer. Regensburg: Pustet.

Bickell, G. 1866. *S. Ephraemi Syri Carmina Nisibena: Additis prolegomenis et supplemento lexicorum syriacorum*. Leipzig: Brockhaus.

Botha, P. 1993. The Theology of Totality: Ephrem's Use of the Particle *Kul* (All). Pages 223–28 in *Papers Presented to the Eleventh International Conference on Patristic Studies Held in Oxford, 1991*. Studia Patristica 25. Edited by E. A. Livingstone. Leuven: Peeters.

———. 2000. Social Values and Textual Strategy in Ephrem the Syrian's Sixth Hymn on the Fast. *Acta Patristica et Byzantina* 11:22–32.

Bou Mansour, T. 1988. *La pensée symbolique de saint Ephrem le Syrien*. Bibliothèque de l'Université Saint Esprit 16. Kaslik: Université Saint-Esprit.

Brock, S. P. 1975–76. The Poetic Artistry of St Ephrem: An Analysis of H. Azym. III. *Parole de l'Orient* 6–7:21–28.

———. 1976a. St Ephrem on Christ as Light in Mary and in the Jordan: H. de Ecclesia 36. *Eastern Churches Review* 7:137–44.

———. 1976b. Ephrem's Letter to Publius. *Le Muséon* 89:261–305.

———. 1982. Clothing Metaphors as a Means of Theological Expression in Syriac Tradition. Pages 11–38 in *Typus, Symbol, Allegorie bei den östlichen Vätern und ihren Parallelen im Mittelalter*. Edited by M. Schmidt and C. F. Geyer. Regensburg: Pustet. Repr. in *Studies in Syriac Christianity* (Ch. XI). Collected Studies 357. Aldershot: Variorum, 1992.

———. 1983. *The Harp of the Spirit. Eighteen Hymns of St Ephrem*. Studies Supplementary to Sobornost 4. 2nd ed. London: Fellowship of St Alban and St Sergius.

———. 1986. Two Syriac Verse Homilies on the Binding of Isaac. *Le Muséon* 99:61–129. Repr. in *From Ephrem to Romanos: Interactions between Syriac and Greek in Late Antiquity* (Ch. VI). Collected Studies 664. Aldershot: Variorum, 1999.

———. 1987. A Hymn of St Ephrem on the Eucharist. *The Harp* 1:61–68.

———. 1989a. The Lost Old Syriac at Luke 1:35 and the Earliest Syriac Terms for the Incarnation. Pages 117–31 in *Gospel Traditions in the Second Century: Origins, Recensions, Text, and Transmission*. Christianity and Judaism in Antiquity 3. Edited by W. L. Petersen. Notre Dame, IN: University of Notre Dame Press. Repr. in *Fire from Heaven: Studies in Syriac Theology and Liturgy* (Ch. X). Collected Studies 863. Aldershot: Variorum, 2006.

———, trans. 1989b. *A Garland of Hymns from the Early Church*. McLean, VA: St. Athanasius' Coptic Publishing Center.

———. 1990a. A Brief Guide to the Main Editions and Translations of the Works of St Ephrem. *The Harp* 3:7–29.

———, trans. 1990b. *St. Ephrem the Syrian: Hymns on Paradise*. Crestwood, NY: St. Vladimir's Seminary Press.

———. 1991a. Come, Compassionate Mother . . . , Come Holy Spirit: A Forgotten Aspect of Early Eastern Christian Imagery. *ARAM* 3:249–57. Repr. in *Fire from Heaven: Studies in Syriac Theology and Liturgy* (Ch. VI). Collected Studies 863. Aldershot: Variorum, 2006.

———. 1991b. Syriac Dispute Poems: The Various Types. Pages 109–19 in *Dispute Poems and Dialogues in the Ancient and Mediaeval Near East*. Edited by G. J. Reinink and H. L. J. Vanstiphout. Orientalia lovaniensia analecta 42. Leuven: Department Oriëntalistiek. Repr. in *From Ephrem to Romanos: Interactions between Syriac and Greek in Late Antiquity* (Ch. VII). Collected Studies 664. Aldershot: Variorum, 1999.

———. 1992. *The Luminous Eye: The Spiritual World Vision of Saint Ephrem.* Cistercian Studies 124. Kalamazoo: Cistercian Publications.

———. 1993. From Annunciation to Pentecost: The Travels of a Technical Term. Pages 71–91 in *Eulogema: Studies in Honor of Robert Taft, SJ.* Studia Anselmiana 110. Edited by E. Carr. Rome: Centro Studi S. Anselmo. Repr. in *Fire from Heaven: Studies in Syriac Theology and Liturgy* (Ch. XIII). Collected Studies 863. Aldershot: Variorum, 2006.

———, trans. 1994. *Bride of Light: Hymns on Mary from the Syriac Churches.* Mōrān 'Eth'ō 6. Kottayam: St. Ephrem Ecumenical Research Institute.

———. 1996. *Syriac Studies: A Classified Bibliography (1960–1990).* Kaslik: Parole de l'Orient.

———. 1997. The Transmission of Ephrem's *Madrashe* in the Syriac Liturgical Tradition. Pages 490–505 in *Papers Presented at the Twelfth International Conference on Patristic Studies Held in Oxford, 1995.* Studia Patristica 33. Edited by E. A. Livingstone. Leuven: Peeters.

———. 1998. Syriac Studies: A Classified Bibliography (1991–1995). *Parole de l'Orient* 23:241–350.

———. 1999a. "The Robe of Glory": A Biblical Image in the Syriac Tradition. *The Way* 39.3:247–59.

———. 1999b. The *Ruah Elohim* of Gen 1, 2 and Its Reception History in the Syriac Tradition. Pages 327–49 in *Lectures et relectures de la Bible: Festschrift P.-M. Bogaert.* Edited by J.-M. Auwers and A. Wenin. Leuven: Leuven University Press (Uiteverij Peeters Leuven). Repr. in *Fire from Heaven: Studies in Syriac Theology and Liturgy* (Ch. XIV). Collected Studies 863. Aldershot: Variorum, 2006.

———. 1999c. St Ephrem in the Eyes of Later Syriac Liturgical Tradition. *Hugoye* 2.1, http://syrcom.cua.edu/Hugoye/Vol2No1/HV2N1Brock.html.

———. 2001. The Dispute Poem: From Sumer to Syriac. *Journal of the Canadian Society for Syriac Studies* 1:1–10.

———. 2004. Syriac Studies: A Classified Bibliography (1996–2000). *Parole de l'Orient* 29:263–410.

Burgess, H., trans. 1853. *The Repentance of Nineveh: A Metrical Homily on the Mission of Jonah; Also, an Exhortation to Repentance and Some Smaller Pieces.* London: Blackader.

Cassingena, F., trans. 1997. *Éphrem le Syrien. Hymnes sur l'Épiphanie. Hymnes baptismales de l'Orient syrien.* Spiritualité orientale 70. Bégrolles-en-Mauges: Abbaye de Bellefontaine.

Cassingena-Trevédy, F., trans. 2001. *Éphrem de Nisibe. Hymnes sur la Nativité.* Sources chrétiennes 459. Paris: Éditions du Cerf.

———, trans. 2006. *Éphrem de Nisibe. Hymnes Paschales.* Sources chrétiennes 502. Paris: Éditions du Cerf.

Cerbelaud, D., trans. 1997. *Éphrem le Syrien. Hymnes sur le jeûne.* Spiritualité orientale 69. Bégrolles-en-Mauges: Abbaye de Bellefontaine.

———, trans. 2004. *Éphrem le Syrien. Le combat chrétien. Hymnes* de Ecclesia. Spiritualité orientale 83. Bégrolles-en-Mauges: Abbaye de Bellefontaine.

———, trans. 2006. *Éphrem le Syrien. Le Christ en ses symboles. Hymnes* de Virginitate. Spiritualité orientale 86. Bégrolles-en-Mauges: Abbaye de Bellefontaine.

Conybeare, F. C., trans. 1939. The Commentary of Ephrem on Acts. Pages 373–453 in vol. 3 of *The Beginnings of Christianity.* 3 vols. Edited by F. J. Foakes-Jackson and K. Lake. London: Macmillan, 1922–39.

Daniélou, J. 1947. La typologie d'Isaac dans le christianisme primitive. *Biblica* 28:363–93.

Darmo, T., ed. 1960–62. *Ḥudra.* 3 vols. Trichur: Mar Narsai Press.

David, C. J., ed. 1886–96. *Breviarium iuxta Ritum Ecclesiae Antiochenae Syrorum.* 7 vols. Mosul: Dominican Press.

De Francesco, I., trans. 2001. *Efrem il Siro. Inni pasquali. Sugli Azzimi, sulla Crocifissione, sulla Risurrezione.* Letture cristiane del primo millennio 31. Milan: Paoline Editoriale Libri.

———, trans. 2003. *Efrem il Siro. Inni sulla Natività e sull'Epifania.* Letture cristiane del primo millennio 35. Milan: Paoline Editoriale Libri.

———, trans. 2006. *Efrem il Siro. Inni sul Paradiso.* Milan: Paoline Editoriale Libri.

de Halleux, A. 1972. Un clé pour les hymnes d'Ephrem dans le ms Sinai syr. 10. *Le Muséon* 85:171–99.

———. 1973. Mar Éphrem théologien. *Parole de l'Orient* 4:35–54.

———. 1974. La transmission des Hymnes d'Éphrem d'après le ms Sinai syr. 10. Pages 21–63 in *Symposium Syriacum 1972: célebré dans les jours 26–31 octobre 1972 à l'Institut Pontifical Oriental de Rome.* Orientalia christiana analecta 197. Rome: Pont. Institutum Orientalium Studiorum.

———. 1983. Saint Ephrem le syrien. *Revue théologique de Louvain* 14:328–55.

Den Biesen, K. 2002. *Bibliography of Ephrem the Syrian.* Giove in Umbria: [Published by the compiler: ephrem_bibliography@hotmail.com].

Dodgeon, M. H., and S. N. C. Lieu. 1991. *The Roman Eastern Frontier and the Persian Wars AD 226–363.* London: Routledge.

Draguet, R. 1980. *La vie primitive de S. Antoine: conservée en syriaque.* CSCO 417–18/Syr. 183–84. Louvain: Secrétariat du CorpusSCO.

Geerard, M. 1974–87. *Clavis Patrum Graecorum.* 5 vols. Turnhout: Brepols.

———, and J. Noret. 1998. *Clavis Patrum Graecorum: Supplementum.* Turnhout: Brepols.

Gelston, A. 1992. *The Eucharistic Prayer of Addai and Mari.* Oxford: Clarendon Press.

Gribomont, J. 1973. La tradition liturgique des hymnes pascales de s. Éphrem. *Parole de l'Orient* 4:191–246.

Griffith, S. H. 1989–90. Images of Ephraem: The Syrian Holy Man and His Church. *Traditio* 45:7–33.

———. 1995. Asceticism in the Church of Syria: The Hermeneutics of Early Syrian Monasticism. Pages 220–48 in *Asceticism.* Edited by V. L. Wimbush and R. Valantasis. New York: Oxford University Press.

———. 1997. *"Faith Adoring the Mystery": Reading the Bible with Saint Ephraem the Syrian.* Milwaukee: Marquette University Press.

———. 1998. A Spiritual Father for the Whole Church: St Ephraem the Syrian. *Sobornost/Eastern Churches Review* 20.2:21–40. Also published as: A Spiritual Father for the Whole Church: The Universal Appeal of St. Ephraem the Syrian. *Hugoye* 1.2 (1998), http://syrcom.cua.edu/Hugoye/Vol1No2/HV1N2Griffith.html.

Gwynn, J., trans. 1898. Selections Translated into English from the Hymns and Homilies of Ephraim the Syrian, and from the Demonstrations of Aphrahat the Persian Sage. Pages 113–433 in *A Select Library of Nicene and Post-Nicene Fathers. Second Series, Vol. 13, Pt. II: Gregory the Great, Ephraim Syrus, Aphrahat.* New York: Christian Literature Publishing Company.

Hage, L. 1987. *The Syriac Model Strophes and Their Poetic Metres, by the Maronite Patriarch Stephen Douayhi.* Bibliothèque de l'Université Saint-Esprit 14. Kaslik: Université Saint-Esprit.

Hemmerdinger-Iliadou, D. 1960. Éphrem (les versions). I. Éphrem grec; II. Éphrem latin. Pages 800–822 in vol. 4 of *Dictionnaire de spiritualité ascétique et mystique, doctrine et histoire.* Edited by M. Villier et al. 17 vols. in 24 parts. Paris: Beauchesne, 1932–95.

Ibrahim, G. Y., and G. A. Kiraz. 1999. Ephrem's *Madrashe* and the Syrian Orthodox Beth Gazzo. *Hugoye* 2.1, http://syrcom.cua.edu/Hugoye/Vol2No1/HV2N1IbrahimKiraz.html.

Jellinek, A. 1967. *Bet ha-Midrasch.* 3rd ed. 2 vols. in 6 parts. Jerusalem: Wahrmann Books.

Jones, S. 2003. The Womb and the Spirit in the Baptismal Writings of Ephrem the Syrian. *Studia Liturgica* 33:175–93.

Kmosko, M., ed. 1926. *Liber Graduum.* Patrologia syriaca 3. Paris: Firmin-Didot.

Konat, A., ed. 1962–63. *Fenqitho d-Ḥudro shattonoyo.* 3 vols. Pampakuda: Mar Julius Press.

Koonammakkal, T. 1998. Ephrem's Imagery of Chasm. Pages 175–83 in *Symposium Syriacum VII: Uppsala University, Department of Asian and African Languages 11–14 August 1996.* Orientalia christiana analecta 256. Edited by R. Lavenant. Rome: Pontificio Istituto Orientale.

Lamy, T. J. 1882–1902. *Sancti Ephraem Syri hymni et sermones.* 4 vols. Mechliniae: H. Dessain Summi Pontificis S. Congregationis de Propaganda Fide et Archiepiscopatus Mechliniensis Typographus.

Lavenant, R., trans. 1968. *Éphrem de Nisibe. Hymnes sur le paradis.* Sources chrétiennes 137. Paris: Editions du Cerf.

Leloir, L. 1963a. Éphrem le Syrien. Pages 590–97 in vol. 15 of *Dictionnaire de spiritualité ascétique et mystique, doctrine et histoire.* Edited by M. Villier et al. 17 vols. in 24 parts. Paris: Beauchesne, 1932–95.

———, ed. and trans. 1963b. *Saint Éphrem. Commentaire de l'Évangile concordant. Texte Syriaque (Manuscrit Chester Beatty 709).* Chester Beatty Monographs 8. Dublin: Hodges Figgis & Co.

———. 1990. *Saint Éphrem. Commentaire de l'Évangile concordant. Texte Syriaque (Manuscrit Chester Beatty 709). Folios additionnels.* Chester Beatty Monographs 8. Leuven: Peeters.

Lieu, J., trans. 1989. Ephrem the Syrian: Hymns against Julian. Pages 105–28 in *The Emperor Julian: Panegyric and Polemic.* Edited by S. N. C. Lieu. 2nd ed. Translated Texts for Historians 2. Liverpool: Liverpool University Press.

Malan, S. C. 1866. *Repentance, Chiefly from the Syriac of St Ephraem.* London: J. Masters.

Mariès, L., and C. Mercier, eds. and trans. 1961. *Hymnes de Saint Éphrem conservées en version arménienne.* Patrologia orientalis 30.1. Paris: Firmin-Didot.

Mathews, E. G. 1994. St. Ephrem, *Madrashe* on Faith 81–85: Hymns on the Pearl I–V. *St Vladimir's Seminary Quarterly* 38:45–72.

———, and J. P. Amar. 1994. *St. Ephrem the Syrian: Selected Prose Works.* The Fathers of the Church 91. Washington, D.C.: The Catholic University of America Press.

McCarthy, C. 1993. *Saint Ephrem's Commentary on Tatian's Diatessaron: An English Translation of Chester Beatty Syriac MS 709.* Journal of Semitic Studies Supplement 2. Oxford: Oxford University Press on behalf of the University of Manchester.

McVey, K. E. 1988. St Ephrem's Understanding of Spiritual Progress: Some Points of Comparison with Origen of Alexandria. *The Harp* 1.2–3:117–28.

———. 1989. *Ephrem the Syrian: Hymns.* Classics of Western Spirituality. New York: Paulist Press.

———. 1990. The Anti-Judaic Polemic of Ephrem Syrus' Hymns on the Nativity. Pages 229–40 in *Of Scribes and Scrolls: Studies on the Hebrew Bible, Intertestamental Judaism, and Christian Origins, Presented to John Strugnell on the Occasion of His Sixtieth Birthday.* Edited by H. W. Attridge, J. J. Collins, and T. H. Tobin. Lanham: University Press of America.

———. 2001. Ephrem the Syrian's Use of Female Metaphors to Describe the Deity. *Journal for Ancient Christianity/Zeitschrift für Antikes Christentum* 5:261–88.

[Miller, D.], trans. 1984. Ephraim the Syrian: A Homily on the Solitaries. Pages 471–80 in *The Ascetic Homilies of Saint Isaac the Syrian.* Boston: Holy Transfiguration Monastery.

Mitchell, C. W. 1912–21. *S. Ephraim's Prose Refutations of Mani, Marcion, and Bardaisan.* 2 vols. London: Published for the Text and Translation Society by Williams and Norgate. Repr. Farnsborough: Gregg, 1969.

Mobarak (Benedictus), P., and S. E. Assemani. 1732–46. *Sancti patris nostri Ephraem Syri Opera omnia quae exstant Graece, Syriace, Latine.* 6 vols. Rome: Ex typographia Vaticana Jo. Mariae Henrici Salvioni typog.

Morris, J. B. 1847. *Select Works of S. Ephrem the Syrian: Translated out of the Original Syriac, with Notes and Indices.* Oxford: John Henry Parker.

Murray, R. 1970. A Hymn of St Ephrem to Christ on the Incarnation, the Holy Spirit, and the Sacraments. *Eastern Churches Review* 3:142–50.

———. 1975–76. The Theory of Symbolism in St Ephrem's Theology. *Parole de l'Orient* 6–7:1–20.

———. 1982. Ephräm Syrus. Pages 755–62 in vol. 9 of *Theologische Realenzyklopädie.* Edited by G. Müller et al. 36 vols. Berlin: Walter de Gruyter, 1977–2004.

———. 1995. Aramaic and Syriac Dispute Poems and Their Connections. Pages 157–87 in *Studia Aramaica.* Edited by M. J. Geller, J. C. Greenfield, and M. P. Weitzman. Journal of Semitic Studies Supplement 4. Oxford and New York: Oxford University Press on behalf of the University of Manchester.

———. 2004. *Symbols of Church and Kingdom: A Study in Early Syriac Tradition.* 2nd ed. Piscataway, NJ: Gorgias Press.

Nöldeke, T. 1904. *Compendious Syriac Grammar.* Translated by J. A. Crichton. London: Williams & Norgate.

Ortiz de Urbina, I. 1965. *Patrologia Syriaca.* 2nd ed. Rome: Pont. Institutum Orientalium Studiorum.

Overbeck, J. J. 1865. *S. Ephraemi Syri, Rabulae episcopi Edesseni, Balaei aliorumque Opera selecta e codicibus syriacis manuscriptis in museo Britannico et bibliotheca Bodleiana asservatis.* Oxford: Clarendon.

Palmer, A. N. 1993a. "A Lyre without a Voice": The Poetics and the Politics of Ephrem the Syrian. *ARAM* 5:371–99.

———. 1993b. The Merchant of Nisibis: Saint Ephrem and his Faithful Quest for Union in Numbers. Pages 167–233 in *Early Christian Poetry: A Collection of Essays.* Supplements to Vigiliae Christianae 22. Edited by J. den Boeft and A. Hilhorst. Leiden: Brill.

———. 1995. Words, Silences, and the Silent Word: Acrostics and Empty Columns in Saint Ephraem's Hymns on Faith. *Parole de l'Orient* 20:129–200.

———. 2002. Akrostich Poems: Restoring Ephrem's *Madroshe. The Harp* 15:275–87.

Parisot, J., ed. and trans. 1894–1907. *Aphraatis Sapientis Persae Demonstrationes.* 2 vols. Patrologia syriaca 1–2. Paris: Firmin-Didot.

Petersen, W. L. 1994. *Tatian's Diatessaron: Its Creation, Dissemination, Significance, and History in Scholarship.* Supplements to Vigiliae Christianae 25. Leiden: Brill.

Possekel, U. 1999. *Evidence of Greek Philosophical Concepts in the Writings of Ephrem the Syrian.* CSCO Subsidia 102. Leuven: Peeters.

Renoux, C., ed. and trans. 1975. *Éphrem de Nisibe. Mēmrē sur Nicomédie.* Patrologia orientalis 37.2–3. Turnhout: Brepols.

Rouwhorst, G. A. M. 1989. *Les hymnes pascales d'Éphrem de Nisibe: analyse théologique et recherche sur l'évolution de la fête pascale chrétienne à Nisibe et à Edesse et dans quelques églises voisines au quatrième siècle.* 2 vols. [vol. 1. Étude; vol. 2. Textes]. Supplements to Vigiliae Christianae 7. Leiden: Brill.

Russell, P. S. Forthcoming 1. *Ephrem the Syrian: 80 Hymns on Faith.* Eastern Christian Texts in Translation 3. Louvain and Washington, D.C.: Peeters.

———. Forthcoming 2. *Ephrem the Syrian: Six Metrical Homilies on Faith.* Eastern Christian Texts in Translation 4. Louvain and Washington, D.C.: Peeters.

S. Ephraem Syri commentarii in Epistolas D. Pauli nunc primum ex Armenio in Latinum sermonem a Patribus Mekhitaristis translate. 1893. Venice.

Salvesen, A. G. 1995. *The Exodus Commentary of St Ephrem.* Mōrān 'Eth'ō 8. Kottayam: St. Ephrem Ecumenical Research Institute.

Shemunkasho, A. 2002. *Healing in the Theology of Saint Ephrem.* Piscataway, NJ: Gorgias Press.

Shepardson, C. 2001. Anti-Jewish Rhetoric and Intra-Syriac Conflict in the Sermons of Ephrem Syrus. Pages 502–7 in *Papers Presented at the Thirteenth International Conference on Patristic Studies Held in Oxford, 1999.* Edited by M. F. Wiles and E. Yarnold. Studia Patristica 35. Leuven: Peeters.

Slim, J. 1967. Hymne 1 de saint Éphrem sur la Resurrection. *L'Orient syrien* 12:505–14.

Srboyn Efremi xorin suri Matenagrut'iwnk'. 1836. 4 vols. Venice.

Tonneau, R. 1955. *Sancti Ephraem Syri in Genesim et in Exodum commentarii*. CSCO 152–53/Syr. 71–72. Louvain: Durbecq.

Valavanolickal, K. A. 1996. *The Use of the Gospel Parables in the Writings of Aphrahat and Ephrem*. Studies in the Religion and History of Early Christianity 2. Frankfurt am Main: Peter Lang.

Wickham, L. 1974. The Sons of God and the Daughters of Men. *Oudtestamentische Studien* 19:135–47.

Widengren, G. 1946. *Mesopotamian Elements in Manichaeism*. Uppsala-Leipzig: Lundequistska Bokhandeln.

Wright, W. 1871. *Apocryphal Acts of the Apostles*. 2 vols. London: Williams and Norgate. Repr. Hildersheim: Georg Olms, 1990.

Zingerle, P. 1869. *Monumenta Syriaca I*. Oeniponti: Wagner.

Index of Scripture Citations

References are to text number and stanza. The addition of n *indicates that the reference is to a note.*

Genesis

Exodus

Index of Names

About the Translators

Sebastian P. Brock was, until his retirement in 2003, Reader in Syriac Studies at the University of Oxford. Among his publications are *The Luminous Eye: The Spiritual World Vision of Saint Ephrem the Syrian* (Cistercian Publications); *St. Ephrem the Syrian, Hymns on Paradise* (St Vladimir's Seminary Press); *Isaac of Nineveh (Isaac the Syrian): "The Second Part," chapters IV–XLI* (Peeters); *The Bible in the Syriac Tradition* (SEERI); *An Outline of Syriac Literature* (SEERI); and four volumes in the *Variorum Reprint* series (Ashgate).

George A. Kiraz is the founder and director of Beth Mardutho: The Syriac Institute, and president of Gorgias Press. He obtained an MSt in Syriac Studies from Oxford University (1991), and an MPhil (1992) and PhD (1996) from Cambridge University. He has written extensively on Syriac and computational linguistics. His recent publications include *A Computer Generated Concordance to the Syriac New Testament* (Brill); *Comparative Edition of the Syriac Gospels* (Brill); and *Lexical Tools to the Syriac New Testament* (Gorgias Press).

A Note on the Type

The English text of this book was set in BASKERVILLE, a typeface originally designed by John Baskerville (1706–1775), a British stonecutter, letter designer, typefounder, and printer. The Baskerville type is considered to be one of the first "transitional" faces—a deliberate move away from the "old style" of the Continental humanist printer. Its rounded letterforms presented a greater differentiation of thick and thin strokes, the serifs on the lowercase letters were more nearly horizontal, and the stress was nearer the vertical—all of which would later influence the "modern" style undertaken by Bodoni and Didot in the 1790s. Because of its high readability, particularly in long texts, the type was subsequently copied by all major typefoundries. (The original punches and matrices still survive today at Cambridge University Press.) This adaptation, designed by the Compugraphic Corporation in the 1960s, is a notable departure from other versions of the Baskerville typeface by its overall typographic evenness and lightness in color. To enhance its range, supplemental diacritics and ligatures were created by Jonathan Saltzman in 1997.

About the Series

To understand Eastern Christianity one must study its literature, a rich and varied resource that is vital to many fields of religious and academic inquiry. Yet scholars and students are often deterred from its study by the lack of accessible and reliable texts and the remoteness of the source languages. EASTERN CHRISTIAN TEXTS provides specialists and nonspecialists with reliable English-language translations of seminal works paired with original-language texts. Each volume is produced to meet the highest academic and editorial standards and is elegantly designed to reflect the dignity of the tradition it represents.

EASTERN CHRISTIAN TEXTS is published by Brigham Young University Press and distributed through the University of Chicago Press.

http://meti.byu.edu/

◆